GUSTAVUS ADOLPHUS
the GREAT

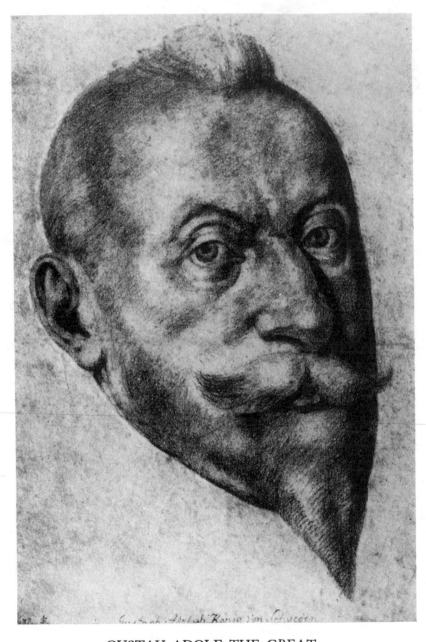

GUSTAV ADOLF THE GREAT

*Original Drawing by L. Strauch, dating from 1632 and recently
discovered in the Schoolhouse in Madenhausen, Bavaria*

GUSTAVUS ADOLPHUS
the GREAT

NILS AHNLUND

Translated from the Swedish by Michael Roberts

Foreword by DENNIS E. SHOWALTER

HISTORY BOOK CLUB
NEW YORK

CONTENTS

ILLUSTRATIONS

FOREWORD

DENNIS E. SHOWALTER

Professor of History, Colorado College

BETWEEN THE SIXTEENTH and the eighteenth centuries three great powers emerged on Europe's northeastern periphery: Sweden, Russia, and Prussia. Each in turn shook the continent; none was an obvious candidate for grandeur. Sweden was a peasant society with neither material wealth nor military standing. Russia was struggling with ephemeral borders, unstable politics, and a government heavily influenced by centuries of Mongol hegemony. Prussia was "an oyster without a shell," existing as much by its neighbors' sufferance as by its own achievements.

Each transformation depended upon a particular ruler. Gustavus Adolphus of Sweden (Michael Roberts prefers the spelling "Gustav Adolf" in his translation), Peter I of Russia, and King Frederick II of Prussia combined their personal gifts and energies with the dynamics of their respective states, then took to the European stage with consequences still perceptible on a global as well as a continental level. Each became a living legend in his own country; each left his mark on Europe.

Gustavus was the first. A fifteenth-century prophecy averred that a series of disasters would end only when a golden lion emerged from the North to defeat the eagle of devastation. Gustavus Adolphus, with his flowing blond hair and unfailing courage, won the title "Lion of the North" among his countrymen, his allies, and his enemies. A symbol of armed Protestantism, he also presided over a synthesis of economic and administrative development that made Sweden a model of a well-governed and prosperous society. Long after his death in battle in 1632, the memory of Gustavus endured both in popular folklore and in councils of state.

Nils Ahnlund's biography was quickly accepted as a classic when it was published in Sweden in 1932. The English edition suffered, however, from the timing of its appearance in 1940; the demands of a world war obscured the deeds of a seventeenth-century king. Ahnlund's scholarship and analysis nevertheless made a lasting impression on the young British scholar who translated the work—Michael Roberts—for the latter went on to write several seminal volumes on the history of early modern Sweden.

Ahnlund presents Gustavus as inheriting and fulfilling a comprehensive tradition of revolution. Sweden itself had been created only in the first quarter of the sixteenth century, at the price of destroying the Scandinavian confederation of Denmark, Sweden, and Norway, the Union of Kalmar, that had stood since 1397. The resulting war of secession was long and expensive. The House of Vasa initially achieved the throne by appealing to the merchants and the lesser gentry in the face of an entrenched high nobility and a wealthy Catholic church, neither of which had any reason to challenge the status quo. Gustavus I, proclaimed king in 1523, sought to introduce centralized administration and centralized financing. He faced opposition from his own supporters, who dominated the Estates and saw no reason to acquiesce in their loss of power. He confronted the challenge of raising cash from an undeveloped economic system, still heavily dependent on barter at its lower levels. And he ruled a land whose climate challenged habitation, let alone development, in the northern regions. It was not surprising that his greatest success was the introduction of Lutheranism as the state church. Even this was a top-down process, reflecting royal determination to assert control over a fractious peasantry rather than any grassroots spiritual awakening.

The turning of this poor and divided land to overseas expansion in the second half of the sixteenth century was a consequence of Denmark's continued hostility to Sweden's independence. Since Denmark, by virtue of its union with Norway, controlled both sides of the Baltic Sound, Swedish commerce with western Europe was painfully vulnerable. However, the eastern end of the Baltic Sea was another story. There a still-amorphous Russia and an overextended Poland struggled for mastery of a littoral that was slipping from the fading grip of the Teutonic Order. Sweden's navy, still not quite a match for its Danish rival, was exponentially superior to anything farther east. As a result Sweden, like Britain in eighteenth-century India, was able to establish and maintain coastal enclaves indefinitely.

Sweden's Baltic expansion also involved a dynastic marriage with the Catholic ruling house of Poland/Lithuania. The son of that marriage, Sigismund, ruled both realms until his Catholic principles led to his deposition by his cousin Charles (Karl) IX in 1599. Sigismund returned to Poland determined to recover the Swedish half of his inheritance. The resulting war strained to the limit a Swedish army that was still a late feudal/early modern compound of peasant levies and hired professionals. Against Catholic Poles and Orthodox Russians, however, Lutheranism came to stand alongside plunder as a focus of morale. And since the Swedes usually fought outnumbered, they tended to cultivate ferocity as a force multiplier, a *furor Suedicus* that neither gave nor expected quarter. Nevertheless, by the century's turn Sweden had learned that it was easier to acquire a sphere of influence than to profit from it.

Charles IX correspondingly emphasized preparing, as comprehensively and as early as possible, his son and heir Gustavus, born in 1594, as both a soldier and an administrator. Ahnlund leaves no doubt that, in contrast to Peter and Frederick, young Gustavus enjoyed a solid, affectionate relationship with a father who provided solid training in the uncertain crafts of kingship. The crown prince combined supervised study of the leading classical and contemporary military and political theorists with heavy doses of practical experience. He grew into a tall, well-built, handsome man—an important asset in an era when crowned heads were expected to look the part and to act it as well. Useful too was Gustavus's ability to choose and trust subordinates. The most outstanding of these was Axel Oxenstierna, chancellor of Sweden until his death in 1654, and a man as remarkable for caution and imperturbability as was Gustavus for spirit and energy.

That relationship still lay in the future in 1611, when Sweden found itself at war simultaneously with Russia and Denmark. In the middle of the conflict Charles died unexpectedly, and Gustavus, not yet seventeen, assumed the throne. He spent the next decade putting out foreign and domestic fires. In the process he demonstrated the proverbial old head on young shoulders. Gustavus negotiated a peace with Denmark that allowed Swedish ships to pass through the Baltic Sound in return for a large indemnity. He ended hostilities with Russia and concluded a truce with Poland. Inheriting an empty treasury, he faced the immediate task of paying Denmark's price for opening the Sound. The young king found Dutch merchants willing to lend cash against the security of Swedish copper, which they imported through the now-open Sound and sold on the Amsterdam market at a tidy profit. Gustavus, making a virtue of necessity, encouraged Dutch investment in Sweden and copied Dutch methods of government administration. In a pattern later used by Frederick II in Prussia as well, Gustavus assigned control over each major department of government to a "collegium" of bureaucrats that reported directly to the king. Turf squabbles restricted collusion; the relatively small scale of Sweden's affairs allowed direct supervision by the king and his chancellor—who developed a taste for bureaucratic oversight disturbing to many of his aristocratic counterparts.

Whatever may have been his private views on the issue of royal power, Gustavus was in no position to take a high hand with his Swedish subjects. He bargained with his noblemen for a charter that affirmed the right of the Estates and the royal council to approve any new taxes, and allowed free speech to royal councilors (an important concession to the aristocracy who provided them). This compromise between royal absolutism and aristocratic constitutionalism was cemented by Gustavus's oath to maintain Lutheranism as the state religion—a gesture securing the firm support of a clergy still uncertain of its place in the Swedish system. Gustavus sought as well to sustain the rights of the peasantry. Although taxes increased, their collection became more honest and more systematic. Aristocratic encroachments on commoners' rights and lands were restrained through the royal courts. The Lutheran church at the parish level became a strong advocate of what might be called the public interest, in the process sinking roots in the rural communities that endured well into the twentieth century. However, Ahnlund points out that Gustavus was no people's monarch. Instead *Gustavus Adolphus the Great* depicts "a feeling of tension" between the crown and its subjects, periodically flaring into open, violent protest against some perceived challenge to law or custom. Gustavus nevertheless succeeded, as none of his predecessors had done, in establishing an emotional link between throne and people. It was his boast that he could sleep safely at any hearth in Sweden. Ahnlund agrees the king was probably right, at least in principle.

Administrative reform and social stability were for Gustavus, as they would be for Peter and Frederick, means to the wider ends of state security and state aggrandizement. Gustavus began overhauling his army by systematizing a still-random domestic conscription system. Each group of ten able-bodied males had to provide one soldier per year. Only in wartime were they paid in still-scarce cash. In peace they were maintained by receiving shares in farms in return for labor. Since conscripts were usually stationed in their home districts, and since farmers were allowed to deduct soldiers' shares from rent or taxes, the system worked as long as the "10 percent rule" was maintained. Even then, as Ahnlund demonstrates, it strained a subsistence economy whose margins in this period remained narrow. Nor could Gustavus's conscription provide enough men to meet the demands of war on a long-term or a large scale. To bridge the gap, the king depended on mercenaries, often attracted to Swedish service by prospects of profit and promotion in the service of a king who paid in cash and rewarded performance. Most were German, though there was a significant leavening of men from the British Isles, especially Scots. In contrast to the later practice of Frederick the Great, they served in separate regiments, often identified by color: the Black Regiment, the Yellow Regiment, and so on. And in contrast to normal European practice, Gustavus took pains to supervise the training of their junior officers in what was becoming a new way of war.

By the end of the sixteenth century, European battlefields were becoming increasingly gridlocked. Gunpowder weapons had checked maneuverability, but firepower was as yet insufficient to decide events by itself. As a result, strategy was fundamental. Princes and generals sought to win wars by maneuver and attrition. In practice this meant wearing down an enemy by exhausting or destroying his resources. The accompanying problem was the risk of exhausting one's own capacities instead. Geography was crucial, and it was no coincidence that the Netherlands, where Maurice of Nassau, prince of Orange, recognized the geographic vulnerability of the small and waterlogged United Provinces, played a key role in the return to decisive battles. It was also no coincidence that Maurice's work was continued by the king of a country whose history and demographics alike highlighted the importance of reaching quick decisions. Like Frederick the Great a century later, Gustavus Adolphus focused on improving the tactical performance of his armies not as an end in itself but as a means of achieving the strategic/political goal of making Sweden a great power.

Gustavus understood, more clearly than any of his contemporaries, that shock was the crucial instrument of victory. He also understood that shock was an element of both fire and movement. The infantry's basic tactical formation was the brigade, organized in three "squadrons," each comprising around five hundred men. While exact proportions varied, about two-thirds of the men in a squadron carried matchlock muskets. The rest were pikemen, trained to maneuver with the musketeers. To improve his infantry's firepower, Gustavus sought as well to develop cannon light enough to accompany the brigades directly. His attempt to make gun barrels from copper tubes covered with leather proved a failure. Eventually, however, an infantry squadron usually included a couple of iron three-pounder cannon, light enough to be drawn by a single horse or a few men, and able to fire eight rounds to the musketeers' six. The heavier Swedish guns were organized into permanent batteries, enabling previously unknown concentrations of fire against selected targets. His cavalry, by contrast, discarded most of its armor, emphasized the sword over the then-fashionable pistol, and was trained to charge at a gallop or a fast trot. What they sacrificed in mass they made up for in speed and ferocity. In particular, the war cry of Gustavus's Finnish troopers, *hakkaa paalle!* (chop 'em down!), meant cold steel and no mercy.

Gustavus's preferred tactics involved deploying his infantry in relatively extended multiple lines, with three or four brigades per line. Cavalry supported by musketeers and artillery formed the army's wings. The infantry advanced to close quarters, covered by the three-pounders' canister, fired one or two salvoes, then charged with pikes and musket butts. The cavalry checked or drove back the enemy horses and exploit-

ed opportunities created by the other arms. The pattern became so familiar over the next two centuries, especially under Frederick the Great, that
its origins in the wars of Gustavus have been forgotten. Like its Prussian
successor, the Swedish army was flexible, able to shift from offense to
defense and defense to counterattack. Like the Prussians, the Swedes,
too, relied on coordination and discipline to throw enemies off balance.

That discipline was not entirely imposed by force. Patriotism for the
Swedes and Protestantism for the mercenaries helped maintain
Gustavus's ranks. And as Ahnlund demonstrates time and again,
Sweden's king was a war captain to follow with pride. He spoke the languages of his men and was a master of soldiers' rhetoric. Powerfully built,
standing over six feet at a time when average heights were a good deal
shorter than today, Gustavus was a warrior as well as a general. In contrast to Peter and Frederick, he habitually led from the front and had a
formidable reputation in hand-to-hand combat. To fight under Gustavus
was to fight under a better man than oneself, and to draw honor from the
service. For his Swedish troops, the king became a symbol of the country, a source of myth and legend quickly taken up by the foreigners in the
ranks.

Sweden's restructured army saw its first extended service against
Poland in 1621. Gustavus's initial aim was to secure Sweden
against invasion by occupying the southern shore of the Baltic. His
appetite grew with eating. The capture of the Latvian port of Riga in
September was a harbinger of the future. The fortress had defied
Swedish efforts for years; Gustavus occupied it in a matter of weeks.
By 1626 Latvia as far as the Dvina River was in Swedish hands. In July
a Swedish army landed at Pillau, in Pomerania—farther west than
any Swedish troops had previously penetrated. By autumn the entire
Vistula watershed was under Swedish control, and Swedish firepower
and mobility were teaching the Poles expensive tactical lessons.

In 1627 Gustavus took his amphibious-warfare show to Danzig,
defeating the Poles at Dirschau but at the price of a serious wound in the
neck—another harbinger of the future. The next two years featured
small-scale campaigning in a region that at the best of times was barely
self-supporting. Both sides became correspondingly drawn toward the
larger conflict to the west: the Thirty Years' War. In June 1628, a Swedish
task force relieved the Baltic port of Stralsund, under siege by the
Imperialists. Emperor Ferdinand's men returned the favor the next year,
when a contingent of Imperialist troopers underwrote a Polish victory in
a swirling, wide-open cavalry battle southeast of Danzig.

By that time, Gustavus perceived the limits of his current strategy.
Poland was too big and too amorphous to be defeated by the blitzkrieg-
style operations at which the Swedish army excelled. The Baltic coastal
area was unable to support large-scale war for any length of time; even in

the well-disciplined Swedish army looting and brigandage were becoming problems. As much to the point, Habsburg power was moving dangerously close to a Swedish sphere of influence that was too new to be considered stable. Increasingly, Gustavus turned his thoughts toward intervention in a war that had reached, if not his strategic doorstep, at least his front yard. The Protestants of northern Germany were appealing to him as a deliverer from an Imperial hand that grew heavier as opposition waned. The stinging defeat of Denmark by the army of Albrecht von Wallenstein in 1629 was the final step in opening a window of opportunity that would have tempted a far more cautious man than Gustavus Adolphus. In June 1630, he landed in Pomerania at the head of 14,000 men.

Contemporaries and historians made much of the religious aspects of Swedish intervention. Ahnlund shows geopolitics as well as piety shaped the king's decision. Intervention in Germany provided a chance to establish a network of allies and clients as buffers against both Polish and Habsburg hostility. The German princes, however, were wary of committing themselves to the kind of war the Swedish king had a reputation for fighting. Not until August 1631 did Gustavus feel strong enough to advance south into Saxony. Even then, he understood that he was on trial, expected to deliver a major victory before he could expect systematic support from his Protestant coreligionists. Looking for a fight, he found it on September 7 near the Saxon town of Breitenfeld. Gustavus had 24,000 men, the pick of his own forces, and 18,000 Saxons haphazardly recruited, trained, and armed, against a veteran Imperial army of about 35,000. The Saxons fled the field at the first shock. The Swedes rallied to protect their suddenly exposed flank, shot to pieces successive Imperial charges, then mounted a series of counterattacks that broke the Imperial flanks and the Imperial army.

At the cost of only 2,000 of his own men, Gustavus accounted for as many as 20,000 Imperialist casualties and provided a battlefield seminar in the use of firepower and flexibility. He followed up his victory by taking the war to the empire's heartland, driving southwest to the Rhine, picking up recruits and subsidies as he went. For the campaign of 1632, the king planned to raise over 200,000 men, organized in no fewer than seven armies, for a coordinated assault against the Habsburg Empire and its Catholic supporters. As it turned out, he came nowhere near those numbers—not least because his own German allies were reluctant to see this northern stranger become too strong. Consequently, Gustavus began once again seeking a decisive, winner-take-all battle. After a frustrating prelude of skirmishes and sieges, costing men, supplies, and time he could ill afford to lose, the king thrust into Saxony once more, in pursuit of an Imperial army whose commander, Albrecht von Wallenstein, was by now no less anxious for battle than Gustavus himself.

The armies that met at Lützen on November 6 counted about 19,000 men apiece. The Imperialists had learned something from past experience. Their tactical organizations were more flexible, their firepower greater, than at Breitenfeld. The Swedish army for its part was worn from campaigning and casualties, its regiments not quite what they had been a year earlier. Add to that the fog that enveloped the field in the engagement's crucial hours, and Lützen's results were in good part consequences of chance. The Swedes eked out a victory but lost a third of their force—and their king, who on this day led one charge too many and was pistolled from his saddle by an Austrian cuirassier.

The death of Gustavus did not remove Sweden from the war. It broke, however, the mainspring of the Protestant alliance. It led as well to the control of Swedish politics by epigoni: Oxenstierna at home, Marshal Gustav Horn and Swedish client prince Bernhard of Saxe-Weimar in Germany. The next sixteen years of broken-backed fighting left Sweden in possession of enough German territory to make it a western European power and secure its Baltic hegemony. These successes were, however, achieved at a financial cost that forced the increased sale of crown lands and sparked an exponential growth in taxation. Both policies eroded the royal authority so assiduously cultivated by Gustavus. Both encouraged the continuation of an aggressive foreign policy in an effort to recoup losses. In 1654, only six years after the Treaty of Westphalia, Gustavus's successor, Charles (Karl) X, began a new round of wars with Poland and Denmark. The resulting "imperial overstretch" brought Sweden to the edge of collapse within a century, clearing the stage for younger powers: first Russia, then Prussia.

Whether Gustavus would have followed other, more prudent courses had he survived remains unanswerable. What is certain is that his achievements set a stamp upon his state and his age. They established matrices that shaped the behavior of both Peter of Russia and Frederick of Prussia. Ahnlund has a fitting last word: "No one who honestly recognizes the importance of the personal factor in history, and the creative force of the human will, can ever remain indifferent" to Gustavus Adolphus, king of Sweden from 1611 to 1632.

INTRODUCTION

INTRODUCTION

I N THE Roslagen district of Uppland, along that Baltic coast
of Sweden from which long ago the Viking fleets set out
upon their expeditions to the east, there flourished about the
middle of the fourteenth century three noble families. They were
all branches of the same line, and must probably have been
closely related to one another, for they all used the same coat of
arms—a faggot or fascine; in Swedish, *vase*. Only one of these
lines was destined to survive the Middle Ages and rise to a position of importance. A series of outstanding personalities among
its members won for the family a distinguished position amidst
the magnates of the country. Among the nobility, and in the
council of the king, they filled offices of honor and dignity; they
were given the wardship of important castles in fee; and thus
they came to play a vigorous part in the troubled politics of the
kingdom.

It will be recalled that this was a period of crisis in Sweden's
history, a period made notable by the struggle for the abolition, or
the maintenance, of the Union of Kalmar. In this struggle the
Vasas played no small part, though they did not invariably take
the same side. One prominent leader of the family, the old High
Steward Christiern Nilsson, was famous as an upholder of the
Swedish-Danish union, and in this capacity he had to suffer much
tribulation before his death in 1442, despite the calculating caution which had always marked his proceedings. In the stormy
period that followed, one of his descendants, Bishop Kettil Karlsson, proved himself a valiant popular leader, with a decided gift
for rallying the peasantry to his side. He ended his days (in 1465)
as regent of Sweden. In subsequent years the Vasas moved gradually over into the camp of the national opposition. During the
whole of the long period towards the end of the fifteenth century
when, with only short interludes, regents of the Sture family ruled
Sweden in practical independence of Denmark, the influence of
the Vasas persisted, though on a diminished scale. Many of them
gave evidence of a passion, a lack of self-control, and unbridled
violence, which provoked the anger of their contemporaries. It is

interesting to observe these characteristics, for they display even at this early date the typical temperamental inheritance of the family. Erik Johansson, Lord of Rydboholm in the Roslagen, and a faithful adherent of the Stures, seems to have been notorious for his irritable and arbitrary temper. He too was a descendant of old Sir Christiern, and from his marriage with Cecilia Månsdotter sprang Gustav Eriksson Vasa, destined to become king of Sweden.

Erik Johansson paid dearly for his loyalty to the house of Sture and his support of independence, for he was one of the many victims of that atrocity which is known to history as the "Blood-Bath of Stockholm" (November 1520). It was by means such as these that Christian II, the Oldenburger king of Denmark, sought to secure his sovereignty and the continued existence of the Union, upon his reconquest of the country after the death of Sten Sture the Younger; and this despite the fact that Sweden had already paid him homage and crowned him king. It was in these dark days, when terror paralyzed the energies of the nation, that Gustav Eriksson took up his work. That work was not to be completed until Sweden was freed, and a new dynasty had been founded by the Vasa family, whose youngest representative he was. There followed a series of events which recall, in their breath-taking rapidity, the Old Norse sagas, and which in popular remembrance are undoubtedly the best-known episodes in Swedish history. The memory of these things was handed down from generation to generation, and made to live again by ever new touches of color: as when it was told how the young noble, scarce escaped from the hands of his foes, turned to the country of the warlike Dalesmen and there unfurled his standard; how he was at first received with suspicion, and only recalled when he had already made his way on skis to the mountains of Norway; how he raised a revolt which swept irresistibly over the country, until on Midsummer Day 1523 Stockholm herself opened her gates—only a few weeks after Gustav had been crowned king of Sweden in the old cathedral of Strängnäs. No doubt it is possible to explain the success of an enterprise, which had at first appeared so desperate, by reference to a fortunate combination of external circumstances; but it is impossible not to do justice to the fiery will, the iron fortitude, the passionate defiance by which a single

man—he was really scarcely more than a boy—achieved the victory
of his people. And this time the victory was enduring. Upon the
great question of national independence there could be no reversal of that verdict.

Yet for Gustav Vasa the day of peace and tranquillity had not
yet dawned. The final victory could only be won after repeated
struggles for power, now against men of his own nation, the
obstinate Dalesmen, now against foreign influences such as that
of Lübeck, his former ally. For two decades the new kingdom
seemed a mere provisional arrangement. Counsellors and admin-
istrators changed and changed again; friends and blood-relations
turned to enemies. From many quarters bitter accusations of
treachery were hurled at Gustav, and he in his turn lamented the
falseness of the world and the incapacity of his servants. But
through all changes and chances the king remained immutable,
and more and more his position came to be uncontested and
incontestable.

The solemn act by which in 1544 the Estates substituted a
hereditary monarchy for the elective kingship of the Middle Ages
initiated a period of less disturbed rule, though the authority
of the monarch showed no signs of relaxing. It was now that the
Reformation, which had been introduced into Sweden in 1527,
really began to strike root in the country. Stockholm had early
embraced the new doctrines, but now they began to gain ground
among the general mass of the population. Gustav, having overset
the medieval ecclesiastical régime and enriched the Crown with
the spoils of the spirituality, would have preferred to convert the
Swedish church into a State church on German lines; but national
idiosyncrasies, especially in regard to the form of service, were
still too vigorous for such a solution to be possible, and some
years were yet to elapse before the purely Lutheran character
of the new confession became clear. Besides, Sweden's relations
to the outside world—whether ecclesiastical or secular—were in
general remarkably limited, being of a purely occasional and
unrepresentative kind. The country still lay on the extreme edge
of the inhabited world, and this remoteness grew rapidly more
pronounced after the fall of the Catholic Church had removed
one of the links that bound her to Europe. To the end of his days

the king retained the outlook of a well-to-do member of the rural aristocracy; and in the rest of Europe he was usually regarded as a sort of Northern Hospodar, rich in landed property and lovely daughters. (It must be confessed that the latter were a source of a good deal of vexation to him—but that is a matter irrelevant to our story.)

In his foreign policy Gustav was decidedly cautious and un-enterprising, and not in the least disposed to give rein to his imagination, or dabble in daring combinations. For years he viewed the policy of the German emperor with a suspicion which was largely explicable by the fact that Christian II was a near relative of Charles V. On the other hand, he also held himself aloof as a rule from the evangelical princes. A Swedish-French treaty of alliance remained barren of tangible results. With Denmark Gustav was able to come to an understanding after Christian II had been deposed, and a new branch of the house of Oldenburg put in his place; though towards the end of his reign the horizon in this quarter was again clouding over. It should be borne in mind that Denmark-Norway at that time still included those parts of south and west Sweden as well as those provinces in the north which were first incorporated into the kingdom in 1645 and 1658. In the last year of Gustav's life the country encountered Muscovite aggression on the eastern frontier of Finland. And though on this occasion the struggle turned out to be of only short duration, the collapse of the Crusading Orders was soon to give rise to a long-drawn-out war between Sweden and Russia.

Popular tradition loves to envisage Gustav as he was in his later years, when the wise old ruler could look back from the calm evening of his days over the long and arduous labors that had filled his life. The broadly charitable outlook to which posterity is always prone softens the harsh colors of his picture and obscures the stormy passions that permeated his political career. He survives as the faithful steward of the kingdom, hoarding bar upon bar of silver in his royal treasury; as the keen-eyed warder who never misses a detail, and who enforces his will in great things and small by means of a mountainous correspondence which reaches to every province of the land. It is not easy to sum up in a phrase the system of government of which King Gustav—

and his sons too, in the main—were the representatives. The closest approximation to the truth is probably to be found in some such phrase as that Gustav's rule was a patriarchal absolutism based firmly upon ancient constitutionalist principles.

Under his successor Erik XIV, the son of Gustav's first marriage with Katarina of Saxe-Lauenburg, Sweden came at a bound into closer relations with Europe proper. Her policy simultaneously took on a bolder and more enterprising aspect which accorded well with the character and inclinations of her ruler. The Renaissance, which at the close of the Middle Ages had found isolated evangelists among the prelates and magnates of Sweden, now swept over the country, and found its chief expression in a court life upon a scale hitherto unprecedented in Sweden; for Sweden was a land of peasants, and her population, excluding Finland, was at this time estimated at about 850,000. Erik's short reign is an act of tense excitement in the drama of Swedish history. Sweden took her first step, a step fraught with consequences for the future, on the road to an active Baltic policy. The occupation of Reval and of some of the lands of the Livonian Knights of the Sword involved her in her historic contest with Poland. Erik was undoubtedly a statesman of wide vision, and even the more curious manifestations of his policy, as for instance his numerous attempts to obtain the hand of a foreign princess, become explicable if they are considered as links in a chain of efforts which the king made to put an end to the isolated situation of his country. In the end he married Karin Månsdotter, a young woman of humble birth whom he really loved. Most of his reign was passed in embittered fighting against Denmark. Otherwise his rule was notable for violent struggles with the nobility of the kingdom, on the one hand, and with his brother Johan on the other.

Erik considered it to be his life-work to secure the hereditary character of the monarchy and the unity of the kingdom. He chose his most intimate advisers and tools from the lower classes. For the historian who seeks to do justice to his memory it is no easy task to separate the spaciousness of his plans from the ill-considered means he so often employed to carry them out. It is, moreover, impossible to ignore the undeniable evidences of a diseased mind shown by some of his actions as king; his intelligence, clouded over from time to time, sank at last into the darkness of insanity. The treatment he suffered during his long captivity, after he had lost both crown and freedom, may have contributed to his mental disorder. He fell a victim to a popular revolt, provoked by his half-brothers Johan and Karl, and supported by the aristocracy. Richly endowed with good qualities, and even with artistic gifts, Erik appears as a kind of prototype of the aspiring and unfortunate prince, in whom certain traits characteristic of the Vasas had been allowed to develop unchecked.

The fact that the two dukes Johan and Karl—like all Gustav's children except Erik—were closely connected by blood with the leading families in the country, was certainly not without influence on the close collaboration between the princes and the nobility at the time of the revolt of 1568. Karl (b. 1550), who at that time was still a mere youth, was kept by his elder brother in the background, but his sturdily independent spirit soon emancipated itself from tutelage. Historical tradition is only too inclined to consider Karl's destiny as clear and settled from the start—a point of view which is the result of limiting observation to the external course of events. Actually, it was Karl, the youngest of the brothers, whom Fate designed to be the defender of the paternal inheritance and of the national monarchy. In this connection it should, however, be borne in mind that as duke of Södermanland, in the course of his disputes with his royal brother, Karl was quite capable of defending—or attempting to defend—the territorial separatism of the princedoms in complete disregard of the natural interests of national unity. The long-drawn conflict between the king and the princes, which now flared up again, runs through the history of Johan III. It presents us, moreover, with the picture of an aristocracy which had a pretty clear idea of its functions, and which, as appointed guardian of the unity and indivisibility of the kingdom, believed that its proper position was at the side of the throne. And the Swedish nobility at this period could already count many dignitaries cast in an ampler European mould— men of character and talent, well versed in the art and science of their day; men such as Erik Sparre, Hogenskild Bielke, and others. In such counsellors the vacillating King Johan found a firm support in the unceasing fight for his rights which he was forced to wage with Duke Karl. But they showed themselves equally ready to resist if Johan attempted to extend his royal sovereignty beyond those limits which they had set as the boundaries of their inherited rights—rights which they were concerned to place upon a secure footing.

It is no matter for surprise that this generation of the greater nobility should have anticipated their descendants in the idea of a division of powers in a constitutional sense. The strongest influence upon their political theories had, however, been received through the free interchange of ideas in the course of their tours overseas, though they had linked the conceptions which they had then formed with the traditions of their own people. All the sons of Gustav I were possessed by the constant fear that the nobility might one day free itself from the obligations it had assumed when it consented to the establishment of the hereditary monarchy, and might attempt to restore the practice of free election to the throne, with all the possibilities of legal limitation which that would involve. And so it happened that when in 1589 Johan came to a decisive breach with his Råd (Council), king and duke joined forces without delay to form a common front.

On the other hand, it was mainly round the person of Karl that the opposition gathered in its fight against Johan III's ecclesiastical policy. That policy, which was the clearest expression of his character, and especially of his markedly esthetic tastes, inclined perceptibly towards Catholicism. In questions of doctrine he observed a certain caution, and he was always careful to base his course in some sort upon the feelings of the people, but he was nevertheless heading straight for Rome. Simultaneously Johan's political adventures were drawing him into the orbit of Spanish influence. The last ten years of his life were marked by a constant alternation of withdrawal from and approach to this quarter, though no irrevocable step was ever hazarded. To the alarm of the strict Lutherans, Johan obstinately persisted in his efforts for a revision of the church service, and he never seems to have felt himself in any true sense a member of the Protestant community. His brother Karl was in these respects his exact opposite; he too was in a theological sense inclined to irenist opinions, but with him, in view of his strong Calvinistic tendencies, they operated in a precisely contrary direction. It was only later, however, that this aspect of his theology aroused the attention of the zealots for the church, since at this time it seemed probable that without the support of the duke they might find themselves the victims of the Romish practices of his royal brother. In all these questions the interest of the nobility was distinctly tepid.

The marriage of King Johan with Katarina Jagiellonica, the daughter of Sigismund I of Poland, was to prove of fateful import. In Erik XIV's time Katarina had shared her husband's long imprisonment in Gripsholm Castle, and it was in Gripsholm that their son, Sigismund, was born. A fervent Catholic, she remained a stranger to most of her subjects, although in the country districts many still clung to the old faith. The ancient monastery of Vadstena, for instance—a foundation of St. Birgitta—still survived, though only the shadow of its former greatness now remained. From all that we know of her, Queen Katarina possessed a stronger and more purposeful will than her lord and master. The heir to the throne, Sigismund, was educated in her faith, without consideration for the obvious danger to his position in Sweden which this involved. And in Sigismund, the true son of his mother, the Catholic faith struck deep roots. In reality the religious question was decided by the prospect that one day the Polish throne might fall to the Vasas. Katarina's death (1583) seems to have had a tempering effect on Johan's leaning to Catholicism, but to Sigismund it appeared as true as ever that the appointed road to his goal lay through Rome. After an embittered contest with other candidates Sigismund was elected king of Poland in 1587, and the respective territorial claims of Poland and Sweden, which had been brought forward at the time of the election, were thereby compromised in a most ambiguous fashion. It was not long before Sigismund, daunted by the difficulties which beset him in Poland, began to wish to abandon his new kingdom.

The curt refusal of the Swedish Råd to comply with his father's wishes and sanction Sigismund's return to Sweden caused in 1589 the breach, which had long been impending, to become open, and cleared the way for the influence of Duke Karl. There followed a hot persecution of the magnates of the country, a persecution highly characteristic both of the violence and of the indecision of Johan's nature. The king had now, by his marriage with a woman of the high nobility, Gunilla Bielke, another son—that Johan of Östergötland who was to play a part in the history of Gustav Adolf. The treaty with Poland, however, remained in force in spite of all the king's efforts to the contrary, and after Johan's death it was to become a reality. Soon afterwards, in 1592, he died.

The most important event in the time following Johan III's death was the Church Assembly at Uppsala in 1593, the results of which were not limited by their effect on Sweden and Finland. The Assembly was an impressive proclamation of the restoration of doctrinal unity, which now at last was realized in the form of the uncontested domination of the pure Lutheran confession. It was at Uppsala that the Swedish Reformation reached its conclusion and received its characteristic imprint, in a form which, outlasting the centuries and defying the ravages of time, is still clearly perceptible in the mental attitude of the people. Duke Karl took a leading part in the work of the Assembly, though in matters of dogma he kept to a certain extent in the background. This synod marked also the beginning of what we may call the golden age of the spiritual Estate, which henceforward was to remain for many years one of the most important driving forces in the nation.

All these events took place while the young king was absent in his other kingdom, Poland. Sigismund's protests went unheeded, and when soon after he made his entry into Stockholm in order to make good his claim to the full control of his inheritance, he found his hands tied. He was accompanied by the papal nuncio, Malaspina, who was burning with zeal to prepare the way for the redemption of the country from schism. Sigismund himself was too well acquainted with the situation not to be a good deal more moderate, but he was resolved to do everything in his power to protect the freedom of his own church and its adherents on Swedish soil. In the long and bitter strife which now began, the king, in form at any rate, stood for liberty of conscience against the demands of a ruthless totalitarianism which stuck at nothing in its attacks. Objection was even made to the king's using his own chapel during his residence in Sweden. The national league, which had been joined by the duke, the Råd, and all the Estates, would not yield an inch. At the stormy coronation Riksdag in Uppsala, Sigismund was compelled, after the most desperate resistance, to give way, and to reinforce his renunciation with a solemn declaration which was tantamount to an irrevocable Charter.

In order to quiet his conscience he communicated a secret assurance to the Roman curia. He soon showed, moreover, an alarming tendency to a very free interpretation of the Charter which had been extracted from him before his coronation, and which was generally considered by the Swedes as an unalterable fundamental law. It seems, however, that this attitude on the king's part was not the direct cause of that renewal of the struggle which now took place. The immediate cause lay rather in the obscurity of the arrangements for the division of powers between the organs of government during the king's absence. There were clashes which Sigismund, in the interests of his sovereign control, deliberately sought to provoke. He did in fact appoint lords lieutenant to the provinces, without consultation with the central government in Stockholm (which consisted of Duke Karl and the Råd), and these lords lieutenant were directly subject to his orders. The result was serious friction, especially between the duke and the lord lieutenant of Finland, Klas Fleming, who considered himself as in reality viceroy of that vast country. A division of the kingdom into two halves seemed well within the bounds of possibility.

Duke Karl of Södermanland was a man of forty-four when his marriage with Kristina of Holstein was blessed with a son, and his dearest wish thus fulfilled. Of the children of his first marriage with Maria of the Palatinate all, except a daughter, Katarina, had died in early childhood. In his memorandum-book the duke noted: "In the year 1594, on December 9, my son Gustav Adolf was born in Stockholm Castle. God the Almighty grant that he may live his life with praise, glory, and honor, and to the satisfaction and joy of his parents. He was born between 7 and 8 o'clock in the morning." As chance would have it, his parents were at that time staying in the capital, and not in Nyköping which for the past decade had been the seat of the duchy.

That duchy Karl had defended with the stoutest determination when King Johan and the Råd had sought to curtail his ducal rights. But now he rose quickly to the measure of his new position as guardian of the threatened unity of the realm. His collaboration with the great nobles of the Råd—men such as Erik Sparre and Hogenskild Bielke—had for some time been marred by distrust. It will thus easily be realized that in these circumstances the joint government which Sigismund had set up was subjected to a severe strain. At first, indeed, it seemed that they would be able to work hand in hand, and Gustav's baptism was the occasion for a friendly, indeed almost cordial reunion of Karl and the Råd. What made the situation intolerable in the long run was, in the first place, Sigismund's continued endeavor to split up the local government among as many authorities as possible, and in the second Karl's insistent demand for a real primacy in the government appointed by the king. This government he sought to raise to the position of a real central administration subordinate only to the king, and dealing directly with him. In the course of the disputes which at once arose, Karl was able to overcome opposition in a manner which was to a large extent consonant with the historic character of the Vasa monarchy, for he appealed to the Estates, and from them received the plenary powers he required. He summoned a general Riksdag to Söderköping for the autumn of 1595 without having received Sigismund's leave to do so. The Råd members followed him hesitatingly and half unwillingly. Under the duke's determined leadership the lower Estates—peasants and burghers—now clearly began to assume an increased importance. This Riksdag at Söderköping, which Sigismund declared to be illegal, raised Karl to the dignity of regent for the period of Sigismund's absence, with the obligation to collaborate with the Råd under legally determined forms. Under an appearance of fidelity to the throne it was now hoped to be able to proceed against the "unruly and rebellious members"— which meant, in reality, against the king's lord lieutenants.

Finland was the first object of attention. But Klas Fleming, a rough but faithful servant of the old type, did not yield to their threats. His hand fell heavily on the Finnish peasants, who set their hope upon the duke as a known friend to the people. In north Finland it came in the end to an armed rising of the peasantry, the famous Club War of 1597, which was bloodily suppressed.

The paths of the duke and the Råd had by this time already diverged. When he demanded armed action against "rebellious" Finland, they refused to accompany him, for they believed that such measures must inevitably lead to civil war. Nor would they come to the Arboga Riksdag in the spring of 1597, at which the duke, supported by the "grizzled multitude" of the lower Estates, again carried his proposals. This Riksdag had been summoned in defiance of the express prohibition of the king and the flat refusal of the Råd to attend, and it was undoubtedly a breach of the custom of the constitution in regard to the proper method of cooperation between government and people. The whole country was in the grip of a powerful agitation. The disunion was great, not only as between the several Estates, but also among their members; not only as between one province and another, but also within the individual provinces. On the whole, the Swedish peasantry made common cause with Duke Karl. Above all the Dalesmen came down decidedly on his side. New negotiations were now begun, but without success. Riksdags and other assemblies followed in continuous succession. The duke-regent appeared surrounded by his adherents, exhorted them to hold together, constantly encouraged them, and sometimes deliberately incited them, but he invariably took care to emphasize that no one was desirous of depriving the king of his constitutional rights. It was, however, precisely upon this point that the split occurred. Even after the majority of the Råd had fled to Poland, Karl was repeatedly encountering resistance which it was not easy to break down. And he never succeeded at this time in making himself undisputed master of Finland, where the royalists held out for several years.

In 1598 came the decisive struggle. When at last Sigismund returned to Sweden, he appeared at the head of a foreign army of some considerable size. He landed in Småland, and a considerable proportion of the nobility of the southern provinces flocked to his standard. At first, too, the fortunes of war favored him rather than his uncle, but soon his feeble generalship destroyed his chance of a quick victory. The battle of Stångebro (near Linköping) was a defeat which cost him the throne of Sweden. True, the capitulation which he was made to sign contained no renunciation of the crown; but it did have the inevitable result of forcing him to abandon his Swedish partisans, above all the returned members of the Råd, who were now handed over to Karl's keeping. It was agreed that at the approaching Riksdag the whole quarrel should be submitted for arbitration. There could be no doubt what the result would be. Rightly interpreting the situation, Sigismund preferred to sail for Poland soon afterwards. Great numbers of his friends, especially of the nobility, hastened to leave the country; we shall meet many of them later in Poland. A year later (1599) the Swedes formally deposed Sigismund, though it was left open to his eldest son Wladislaw to return to the kingdom within a limited time, and eventually to assume the crown. No answer was ever returned to this proposal. Sigismund continued to regard himself as *de jure* king and regent of Sweden —and, what was more important, a large proportion of the European powers shared his opinion.

If a terminal point must be fixed for this fateful drama, the most appropriate place would certainly be the Linköping Riksdag of 1600. Erik Sparre, Gustav Banér, and two other nobles went to the scaffold upon a judgment of the Estates which has found scarcely a single defender among later historians. Of such stuff was Gustav Adolf's father. Yet his inflexible determination was not his only characteristic. It was equally typical of the man that he should have hesitated so long to assume the crown. In a later chapter an attempt will be made to delineate his character more at length, in connection with the circumstances in which his son grew up. Not only is Karl IX the principal figure in the first portion of Gustav Adolf's history, but his deeds are also the necessary prelude to his son's achievements. Hence the tension which gives a special character to Sweden's history in the following years. The Swedish-Polish war, which broke out in 1600 and was not formally ended for another sixty years, is only one element, though an important one, in the evolution of the kingdom, and it takes second place to the fundamentally significant dynastic rivalry within the Vasa house. This rivalry is, in its political and religious effects, the animating force behind all these events. That this is particularly true for the age of Karl IX, is only natural; but we shall soon see that the uncertain situation it created gives us in many respects a key to the understanding of the history of Gustav Adolf, especially in its opening period, when the lines of his statecraft were laid down. In the words which begin the inscription on his tomb in the Riddarholm church in Stockholm, *in angustis intravit.*

THE WAY TO THE THRONE

GUSTAV ADOLF
THE GREAT

THE WAY TO THE THRONE

[1]

IT was the beginning of October 1595, and Duke Karl of Södermanland was setting out from Nyköping, his town of residence, with a cavalry escort of some five hundred men. His way lay over rough roads, southwards towards the heights of Kolmården. The cavalcade no doubt included a number of "women's carriages," for his Duchess Kristina accompanied him, and with her went her first-born, a little fair-haired lad scarcely ten months old, who was, perhaps, just taking his first steps at this time. The accounting clerk who made daily notes of the ducal expenses refers to him respectfully as "my gracious lord, Duke Gostavus Adolphus." On their way they stopped at the royal manor of Skenäs, on the southern shore of Bråviken; and on Saturday, October 4, they reached their journey's end. This was Söderköping, at that date one of the most considerable market towns in the kingdom, and just then presenting a more animated appearance than usual. For it was at Söderköping that the duke and the Råd had appointed the Estates of the kingdom to meet, to devise remedies for the disturbances which had upset the even tenor of government during the absence of King Sigismund in Poland.

It is tempting to see a symbolic significance in Gustav Adolf's presence in Söderköping during those autumn weeks when the national Regency was once again established and the fundamental conditions laid down for the political struggle with which his life and work were to be concerned. But at that early and peaceful age he was scarcely likely to have had any inkling of these events which were to be so decisive for himself, or to have retained any memory of this his first visit to the little Östergötland town; and we, who derive from these old accounts the knowledge that his parents had a new cradle made for the "young lord" in Söder-köping, are presumably better informed upon that point than he was himself. Among those who may have bent over that simple cradle—it cost one daler—we think especially of the chancellor, Erik Sparre; for at the beginning of the new year he had been honored by an invitation to stand godfather to the boy. At the Söderköping Riksdag[1] of 1595 Sparre was still one of Karl's ad-herents, though with inward misgivings. This brilliant noble, the ornament and intellectual leader of the Råd families, did more than anyone on this occasion (Duke Karl himself excepted) to preserve that unity to which the Riksdag's resolution bears wit-ness, at a moment when internal divisions were threatening.

It seems doubtful whether he ever saw his godson again; for the breach was soon complete between the duke-regent and the increasingly suspicious Råd party. With Erik Sparre at their head, the lords refused to defy the veto of their absent king by attend-ing the Riksdag which, upon his own responsibility, the duke summoned to Arboga early in 1597—a Riksdag which formed the prelude to a period of revolution in which all regard for the constitution was thrown overboard. At this Riksdag, as at the preceding one, Karl was accompanied by his wife: it is not re-corded whether this time Gustav Adolf was allowed to go with them. But it is certain that the duke's family viewed only from a distance the events which succeeded it, and which led to Sigis-mund's defeat at Stångebro in 1598, and to the great judicial massacre of Linköping in 1600—of which the foremost victim was Sparre himself.

Contemporaries were generally inclined to fix much of the re-sponsibility for the ruthlessness which characterized Duke Karl's proceedings upon his wife, Kristina of Holstein. The writers of the defeated party hurled invective against her with unmeasured bitterness. They were in the habit of likening her to Jezebel, the Queen of Ahab, the Princess of Sidon, who by false witness com-

---

[1] Riksdag, a meeting of the Estates. A parliament. The Riksdag was held some-times in one city, sometimes in another.

passed the condemnation of Naboth. This odious comparison was in itself a hint of their belief in the certainty of imminent misfortune for the whole of Karl's family, according to the word of the prophet Elijah: "Behold, I will bring evil upon thee, and will take away thy posterity, and I will cut off all the sons of the house of Ahab."[2] Lampoons made free use of the Biblical *motif* in their appeals to the Almighty:

> *May Jezebel never present him with twins*
> *To follow their parents and rival their sins!*

If the passionate hatred behind such attacks provides some measure by which to estimate their validity, it is on the other hand a well established fact that Kristina was by many considered to be the help and stay of her husband. The world was prompt enough to expect intercessions and appeals for clemency from a woman in her position. What she did or left undone in this respect no man now can say. But what we do know of her attitude during these dark years of strife does not give us the impression that she was as heartless as hostile pamphleteers would have us believe. For instance, when the forlorn wife of Gustav Banér (a member of the Råd) was brought to bed of a son during her husband's last imprisonment, Kristina took her under her care, and offered to stand godmother to the child—actions which won the warm commendation of a contemporary family chronicler, though as a rule this author writes in language of burning indignation. It is difficult, then, to avoid the suspicion that those who judged Kristina so hardly were not acquainted with her real disposition. But she was always more stable temperamentally than the majority of women, and less susceptible to gusts of sentimentality. She demanded submission before she showed herself gracious. Axel Oxenstierna's remark, in his memorial oration over her, that she set herself against the proud, but spared and protected the humble, gives us an insight into her true character. And her relations with her eldest son were to bear emphatic witness to her unsentimental nature.

There was a rumor current that Kristina harbored a purely personal grudge against King Sigismund, and was anxious to

[2] 1 Kings xxi. 21.

avenge a humiliation to which he had once subjected her. The story went that he had courted this princess of Holstein when she was still a mere girl, and had reached the stage of sending her presents in token of his troth, before the affair was finally broken off at his instigation. The tale is substantially true. When Prince Sigismund was chosen king of Poland in 1587 (by which time Kristina had reached the age of fourteen) he was still to all intents and purposes betrothed to her. The match was viewed with favor by Sigismund's sister, Princess Anna, and by his aunt, Elisabeth of Mecklenburg; and from the Swedish point of view it appeared eminently desirable, since the girl was a good Protestant, and was, besides, cousin to the reigning king of Denmark. But the former of these reasons became of dubious validity after Sigismund ascended the throne of Poland. Nevertheless, in spite of his strong Catholic convictions, Sigismund seems for a time to have felt some hesitation about retracting his promise; no doubt the uncertainty of the position in Poland had its influence upon him. It is thus understandable that the pride and patience of Kristina should have been sorely tried. Several years passed; Sigismund, still uncertain of his crown, made advances to the house of Habsburg, with which his relations had hitherto been unfriendly. His marriage with the Archduchess Anna, which was celebrated in the spring of 1592, signified a not inconsiderable success for the policy of the Papacy. But Kristina was not far behind him in entering the haven of matrimony. In the late summer of the same year she knelt before the altar with the duke of Södermanland, then a widower of three years' standing.

Johan III was informed that the now despised fiancée of his son had "neither wit nor beauty." The judgment stands in irreconcilable opposition to the opinion of Axel Oxenstierna that she was "in her person fair and of good stature, in her mind and spirit lofty and noble." Her father, Duke Adolf of Holstein-Gottorp, the founder of one of the most famous dynasties in the history of the North, had made a name for himself as a valiant prince and a patron of the arts. He was a man whose restlessness abated only with old age; a Nordic type of the Renaissance man, full of the joy of living, with a strong taste for the beautiful, but with no very firm convictions in matters of religion. From her mother's family, on the other hand, Kristina had inherited a strong tradition of the theological seriousness of the Reformation era; indeed, the estimable and upright duchess whose name she bore was herself the daughter of Philipp the Magnanimous of Hesse, who had been the friend of Luther and Melancthon.

Such an ancestry necessarily exerted a powerful influence upon Karl and his young wife. Hesse stood in the forefront of that wing of German Protestantism to which Karl early felt himself inclining—the group which may be called the party of action, whose distinguishing feature in history was perhaps its vacillation between the Lutheran and Reformed Confessions. Prominent in its ranks was the Palatinate house, from which Karl had taken his first wife Maria—herself a granddaughter of Landgraf Philipp. Already, then, Karl's ecclesiastical politics were friendly towards the Palatinate of Hesse. At this period each of these States was governed, sometimes by Lutheran, sometimes by Calvinist princes; though in both—first at Heidelberg, afterwards at Kassel—Calvinism ultimately obtained the upper hand.

It was not long before Karl's Swedish contemporaries suspected him of entertaining purely Calvinistic doctrines—an insidious and dangerous accusation in an age when many Lutherans found the road to Rome shorter than the road to Geneva. Karl kept his own counsel as to his religious views, but his standpoint seems to have been not so much that of Calvinism as the expression of a theology which aimed at a general reconciliation between Protestants, while discriminating sharply against all forms of popery. If he were really a Calvinist, he remarked on one occasion, his "princely self-respect" would compel him to avow it. Nevertheless, he always stood rather nearer to Calvin than to Luther. It was therefore all the more inevitable that his theological opinions should widen the breach between himself and that convinced adherent of the Counter-Reformation, his nephew Sigismund.

When, on December 9, 1594, Gustav Adolf was born in the castle at Stockholm—at that time the residence of his parents—Sigismund's marriage had not yet been blessed with an heir. Just six months afterwards there was born in Cracow a Prince, Wladislaw. The succession in both lines seemed secure; and between these two almost contemporary scions of the house of Vasa there stood also—in virtue of the Succession Agreement—Sigismund's half-brother Duke Johan, who at the time of Wladislaw's birth was six months old. Karl had on numerous occasions solemnly disavowed any intention of deviating from the Succession Agreement, and he continued to manifest scruples in this respect even after Sigismund's deposition. Fundamentally—despite his resort to revolution—he was a legitimist *pur sang,* above all where the house of Vasa was concerned. He stood stiffly upon his own rights as hereditary prince. Yet it is scarcely to be wondered at if the doubtful prospects which lay ahead should have awakened in him and his wife the hope that their eldest son might one day be destined to ascend the throne of Sweden.

At all events it is clear that the duke took it hardly when in the summer of 1595 he received the news of Wladislaw's birth. A form of Thanksgiving was drawn up by Erik Sparre and handed over by him to the archbishop to be read from the pulpit. The duke demanded the return of the paper. The original form of Thanksgiving had contained a prayer that the prince might grow up to be a blessing to his land and people "and especially to the Kingdom of Sweden." Karl resolutely struck out the last clause, but ostentatiously added a sentence—obviously under the influence of conflicting feelings—concerning the prince's education in the pure evangelical faith. The episode, which is well attested from a contemporary source, throws a flash of light upon his secret thoughts.

When Sigismund was deposed, Karl and the Riksdag (which was wholly under his control)[3] offered to receive young Wladislaw into Sweden. It was a scheme that had grown up gradually in Karl's mind during the preceding years of conflict—it can be traced back to the months after the Arboga Riksdag, a full year before Sigismund's disastrous campaign. What the duke wanted for himself was, quite simply, the control of the kingdom, not the title of king. As it was his intention that the prince of Sweden and Poland should be given full regal powers only when he had reached the age of twenty-four, he was in reality reserving to

[3] At Stockholm, July 1599.

himself the direction of affairs for the rest of his lifetime. Even after Sigismund had made it clear that he considered that this was too high a price to pay for the retention of his son's rights of succession, Karl hesitated to sever this strand in his policy.

At the Riksdag of Linköping (1600), which completed the revolution and laid the foundation of a new order, the Estates were quite prepared to place the crown upon Karl's head. They recognized Gustav Adolf, as his eldest son, to be heir to the throne in preference to Duke Johan as representative of the senior line; but in spite of this fact, the Riksdag's resolution, thanks to Karl's intervention, was framed in terms that were decidedly ambiguous. Karl could not bring himself to take a decisive step with regard either to Wladislaw or to Johan. For his part, he compared the resolution to "a knot stronger and more complicated" than any he had previously contrived. And it proved in fact to be an intricate series of knots, which had to be unravelled one by one.

Wladislaw was first eliminated. Another year or two were needed, even yet, before Karl considered him as out of the hunt. Next, the case of Duke Johan engaged his serious attention. As far as he personally was concerned, Karl was hardly ever quite ready to untie this knot. He tried at all events to avoid taking any part in a decision which would deprive his nephew of his hereditary right. Time after time he threatened to lay down the government in Johan's favor. At the Riksdag of Norrköping in 1604, which both the young dukes attended, Johan solemnly renounced all claim to the throne; but that did not prevent Karl from repeating, at several later meetings of the Riksdag, declarations of abdication which were exceedingly trying to the patience of the Estates, nor did it prevent him from drawing up a will based upon the assumption that on his death the nation would be free to choose between Johan and Gustav Adolf. His coronation, which at long last took place in 1607, practically put an end to this condition of uncertainty, although even after that the king does not seem to have laid aside all thoughts of Johan as his successor. In his heart of hearts, no doubt, he desired all the time to prepare the way for his own son. By the Succession Agreement of 1604 Gustav Adolf's right to the crown of Sweden was clearly recognized, in so far as the will of the people could affect the issue. Karl IX's nervous reservations, his inconsequence, his apparent revocations of decisions already taken, were attempts to test the solidity of his work. Perhaps, too, they were prompted by the necessity for considering European opinion.

[2]

A VERY marked trait in Karl's character—and it grew more conspicuous with the passing of the years—was his mistrust of human nature, and in particular of the faithfulness and loyalty of the Swedish people. He found confirmation for this pessimistic view everywhere: in his deep religious conviction that the world was thrall to sin; in his study of the history of his fatherland, with its many examples of swift changes of rulers; and—not least—in his experience throughout life, which he interpreted in the light of his personal prepossessions. His writings and speeches give abundant evidence of his belief in the shabby inconstancy of the world.

Karl had to the full the suspiciousness of the earlier Vasas, but in him it seems to have been blended more than in any other of his race with a defiant misanthropy. His appearance, as it is known to posterity, seems indeed to give indication of this side of his character: the face appears ravaged by the storms of life; the brows shade prominent, searching eyes which speak eloquently of their ability to flash fire. It was indeed no age to foster in a man in his conspicuous position that benevolent assurance which had always been sufficiently foreign to his nature. In the eyes of practically the whole of Europe he was at first no better than a rebel, an interloper, a usurper; and he never completely succeeded in breaking down this barrier of coolness and disapproval; even his son was made to feel its strength after he came to the throne. Karl was the more sensible of this feeling since even his closest friends in the most advanced camp of Protestantism sometimes shook their heads over his proceedings. When in 1604 he gave way to the wishes of the Swedish Estates, and brought himself to accept the crown, neither the Elector Palatine nor the Landgraf of Hesse made any secret of the fact that they considered this step to be rash and premature. His position still appeared—as in fact it was —anything but secure.

Still, it was to this group of princes that Karl looked mainly for assistance; and it was this line of policy which he inculcated into his son, as soon as the boy was old enough to get some sort of grasp of world affairs. The first act of State to which Gustav Adolf put his signature impresses us clearly as harmonizing with his father's efforts. It dates from the summer of 1602, when Gustav Adolf was in his eighth year, and it is addressed to young Friedrich, Count Palatine—later to be famous in history as the Winter King.[4] It bears small resemblance to a child's letter, being couched in the prolix and artificial style of the German chanceries: it was in the chancery, naturally, that it had its origin; but it purports, at least, to give suitable expression to the prince's sentiments for the elector, who was a boy of much the same age as himself. Gustav Adolf writes that he has heard of the elector's exceptional intellectual gifts and truly princely virtues. He would now remind him of the mutual confidence which has subsisted between their fathers, in the hope that they too may have an opportunity to cultivate equally good relations to their common advantage. For his part the writer will employ all his endeavors to follow in the footsteps of his gracious and well beloved father. Friedrich of the Palatinate replied in the same style.

Karl's connection with his German "in-laws" became for him as time went on a kind of sheet-anchor in the storm. In his will (1605) he enjoined the Elector Palatine and Landgraf Moritz to stand by his widow and children, though they were not to meddle with the internal affairs of the kingdom. He solemnly exhorted his children to cherish the bonds of friendship with these and other evangelical princes of Germany. There was about this time some discussion as to whether Gustav Adolf's elder half-sister Katarina should go to Heidelberg to complete her education. However, the idea was not followed up: the wise and tactful Katarina stayed at home, where, from all we know of her, she seems to have exerted a very gracious influence. One of King Karl's dearest plans had been that his sons and nephew should at some time stay at one of the evangelical courts on the Continent with a view to acquiring their "manners and customs."

[4] Friedrich V, *ob.* 1632, King of Bohemia 1619-1620.

But this plan too remained unrealized; and it was not until 1618 that Gustav Adolf first set foot on German soil.

His first trip across the Baltic, at midsummer 1600, took him with his parents to Estland. The expedition was an important one. Karl's task was to try to preserve for Sweden her possessions south of the Gulf of Finland, which seemed at this time to be slipping from her grasp. After signing a message to the Estates strongly urging them to take steps to counteract popish plots and to unite to maintain order in the country, the king boarded the fleet with his family. Besides Kristina, Katarina, and Gustav Adolf, he took with him on the journey Duke Johan, and one of his nieces, a princess of Mecklenburg. During their stay in the Baltic provinces, which ultimately extended to more than a year, Karl's household lived for the most part in the castle at Reval, and there in the spring of 1601 his younger son Karl Filip was born. Karl himself was away for long periods campaigning against the Poles, and he had besides much else to occupy his attention. On one occasion, when the royal family was residing in the fortress of Weissenstein (soon to be retaken by the enemy) Magnus Brahe, who managed the court's housekeeping, complained with some acerbity of the difficulty of obtaining provisions: Her Grace and the noble young princes had, alas, been "on pretty short commons." After Karl had achieved the object of his expedition, and had handed over the government of Livland to his brother-in-law Duke Johann Adolf of Holstein, he started in the late autumn upon his homeward voyage, in some perturbation at reports of the attitude of Denmark.

This autumn journey, which at first led north over the Gulf of Finland, came near to costing the duke and his family their lives. "When they came to the Finnish skerries," says a contemporary narrative written in Reval, "the ice barred their way, so that they could not make land. The prince with four ships put out to sea again; eight of the others are known to have sunk with all hands; two sloops returned three days later, having lost more than half their company—where the rest were, they knew not." During the winter the news spread through Poland that Duke Karl and his duchess, together with the young princes and princesses had all "lost their lives in Finland through suffering shipwreck on their way home to Sweden." Karl Karlsson Gyllenhielm, the duke's illegitimate son, who had recently been taken prisoner by the Poles, heard the tidings with anguish in his heart. In reality, the travellers had made land near Ekenäs on November 20 "with great danger, in a thick mist and much pack-ice," as Karl himself described it in a letter he sent off the following day. Long afterwards, Axel Oxenstierna set down the particular circumstances, as they had been described to him: "It happened that after the duke's ship came into the harbor in the evening, it froze so hard during the night that on the following afternoon he and his companions were forced to make for the shore over the ice." That year the duke and his family kept their Christmas in Åbo castle. By March 1602 they were back in Stockholm after a sledge trip round the Gulf of Bothnia, with regular halts for the night at the parsonages along the coast, which by the exchequer in Stockholm had been provided with flour and malt to facilitate the entertainment of the royal party.

[3]

IT WAS not long before Gustav Adolf began to show traits of a vigorous nature. Typical little incidents dating from the years just preceding this great excursion, and recalled in old age by his half-brother Gyllenhielm, are familiar to us all:[5] the ship with its full complement of guns, the encounter with the snakes in the meadow at Nyköping, his pleasure when a peasant from Öland presented him with a horse. . . . Courage and generosity and high aspiration reveal themselves in such of his youthful utter-

[5] Once when Gustav Adolf was about five years old he was walking with his father in a meadow near Nyköping. When he was warned not to go into the bushes, because there were adders there, he at once replied: "Give me a stick; I'll kill them!" His father smilingly asked his companion: "Did you think he would be frightened?" On another occasion at Kalmar he was shown the Swedish fleet. The boy was then asked which ship he liked best. He pointed to the *Black Knight*. When they enquired why he preferred this ship in particular, he instantly replied: "Because it has most guns."

A peasant from Öland brought the little prince one of those ponies peculiar to the island. "I shall pay you for this horse," said the prince, "for I imagine you could do with some money." At that he drew a little purse from his pocket and shook some ducats into the hands of the delighted peasant. —*Gyllenhielm's Memorials*

ances as have been preserved to us; and these were qualities which must have appealed to the most accessible side of his father's rugged nature. We can discern, too, an easy self-assurance: "Get out of the road; don't you know your betters?"

Like his daughter Kristina, Gustav Adolf early gave evidence of a rich intellectual endowment. With regard to his academic education, however, his parents do not seem to have made any attempt to force the pace of his natural development. As far as we know, it was not until they returned from Estland and Finland that they made any arrangements to keep him regularly at his studies. Thereafter he entered upon what we should call his schooldays, though he had already acquired, mainly from his mother, certain necessary rudiments. It was at her knee, for instance, that he began an acquaintance with the German language which was gradually to develop into a perfect mastery of it. He could write German before he could write Swedish, and it was, in the literal sense of the expression, his mother-tongue. In all his private communications to his mother, whether verbal or epistolary, he invariably made use of German; but for official business they addressed each other in Swedish—and very pointed and emphatic Swedish it was, upon occasion.

Naturally the young prince's tutors did not fail to give him an early and thorough grounding in the truths of Christianity. This was a most important side of his upbringing, but it was not always by any means the easiest. From the strict Lutheran point of view his father's convictions fell something short of orthodoxy, and the clergy did not hesitate to say so, particularly when Karl on his return in 1602 brought back with him as court preacher a Calvinist divine, one Theodorik Micronius, whom he had picked up in Livland, and whose companionship he had learnt to value. Archbishop Olaus Martini, a zealot for the purity of the faith, and no respecter of persons, immediately took steps against this intruder, and cited him to appear for examination early in the summer of that year. When in due time the examination took place, it demonstrated conclusively that the much-favored preacher harbored heterodox opinions. A deputation of bishops and rural deans, drawn from the Estate of the Clergy in the Riksdag (which had just met) accordingly waited on Karl with a petition demanding his expulsion.

Karl was furious; but the Clergy stood their ground. Their next step showed that they were less anxious for Karl than concerned to protect his eldest son and Duke Johan from influences which from their point of view they honestly considered to be pernicious. They induced all four Estates to concur with them in a blunt demand that "the German preacher at court, with whom we are at issue upon the question of the form and order of Service, may without delay be removed out of the country, so that the young princes upon whom the government of the country will one day devolve be not corrupted with his evil leaven." There is no mistaking the general uneasiness. What Karl answered to this request, or whether indeed he answered it at all, we do not know; but at all events the Estates did not recede from their position, and the struggle was resumed later in the year. By this time Karl's anger with the Clergy knew no bounds. If he had been driven to shed blood, that was their fault; and this was how they requited him! In any case, he did not give much for these alleged differences in doctrine. "If only," he remarked to the archbishop with a pointed glance at his bald pate, "you had as much hair as Micronius, I would take a small boat, and a good stout sailor to row it, and hold you both by your hair, one on each side of the boat. And when the boatman was rowing as hard as he could, I would let go of the two of you, and then, perhaps, you might find yourselves in agreement for once." But in spite of this characteristic outburst the Clergy refused to give way.

Unity in religion was the great watchword of the age. The resolution of the Riksdag of Söderköping had declared that nothing so firmly binds the hearts of men together as religious unity. It was well known that the duke had concurred only reluctantly in the orthodox solidarity of the Assembly at Uppsala. And now he was beginning to make difficulties about the Confession of Augsburg. The more reason, then, for the defenders on the walls of Sion not to yield an inch! As regarded Micronius the controversy was to all intents settled when some time later he quitted the country on some convenient pretext. The young princes at court were thus removed out of range of Calvinist propaganda—at all events from the pulpit. But for some years to come there continued to be controversy as to the Confession of Augsburg and its relations to other confessional documents to which Karl was inclined to attach more importance.

There is an unconfirmed statement, dating from a later period, that Johan Skytte's appointment as Gustav Adolf's tutor, in May of this year, was approved by the Riksdag. It is by no means impossible that the selection of a new tutor was communicated in some form to the assembled Estates as proof of the fact that the young prince had been entrusted to the best hands. Skytte—at that time he still went under the name of Schroderus—was a good Lutheran, though not of the inner circle of orthodoxy as that age conceived it. Certain of his later utterances imply that he felt himself drawn towards German mysticism, and that he cherished an innate dislike for theological rationalism—a type of creed which at that time was strongly supported, and which was not considered to be inconsistent with the most rigid orthodoxy. The information that Skytte read Thomas à Kempis with his pupil fits in well with this supposition; and it is worthy of note that Gustav Adolf's religious instruction during his years of adolescence should have been in the hands of a man whose views were, by contemporary standards, comparatively latitudinarian. When Skytte took up his post as preceptor to the heir apparent, he had to subscribe to an undertaking which bound him primarily to improve his pupil in Christian doctrine as set forth in the prophetic and apostolic books. The Confession of Augsburg was not mentioned at all.

Johan Skytte, at this time twenty-five years old, was a peasant's son from Nyköping, and one of contemporary Sweden's rather sparse intellectual luminaries. It need scarcely be remarked that he owned himself a convinced supporter of the political system which Karl had even at this date hardly succeeded in stabilizing: to the end of his life, in fair and foul weather alike, he remained true to his political faith. His enemies even spread the rumor that he was the duke's bastard. It is at all events certain that his appointment to be Gustav Adolf's tutor was the first step to a brilliant career, though that career never seems to have brought him spiritual harmony or peace of mind. As mentor to Karl's eldest son he seems, as far as we can tell, to have been equal to every requirement, though it is not clear that any very deep personal regard ever existed between him and his pupil. In a purely human point of view Gustav Adolf perhaps preferred another of his instructors, the eccentric but talented Johan Bure, who assisted Skytte in the prince's education. The greatest Runic expert of his day, Bure had a brooding and inquiring mind of marked originality, and he knew, as none other did, how to stimulate Gustav Adolf's taste for old Swedish history, and for the traditional sagas and visible memorials of his native country. In spite of his doctrinal fantasies Bure always stood on terms of mutual sympathy with Gustav Adolf after he became king. Now and then, indeed, the king would make fun of his old friend and twit him with having been "a greybeard from birth," but we know also that sometimes he took his advice on serious questions of conscience.

One observation may be made here. When Gustav Adolf was put under Skytte's care, he was much more practised in sporting activities than in book-learning. In August 1602 an embassy from Hesse-Kassel visited Stockholm, and in its honor a tournament on foot was arranged which lasted some four hours. "Then Duke Gustav Adolf and Duke Johan strove valiantly together, so that it was a pleasure to see them," notes Bure with satisfaction in his diary. One might have thought that the contest would have been sufficiently one-sided: the one champion aged thirteen, the other still short of eight. With such strenuous pastimes were the labors of the schoolroom relieved.

In 1604 Swedish literature produced its first printed treatise on pedagogy: *A Brief Instruction in such Arts and Virtues as a Prince shall practice and use, who would anon rule Land and People prosperously*. The book was the work of Johan Skytte, and it was probably written at the suggestion of Karl IX, since it appears very much as though it was by design that it first saw the light in the year of the Succession Agreement. From it, we may deduce what sort of training the king wished to be given to his son in order to fit him for the position he was soon to occupy; for there can be no doubt that the work was approved in all its main principles, and was probably actually censored, by him. Although the author-preceptor makes use, naturally enough, of foreign writers and classical sources, his work contains a number of independent contributions of his own. It is penetrated through and through by a strongly marked moral tone, and its chief object is to induce a lively sense of duty. The prince has received his power from God, and his mission is to take care of the welfare of the common man. But the commonalty is of its nature fickle and unstable: it is "well content that the rulers of the land be changed and overset." This is Karl, speaking from the heart; for such, precisely, was his opinion. A fundamental inclination towards peaceful methods pervades the author's exposition, though he is fully conscious that a ruler must know how to set an army in battle array. The nobility, for their part, should give the commonalty a good example, if there should be need of special tax-grants to the Crown. Now and then we detect lines of thought and turns of phrase which might be interpreted as discreetly veiled warnings against Karl's characteristic failings: as when it is emphasized that a good prince must contain himself in patience while transacting business with his council. However, the sentence is given with protecting quotation marks around it; and as a general principle its validity was of course undeniable. Again: they are unworthy counsellors, "who say yea, when their Lord says yea, and say nay again, when their Lord says nay." Skytte's instructions had incontrovertibly a pretty strong flavor of realism.

The training for kingship set out in this program was to be crowned by the study of "politics"—here conceived as the knowledge of practical statesmanship, history, and law. History is valuable mainly to demonstrate how good and evil governments bear fruit after their kind. The same pragmatic conception was later maintained by Johannes Rudbeckius in his sermons before Gustav Adolf as king, and it emerges with undiminished force in Gustav's sketch of his own history, though unfortunately this broke off at 1597, and thus progressed no further than the introduction.

Gustav Adolf's tutors attached especial importance to knowledge of languages and oratorical fluency. Skytte, himself a master of these accomplishments, held out as examples in this respect Elizabeth of England—"that goddess among women"—then not

long dead, and Landgraf Moritz of Hesse, whom Skytte had himself extolled in a formal oration during his study-years in Germany. The results were to show that these exhortations had been
taken to heart. "In his youth," says Axel Oxenstierna, "he obtained a thorough knowledge and perfect command of many
foreign tongues, so that he spoke Latin, German, Dutch, French,
and Italian like a native, understood Spanish, English, and Scotch,
and had besides some notion of Polish and Russian." Spanish, a
language important for the knowledge of military literature, we
know that he studied with Skytte. Greek he knew less well, if
we may judge from fact that as late as 1627 he was taking
lessons in it from Bure. Of modern languages, other than his two
mother-tongues, he seems to have been most at home in French,
though it had not then attained its full stature as the language
par excellence of diplomacy and culture. Latin, at that time the
staple language of diplomacy, he spoke and wrote with ease, con-
trasting in this respect with his father, though sometimes he
would profess to be getting rusty in it, if he saw his interlocutor
fumbling for a word.

Exercises in Latin rhetoric came into the curriculum at an early
stage. We know from the notebooks of Bure that upon some
state occasion or other in the later summer of 1604 Gustav Adolf
and Johan delivered public orations: possibly as an exercise before
the Råd, then assembled in Stockholm castle, or possibly in honor
of Skytte, who was raised to the nobility just about this time. Bure
seems to have lent the youngsters a hand with their *opus*. From
the following year comes an imaginary Philippic, composed by
Gustav Adolf in the style of Cicero, and corrected by Skytte,
against Councillor Hogenskild Bielke, who had come before the
judgment of the Riksdag, and was afterwards to share the fate of
the magnates executed at Linköping. The speech is noteworthy
only as witness to the atmosphere in which Gustav Adolf grew up.
Of course he practised rhetoric in Swedish too, and when Johan
Skytte was married in the spring of 1606 Gustav Adolf made the
usual speech on behalf of the bride.

In addition to this training for kingship, with its strictly practical aims, he also—and especially after his tenth year—attended
council meetings and audiences to watch and listen to the pro-

ceedings. We have referred already to his presence with his father
at the Norrköping Riksdag of 1604. At the great meeting of the
Committee of the Estates at Örebro in the spring of 1606, he was
for the first time given an official function to perform—that of
presenting to the Estates the King's written declaration touching
a matter which was once again giving rise to anxiety. Karl was
threatening to abdicate in favor of Duke Johan, and on this occasion the threat seemed to be more seriously intended than formerly. "The regal office and government are a heavy burden,"
said Karl in his declaration, "and, contrary to received opinion,
more is required for their assumption than a store of fair words
and fine raiment." However, the Estates strove to outdo one
another in assurances of fidelity, and in the end Karl promised
to resume his thankless task.

[4]

THESE were difficult, turbulent years. The new monarchy stood
on no very sure ground. Abroad, it had a stiff task to win recognition. At home, the situation was disquieting, particularly after
the heavy defeat at the hands of the Poles at Kirkholm in the
autumn of 1605. The proclamations of Sigismund urging his
deluded people to return to their rightful "Christian" sovereign
were read from the church steps of Småland. Again and again
the rumor went round that fresh plots and new attempts upon
the king's person had been discovered. Trials and executions followed hard upon one another. The leading noble houses, brooding over their unhappy memories, were the objects of Karl's deepest suspicion: Barbro Bielke, the mother of Axel Oxenstierna,
was even subjected to a domiciliary visit. The Clergy wrangled
with the king on points of doctrine and the order of service. The
people murmured at the war in Livland, which had been going
on since 1600, and which they considered could have been brought
to a conclusion if Sigismund had not been attacked in his Polish
dominions. And the state of Karl's temper made him at times a
positive danger to his *entourage*.

It is scarcely to be wondered at that in all these questions
young Gustav Adolf should have unreservedly taken his father's
part. Never, as long as he lived, did he permit himself a word

which could be interpreted as a criticism or censure of his father, although his own policy was to be based upon quite other principles. His speech against Hogenskild may have been a mere exercise, but it must also be taken to represent a genuine expression of the lad's outraged feelings: the imprisoned councillor had, in letters to his relations which were afterwards made public, called down the wrath of Heaven upon the "impious offspring" of the tyrant and his Jezebel. The opposition felt reasonably sure that "the hawk would hatch no dove." The exiled Count Axel Leijonhufvud, Karl's cousin on his mother's side, and at one time high in his confidence, had been heard to observe that the son had already given signs of his father's "savage fury." It is Axel Leijonhufvud who tells the story of how Gustav Adolf did not shrink from mimicking the tragedy of Linköping in his boyish games. The other boys had to kneel down in front of him, while he with a wooden sword struck off their hats or caps, crying: "There falls Gustav Bauér's head—the traitor!—and Erik Sparre's—and Hogenskild's—!"—and so on. Our informant, with his passionate craving for vengeance, is perhaps hardly a calm or impartial witness; but the story is not altogether improbable, for Count Axel gives it as a matter of common knowledge. If the story is true, it forms a striking proof of the absolute, unreflecting identification of himself with his father's work carefully inculcated into Gustav Adolf in his formative years.

An attentive observer of Gustav Adolf in his maturity cannot but perceive that there are moments—usually brief—when the primitive substratum of his being seems to be laid bare, and volcanic torrents surge upward. At such moments he resembles his father. As a general rule his firm grip upon his self-control enabled him, with the help of happier traits of character which had been wanting in Karl, to master this troublesome temperamental inheritance. Yet a trace of it remained, a testimony to his Vasa blood. In Gustav Vasa, and in almost all his children—sons and daughters alike—there was an element of disharmony, a lack of balance about their personality. It appeared at times very clearly in the founder of the dynasty; and in the Vasa family, so richly endowed with talent—one might even say genius—it can be traced a good deal further back. There is a view of history which loves to idealize Gustav Adolf as a man whose character was as it were moulded and set in its final form from the very beginning. There are incontrovertible reasons for rejecting this conception. As a man, no less than as a king, he was what he was only as the result of gradual development.

When Gustav Adolf reached his fifteenth year, or thereabouts, he refused to be "disciplined" any longer, and turned for companionship to those who were prepared to allow him to follow his own inclinations towards female society, card-playing, hunting, and military exercises. This information is derived from Otto Mörner, the court chamberlain, who could observe his development at close range, and whose brother Bernt Didrik Mörner was incidentally Gustav Adolf's own tutor, and had assisted in his upbringing. It looks as though these zealous lords in waiting were experiencing a certain amount of anxiety. Skytte, who in the spring of 1610 had laid down his post as Gustav's principal tutor to go off on a long embassy abroad, took the opportunity to make a parting speech to the queen, and in it expressed his earnest desire that his royal pupil might "for a brief while longer" devote himself to his studies. Presumably Gustav Adolf had not come up to the expectations of his conscientious mentors. But, as we shall see, he began just about this time to be increasingly employed to deal with public affairs.

It would be unfair to blame too hardly a healthy young man, innocent of introspection, for these evidences of dawning self-indulgence, though it would seem from Mörner's testimony that some doubts were felt as to his stability and sense of responsibility. It is likely enough that Gustav Adolf felt himself attracted by the young women about the court; he developed early, he was by nature hot-blooded, and he had an appreciative eye for feminine beauty. That he made a reputation in his youth as a safe shot and a good horseman is confirmed in the verse and prose of contemporary eulogists, and certainly his prowess as a hunter lived long in the memory of the people. As late as the middle of the last century the peasantry of the Mälar district would speak of "Gösta Hooknose" and his generosity to the poor country-folk with whom he took shelter incognito on his hunting-trips through the woods.

If Gustav Adolf manifested an insatiable appetite for the society and conversation of experienced soldiers, he was in this respect only acting in obedience to his father's instructions. When he was only eight he was present at the farewell audience of Count Johann of Nassau, upon his resigning the command of the Swedish army in Livland. Gustav Adolf saw him again in 1620 on his tour through Germany; and on that occasion the old general, famous throughout Europe, brought out his model soldiers and illustrated a tactical problem. Gustav Adolf had learnt the elements of the military art in Skytte's study—it was Skytte who first aroused his interest in Dutch tactical methods. According to Oxenstierna, he resolved from the first to take Prince Maurice of Orange[6] as his model. Distinguished professional soldiers of various nationalities were often to be seen at the Swedish court, and swarms of veterans came to Sweden, especially after the conclusion of the truce between Spain and the Dutch in 1609. There were thus opportunities for discussion of "the wars, battles, and sieges of other nations; their discipline by sea and land; their ships, and their methods of navigation." Questions and answers might go on all day. It was only for a very short period that Gustav Adolf was able to obtain any more consecutive and specialized training in warfare; and that was for a few months at the end of 1608, when he had the advantage of the instruction of Jakob de la Gardie, then lately returned from several years' service under the banners of Prince Maurice.

In his relations with his children, and with Gustav Adolf in particular, King Karl exhibited simultaneously solicitude and strictness—two of his most admirable characteristics. He felt it to be his imperative duty to advance the temporal and spiritual welfare of his children. His well known *Memorial* for his eldest son is lasting proof of this. Now and then, we can detect a tinge of anxiety in his paternal admonitions, and they easily took on an emphatic, almost minatory, tone. Thus on one occasion he writes to Gustav Adolf: "We strictly charge and command you to keep God ever before your eyes." Karl's prophecy, *ille faciet,* which is usually considered as being especially illuminating for

[6] Statholder of the United Provinces, 1585-1625.

their relationship, was certainly not committed to paper until long after his death, and it is impossible at this date to decide whether in fact it was ever made; but there is no very good reason against it, and in appearance it bears the stamp of essential truth.[7]

Otto Mörner's apprehensions proved to be groundless. This light-hearted pleasure-seeking was merely a transitory phase of the years when the boy was ripening to manhood. The Court, moreover, lived as a general rule in an extremely modest style. Queen Kristina was economy itself: as the years passed, indeed, her careful management seems to have verged on parsimony; and the atmosphere at Court must frequently have been depressing. Johan Skytte tells a story which gives us a vivid glimpse of Gustav Adolf's boyhood. One day the prince—he was still, we are told, a mere boy—was found weeping bitterly. They asked him what was the matter, and at last elicited the reply that he was miserable because of the country's troubles, and frightened at the thought of what would happen after his father died.

[5]

AFTER Karl IX had assumed the royal style his eldest son bore for some years the title of duke of Södermanland. In his evident vacillation between various plans for regulating the succession, the king for a moment toyed with the idea of dividing his former duchy between his two sons. In a draft ordinance he had a provision inserted to the effect that there were to be three territorial principalities in the kingdom, Finland, Södermanland, and Östergötland: beyond these, no further partitions were to be permitted. Finland had once been Johan III's duchy, and he had designed it for his youngest son; but Karl preferred to subject this arrangement to an alteration which was not without importance. At the coronation festivities in Uppsala in the spring of 1607, he invested Gustav Adolf with Finland, Karl Filip with Södermanland, and Johan with Östergötland. One by one the

[7] Little Gustav Adolf was often in the room when the Råd came to consult with his father. When on one occasion they were dealing with a question of great difficulty, Karl IX is said to have laid his hand upon the boy's head and uttered the words: *"Ille faciet."*—The anecdote has been preserved in various forms. It first appears in a work by J. Loccenius dating from 1676.

three young princes were called up to the king's throne in the cathedral, and from his hands received three banners, the symbols of their seizin. Gustav Adolf was also permitted by his father to use the title of duke of Estland and Livland, as well as that of grand duke of Finland. This was a measure designed to establish in the eyes of the world the extent of the lawful claims of the heir-apparent, and also the essential integrity of the kingdom: to him, and to none other, pertained the overseas provinces, the threatened outposts and bastions of the Swedish realm.

Yet the prince did not thereby acquire any administrative rights in these territories as long as he remained a minor. It was a mere formality when de la Gardie at the beginning of the Russian campaign (1609) was styled "Duke Gustav Adolf's lieutenant-general for all the forces in Finland." A little later Gustav Adolf was given portions of Västmanland, together with the royal revenues derived from them, and in 1600 this enfeoffment (in virtue of which Gustav Adolf now signed himself duke of Västmanland) was rounded off by the gift of most of the rest of the province, and some Dalecarlian parishes in addition. Gustav Adolf kept up a particularly close connection with this district even after his accession, and loved to stay in its castle or on one of the royal manors there. Mention of Västerås, Väsby, or Ulvsund (the later Kungsör) frequently recurs in his history.

Of the carefully delimited rights which Gustav Adolf acquired with these dukedoms, none perhaps was more important than the competence to hear and remedy the various grievances of his people. It was training in practical statesmanship, and King Karl, with his paternal theories of government, attached great importance to it. As early as 1608 Gustav Adolf had been entrusted with tasks of this sort while proceeding on a trip to Kalmar. "Be gracious," urged his father, "to such as need your help, so that they depart not from you comfortless." And so it was that Gustav Adolf was bred up in the spirit which from the beginning had animated the Vasa dynasty.

It was not long before heavier responsibilities were laid upon him. At Stockholm, on August 15, 1609, he made his first speech to the national Estates, when he dismissed them at the close of a rather stormy session. Karl IX, his health shattered, had been lying speechless for some days upon a bed of sickness. The opposition which he had met with at this Riksdag had been responsible, according to some apparently trustworthy accounts, for bringing on a stroke from which he was never fully to recover. It was several months before he could move or speak, so that his enemies could describe him, with ill-concealed relish, as "worse than a brute beast." His health mended by degrees, but he found himself "much handicapped by constant weakness," and he turned once again to the idea of abdication. At the next Riksdag, which was held in Örebro at the end of the following year, it was only by a great effort that he managed to welcome the Estates to the House of Assembly. An eyewitness has described how in short, halting sentences he confessed his infirmities: "'If I could talk, I would; I would speak out properly; but now I can hardly talk at all; for you must know, good people,' said he, beating his breast and looking up to Heaven, 'God hath stricken me.'" It sounded like a self-accusation. The propositions to the Riksdag dealt with the question of appointing a coadjutor to assist the ailing king in the business of government. The Clergy looked towards Gustav Adolf, from whose employment in matters of State during his father's lifetime they expected much future benefit to the kingdom. The Burghers avowed their confidence that the sixteen-year-old prince was "now capable of directing the government to the best advantage of us and of our fatherland." The only resolution taken, however, was one in which the Estates reaffirmed their oath of fealty to the king and to his heirs as determined by the Succession Agreement.

During this, the last Riksdag held by Karl IX, Gustav Adolf habitually addressed the Estates when communications were to be made to them from the government. Various ordinances and instructions dealing with the internal affairs of the kingdom were promulgated in his name; and to all intents and purposes he acted as co-regent with his father. But the circumstances of the moment were giving increased prominence to the Råd, which had hitherto occupied a rather subordinate position, and here the lead was gradually assumed by the young noble who was afterwards to be Gustav Adolf's chancellor. It was already possible to discern a new alignment of constitutional forces, menacing that "rule of secretaries" which is generally considered to be one of the darker sides of Karl's system; menacing too the monarchy itself, which after Karl's death, now clearly imminent, would very probably have to gird itself for a struggle with a domestic opposition in which the nobility would take the lead.

[6]

AT AN assembly at Örebro in the spring of 1611 Gustav Adolf, in accordance with the custom of the age, was declared "worthy," or, as the text ran, "so far arrived at man's estate as to be able to bear armour and weapons." It was a moment for which he had assuredly waited with impatience; for in the preceding year he had ventured to plead with his father to be given a command in the Russian campaign, though without success. But now the tide of battle was pounding at the gates of the kingdom. The War of Kalmar had broken out, and a general levy had been ordered for the defense of the country. Gustav Adolf, having been duly recognized as fit to bear arms, was at once given a leading share in the work of defense.

It was, as a modern author has aptly termed it, an all-in bout. The War of Kalmar may be said to have been the last of the great border wars between Sweden and Denmark, waged on both sides with primeval ferocity, with harryings and frontier raids as comparative interludes in a continuous struggle for the key positions in Götaland. Denmark took the offensive. Christian IV,[8] who had begun hostilities in the style of medieval chivalry by sending a herald with a challenge, had hopes, if all went well, of being able to effect the complete subjugation of Sweden—so weak appeared the basis upon which the monarchy of Karl IX was founded. There were many who criticized Karl for his unwillingness to remove the obstacles to a peaceful settlement. Discontent and discouragement were rife throughout the country. Queen Kristina herself seems to have considered that hostilities should have been avoided: in one of his blacker moments Karl reminded her that she was herself a "Jutish woman." The public danger fanned his vitality into a strong but feverish flame. We

[8] King of Denmark, 1588-1648.

recall his curious challenge to Christian after Kalmar Castle had capitulated; the suggestion being that God should judge between the two nations by the issue of a personal duel—a duel between a broken old man and a man in the full pride of his strength! If hate could have brought victory the result would not long have been in doubt. Karl, moreover, made no secret of his belief that the sands of his life were running out; and it is said that the recent appearance of a comet strengthened him in his presentiments.

Gustav Adolf seems to have taken it very much to heart that the enemy did not show a proper respect for his father. When at midsummer 1611 he took the town of Kristianopel[9] by surprise, a scene was enacted which clearly reflects the young man's indignation and wounded pride. As he stood there at dawn in the market place, with one of the two detachments of cavalry that had carried out the surprise—the other was scattered in search of plunder—the pastor of the place came to him to implore protection for himself and his family. Gustav Adolf took the man roughly by the hand, and held him fast there for close on a quarter of an hour while he addressed him with as much emphasis as if that frightened, half-naked priest had been a plenipotentiary for the whole Danish people, bound to take his words to heart. He made merry at the notion that the king of Denmark, a young, inexperienced warrior, should suppose himself capable of waging war against a commander so old and tried as his father. The Swedes would soon make him look out for himself! He referred to a rumor alleged to be current among the Danes, to the effect that the Swedes were so short of men that they were forced to take women for their cavalry, and expressed his opinion of such malicious tales in a somewhat gross witticism. This story of the conversation with the pastor in the market place of Kristianopel— it ended, incidentally, with his allowing the priest and his family to leave the town—is in every way more probable than the other version whereby Gustav Adolf's troops are said to have captured the place through entering it in disguise.

It is poor psychology to assume, as an early Danish historian does, that Gustav Adolf, when he pinioned the unfortunate

9 In the province of Blekinge.

clergyman, took a certain pleasure in hurting his feelings. He was certainly speaking from a full heart. The sixteen-year-old boy was on his first stirring campaign; and he was in a state of emotional excitement. His feelings boiled over, and he could not refrain from giving vent to them. It was the first time, outside the fighting line, that he had met any Dane who held a position of authority.

The campaign showed, in fact, that he had still a long road to travel to attain the humane equanimity of his later years. He left Kristianopel a reeking heap of ashes. Such was the law of battle, as it was observed in this war: "plunder, burn, and massacre." Still, in comparison with others, Gustav Adolf does not emerge too badly. The Danish garrison in the stronghold of Borgholm, which fell into his hands at the beginning of October, thanked him for his "Christian clemency." This achievement completed the recovery of Öland, and it was the last good news that he was able to bring to his father.

Woods hewn down for ambushes, broken bridges, devastated cornfields, burning towns and villages—these things gave Gustav Adolf an ineffaceable impression of the conditions of such warfare; an impression which he later expressed in the words, "Nowhere are we weaker than within our own borders." Men of the older generation could still remember the Seven Years' War in King Erik's time; and on the Holaveden, close by the great post road, skeletons still visible told of the soldiers who had fallen in battle there. And now fresh horrors were added to the others. These experiences in no small degree explain and illuminate Gustav Adolf's later military policy, and the popular support which that policy could command at critical moments. As the Estate of Peasants remarked in 1629 when supporting a campaign against the emperor in Germany, "the goat grazes where he is tethered."

[7]

ON OCTOBER 22, 1611, King Karl embarked in a sloop at Mönsterås to go to Nyköping. Hostilities had almost come to a standstill for that year. The orders for the next few weeks had been given, the commanders appointed, and Karl turned homewards with a heavy heart, for his efforts in the field had not been attended by the success for which he had been hoping. He had hardly escaped from the daily cares that beset him and put out to sea when he collapsed. The first day out he began to complain of pain, and on his arrival at Nyköping some days later he was so weak that he had to be half carried from the ship up to the castle.

Gustav Adolf was at that time staying with the rest of the royal family at Bråborg in Östergötland; and thither went speedy tiding of the king's alarming illness. The queen and the three young dukes hastened at once to Nyköping. When they arrived Karl was past speech, though he could still recognize them all. The end was now very near. On October 30, at dinner time, he died "worthily, in a Christian spirit, and without a struggle." Among those who stood by his deathbed were Gustav Adolf and Axel Oxenstierna.

In the events which followed, Oxenstierna—still only twenty-eight—undoubtedly played a part that was in many ways decisive, although as a rule he kept himself in the background. He was the rallying point of the Råd, which upon Karl IX's death was hastily summoned to meet the queen, Duke Johan, and Gustav Adolf to decide on plans for the necessary negotiations with the Estates. It was his hand that pulled the strings at the remarkable Riksdag which met in December at Nyköping. His aims are clear enough. He proposed to stand guard over the work of Karl IX, and to preserve the crown for Karl's dynasty: any other course was out of the question. But in place of a strong personal monarchy, such as the late king had embodied, he wished to place a constitutional kingship modelled as far as possible upon aristocratic lines. He had in fact much in common with those councillors who had once rallied round Erik Sparre, and his views were shared by a majority of the nobility. All over the country discontent had become vocal. Råd and nobles, quite apart from the maintenance of their class interests, stood out as spokesmen of the wishes of the common people. The Riksdag of Nyköping, where all Oxenstierna's abilities were applied to securing the demands of the Estates, showed this clearly enough.

Overriding the provisions of the Succession Agreement of 1604, the Riksdag decided that since Kristina and Johan had declined their parts in a regency, the entire and undivided government of the kingdom should be entrusted to Gustav Adolf, although by the terms of the Succession Agreement he was to have obtained it only after completing his twenty-fourth year, that is, not until 1618. As yet he did not even fulfil the requirement laid down in that ordinance as a condition for his sharing the government with the guardians who had been prescribed for him, for he was still a year short of his eighteenth birthday. The Estates, however, declared themselves persuaded that his natural understanding would compensate for his deficiency in years. But as an antecedent step they had put forward claims which may be summed up as a demand that the monarchy be bound by legal obligations more precise than in the case of any preceding king of the Vasa line. These representations, the main object of which was to assert the duty of the new ruler to maintain and respect the rule of law throughout the land, became in all essentials the basis of the Charter which Gustav Adolf was forced to concede in return for his recognition at the end of the year. The new privileges for the nobility, to which he set his signature at the same time, formed in some degree a special charter for the first Estate, which thereby received a very considerable extension of its right to take precedence in the life of the nation.

Gustav Vasa and his two eldest sons had come to the throne without any other pledges being demanded of them than the old regal oath as laid down by the *landslag*.[10] Sigismund and Karl had, in addition, given Charters, but these had in the main been designed to afford security to the established religion. Gustav Adolf's Charter was of a different order. In many respects it approximated in principle, if not in detail, to a precise regulation of the mutual relations between the rights of king and people. It bore within it the seed of a development which might have ended in a supremacy of the Råd reminiscent of medieval practice, if the monarchy had been represented by a *roi fainéant*. As it turned out, events took quite another direction. Without violating the form of the constitution, Gustav Adolf managed to use it for his own purposes. That this was possible is to be explained not least

[10] The common law of Sweden (as opposed to provincial codes) dating from the mid-fourteenth century.

by his unceasing cooperation with the man who soon stood out as the dominating personality among the aristocracy. In January 1612, immediately before his departure for the battle front in the border provinces, Gustav Adolf appointed Axel Oxenstierna his chancellor by a commission whose ample terms are the measure of the trust he reposed in him. Such an appointment was a tacit promise—soon to be redeemed—that the "rule of secretaries" was to be called to account.

The Charter referred the new ruler in many matters of importance to intimate collaboration with Duke Johan of Östergötland. Alterations in the law, and the more important questions of foreign policy, required his concurrence, as well as that of the Råd and the Estates, before a decision could be taken. On the other hand nothing was said in this connection about the queen mother, who had the guardianship of the interests of Karl Filip and the right to govern his duchy of Södermanland until he came of age; but in reality Kristina's wishes came in the next few years to count for almost as much as those of Johan, whose position was always embarrassed in consequence of his close blood-ties with the arch-enemy of the dynasty, King Sigismund.

When Gustav Adolf assumed the government, he took the title of "Elected king and hereditary prince of the Swedes, Goths, and Wends." He left out the title "King of the Lapps of Nordland" which his father had borne, and which Christian IV, scenting a challenge, had included among his grounds for declaring war. The omission was a clear expression of his desire to liquidate the ambitious Northern policy which King Karl had tried so obstinately to carry through at the expense of Denmark-Norway. It is not until Gustav Adolf's coronation, nearly six years later, that we get the final disappearance from his royal style of the word "chosen"—or, as it runs in some documents, "elected"—a form of words which had made it plain to the world that his power as yet lacked solemn confirmation.

[8]

DURING the whole of the first year of Gustav Adolf's reign, the Danish armies stood on Swedish soil; and the young king was engaged incessantly in leading defense and counter-attack. In spite of this, Denmark was one of the powers which went furthest in acknowledging from the start the validity of the new monarch's title. The explanation of this apparently curious circumstance lies in Denmark's political tactics. King Christian had considered it safest when he began hostilities to repudiate Sigismund's claim to the crown of Sweden, for he half hoped that he might be able to bring his Northern neighbor under the "*dominium* and obedience" of Denmark. To cut short any discussion he abruptly refused to concede to the Polish king the title of king of Sweden, which had hitherto always been accorded him. When, some years after making peace with Sweden (at Knäred in 1613) he effected a *rapprochement* with Poland, he found it opportune to restore the Swedish title to Sigismund, under the pretext that it was a matter of equity, and could be conceded without prejudice to the rights of Gustav Adolf. During the peace negotiations in the autumn of 1612, however, the Danes had contended that Gustav Adolf must still be held to be a minor, since he had not yet completed his eighteenth year; and they demanded that the Swedish plenipotentiaries should produce commissions drawn in the name of the Estates. As a matter of fact, the question was adjusted without complications; but it is easy to perceive in what light the young king's position appeared to his suspicious neighbor.

Not for one moment did Sigismund of Poland concur in approving the change of rulers which had taken place in his hereditary dominion. Fear that his emissaries would strain every nerve to win revenge was no doubt among the reasons which contributed to the decision of the Estates at Nyköping not to insist upon a regency, as laid down in the Succession Agreement. It soon became very clear that Sigismund had no intention of deviating from his demand to be considered as the legitimate king of Sweden. To him, Gustav Adolf was, quite simply, Duke Gustav Adolf of Södermanland, the more or less accidental usurper of the throne. The great majority of the Catholic powers of Europe, and in particular the Habsburgs in Austria and Spain, followed his example. Far on into the next decade we find Gustav Adolf alluded to as "duke of Södermanland," or—as sometimes in the Spanish Netherlands—"duke of Finland," or "Gustavus," or "the Swede." There were even a few Protestant princes, for example the elector of Brandenburg, who at first took up the same attitude. All who wished to have diplomatic dealings with the king of Poland gave him what he considered to be the full title which Providence had bestowed upon him, for he never opened letters which did not fulfil requirements in this respect.

No one who knew Sigismund well could imagine that the mere question of title was for him the all-important point. It was characteristic of his unshakeably legitimist standpoint, that in his assumed rôle of father of his country he sought to restrain Christian IV from attacking Sweden, and later laid claim to Älvsborg when the Danes held it in pledge. He never ceased to consider the Swedes as his "subjects," and it was as subjects that he addressed them in those communications which at regular intervals he caused to be smuggled into the country.

In the early days of his reign Gustav Adolf made use—though only rarely and incidentally—of another title, otherwise unknown in Swedish history. The "Troublous Times" in Russia[11] were nearing their climax. In the universal confusion, Poles and Swedes contended to establish their influence in the disintegrating barbarian State. In the early summer of 1611, the Russian national militia assembled in Moscow, despairing of the chances of its native rulers, had chosen Gustav Adolf of Sweden as their tsar and grand duke. Their decision had indeed no effect, by reason of confusion in the conditions attached to it, but immediately afterwards Jakob de la Gardie, as commander of the Swedish auxiliary army, concluded a treaty with the authorities of the captured city of Novgorod.[12] By this treaty, to which it was assumed that the other Russian provinces would agree, it was decided that the "Lordship" of Novgorod should choose the king of Sweden as its "protector," and should elect one of his sons as tsar. This last clause demonstrated the risks of intervention. It had not been foreseen by Karl IX, whose real object had been to check the progress of the Poles; and when Gustav Adolf was

[11] The period (1605-1613) from the death of Boris Godunov to the accession of Michael Romanov.

[12] Novgorod had been an independent republic in the Middle Ages, and the leading trading-center of north Russia. In 1478 it was incorporated into the Grand Duchy of Moscow.

recognized as king in succession to his father the question was still open for decision. The offer was not declined: Gustav Adolf seems to have been ready to accept the crown of the tsars for himself. He transacted State business as grand duke of Moscow; and on the same day that he put his signature to the privileges of the nobles, he granted letters patent enfeoffing a Russian with land in the territory of Novgorod.

There is evidence to show that in the summer of 1612 he was still sticking to this project, possibly for more or less tactical reasons, but in the end he convinced himself that it was impossible, and finally succeeded in overcoming Queen Kristina's objections to the candidature of her younger son: he was indeed the only foreigner (if de la Gardie is to be believed) who had any hope of uniting the Russians behind him. Gustav Adolf openly acknowledged that he did not like the arrangement, "particularly in view of a possible conflict of policy" which might in the future divide him from his brother. But before Karl Filip, after long delays, reached the frontier, events in the east had taken a turn[18] which destroyed the basis for any dreams of establishing a Swedish junior line on Muscovite soil. Sweden found herself in consequence involved in fresh struggles, which were not ended until peace was signed at Stolbova in 1617.

In the autumn of the same year Gustav Adolf's long-delayed coronation was performed in the cathedral church of Uppsala.

[18] By the election of Michael Romanov (1613-1645) as tsar.

GUSTAV ADOLF'S MARRIAGE

GUSTAV ADOLF'S MARRIAGE

[1]

WHILE Gustav Adolf was still in his cradle, his mother, as the custom was in those days, had arranged for the casting of his horoscope in accordance with the relative positions of the heavenly bodies at the hour of his birth. This nativity, which was kept secret from the world at large, contained among other things particularly explicit prophecies concerning the date of his marriage and his personal reactions to matrimony. When Gustav Adolf should have reached the age of twenty-five, he was to take a bride of his own choosing, regardless of the opinions and preferences of others. We have the information from Queen Kristina herself, for at the beginning of 1615 she let one of her confidential servants into the secret.

The young prince's parents had, however, no intention of allowing their respect for the science of astrology to deter them from concerning themselves with his future marriage. As early as 1605 we find his name mentioned in connection with political schemes designed to give increased security to the younger branch of the house of Vasa in their legitimate occupation of the Swedish throne. Karl IX would have been best pleased if his son could have married an English princess, though he also turned his thoughts from time to time to the princely houses of Saxony, Brandenburg, and Württemberg. The advantages of a dynastic union with the leading Protestant power in Europe were obvious, and Karl did not abandon hope that one day such a union might be realized. From other points of view, moreover, James I's only daughter Elizabeth might seem to be a most desirable match. She was rather younger than Gustav Adolf, and she had considerable personal attraction. Karl had taken soundings in London, and had obtained the impression that the English court was not antipathetic to the idea of such a marriage. This impression was not shaken by the reports of Johan Skytte and Gustav Stenbock, who had had an opportunity to prosecute enquiries in the course of their embassy to England in the summer of 1610. The charming young princess, in the opinion of these Swedish visitors, showed clearly that "she was more inclined to Duke Gustav than to any other prince in the world." On the whole, there seemed every reason to expect a "gratifying success" from the affair. The embassy had, indeed, apparently no formal commission to propose the suit, but the English interpreted their too lively interest as a request for the hand of Elizabeth on behalf of the heir to the Swedish throne. Shortly after their departure, moreover, James I informed his brother-in-law of Denmark that King Karl of Sweden had proposed a marriage between his son and James' daughter, and had even declared himself prepared to make considerable sacrifices to obtain it.

A thorny problem with regard to young Elizabeth's marriage was whether it would be possible to secure a husband of the correct religion and of sufficiently exalted rank. Apart from Gustav Adolf there was in fact no Protestant prince of royal parentage available, and it was only with extreme reluctance that James could contemplate the wedding of his daughter to a papist. Karl IX's position was certainly hardly on a par with that of a legitimate monarch, but this was not an insuperable obstacle. Upon the visit of the Swedish embassy in 1610 James declared that he was willing to recognize him as king of Sweden in virtue of the choice of the Estates. It is probable that he then had the projected marriage in mind. However, the scheme met with strong opposition from his queen, Anne of Denmark, a sister of Christian IV, and anything but well disposed towards Sweden. The scruples which she entertained soon derived increased weight from subsequent developments in the relations between the two Northern nations. The War of Kalmar put a stop to the whole project. It does not seem to have been followed up even from the Swedish side.

Other suitors for Elizabeth's hand appeared in rapid succession. While in his own country Gustav Adolf was rushing from battlefield to battlefield, Elizabeth was celebrating her betrothal to Friedrich V of the Palatinate. The union had latterly been warmly recommended by Christian IV, but it was less agreeable to Queen Anne, who would have preferred to see her daughter queen of Spain. But the whole of Puritan England held such a union in abhorrence, and counted it unto James for righteousness that he had in this matter steered a clear anti-papist course. The Palatinate

EBBA BRAHE

Miniature by an Unknown Artist

QUEEN KRISTINA THE ELDER,
MOTHER OF GUSTAV ADOLF

Detail from a Silver Medal

was generally considered to be the home of the most resolute section of Protestantism. The young elector was still under the tutelage of his guardians; but already there were many who speculated on the chances of his acquiring the crown of Bohemia. This hope may or may not have told in his favor in England. At all events, it was not disappointed; for in 1619 the Bohemians, in revolt against the house of Habsburg, chose the elector as their king. The battle of the White Mountain brought his reign to an abrupt conclusion, under circumstances which have become familiar, and it was not long before the Palatinate also was wrested from him. So that the bride of the Winter King became for her countrymen the martyr *par excellence* for the Protestant cause.

Through all her chequered career she never succeeded in meeting Gustav Adolf. But the youngest son of the exiled pair, born at the Hague in 1632, was by her desire given the name of the Swedish king in baptism. Friedrich had wished to call him after their first-born, a youth of promise who had been drowned some years earlier; but Elizabeth had her way. Her weak state of health prevented her from accompanying her husband when he paid a hopeful visit to Gustav Adolf's headquarters about the same time. She never saw him again alive. Some days after the battle of Lützen Friedrich of the Palatinate followed his protector to the grave. Elizabeth lived on for three adventurous decades; the little Gustav Adolf survived for only nine years.

[2]

IN THE reports of Stenbock and Skytte upon their English mission there are very plain hints that Gustav Adolf's own "will and pleasure" might be a decisive factor in the prosecution of negotiations with the house of Stuart. We recall Otto Mörner's words regarding his early-awakened interest in certain of the young women about the Court. It is not clear whether Ebba Brahe had at that time been launched into Court society. According to an old tradition—and it seems inherently probable—Queen Kristina took over her upbringing after the death of her mother in the spring of 1611. She was then hardly more than a child, for she had just turned fifteen. It soon became sufficiently clear that she was the object of Gustav Adolf's knightly devotion.

A miniature portrait of Ebba Brahe dating from a rather earlier period shows us a soft, amiable face with aristocratic features and large, mild eyes. Her social position was above criticism. According to traditional Swedish ideas there was no reason *a priori* why the king should not take her as his bride. Her father, Magnus Brahe, count of Visingborg, was Lord High Steward.[1] In point of rank he was the first dignitary in the kingdom, and he was also one of its greatest landed proprietors. Both on her father's and on her mother's side she could claim relationship to the royal family. The old queen dowager, the pious widow of Gustav I, was Brahe's aunt, and was still, in spite of her advanced age, managing her estate at Strömsholm. And had not King Johan taken his second wife from among the Swedish higher nobility? Indeed, was there not still living on a manor somewhere up in Tavastland an aging woman who had once worn the crown of a queen, for all that she was only a poor soldier's daughter? At the time of Gustav Adolf's accession both Katarina Stenbock and Karin Månsdotter[2] were still alive: indeed, the former lived long enough to see his young queen—and, incidentally, to give her a handsome wedding present.

Karl IX, who was himself of noble Swedish blood as pure as that of any of the nobility whom he summoned to his service, was too much of a realist, for all his old-fashioned ideas in some other respects, to allow any considerations to influence him other than those of dynastic policy. He had condemned Johan's choice of Gunilla Bielke as quite unsuitable, and had pointed his disapproval by absenting himself from the wedding. The distinction between a sovereign and a subject must never be suffered to be obscured. He might now and then toy with the idea of a marriage between his daughters Katarina and Maria Elisabeth and his deadly enemies the Polish Vasas; but certainly he never for one moment entertained the notion of one of his sons wedding a woman from the Swedish nobility. Yet they both came very near to doing so. Before his premature death Karl Filip had managed to contract a secret morganatic marriage with a young lady of the

[1] In Swedish, *riksdrots*. The *riksdrots* was president of the supreme court. Cf. the functions of the High Steward in regard to trial by peers, in England.

[2] See genealogical tree, p. 307.

name of Ribbing. The furtive nature of the connection is no doubt to be explained by the twenty-year-old duke's respect for the strictness and worldly wisdom of his mother. Her capacity for getting her own way in affairs of this sort was a matter of common knowledge. In flat contradiction to current ecclesiastical ideas, which considered the union of cousins to be a thing forbidden, she had in 1612 brought about the marriage of Johan of Östergötland to Maria Elisabeth, in spite of the fact that the whole body of the clergy had put in an exasperated protest, and in spite of the obvious lack of any mutual inclination on the part of the contracting parties. It was a matter of course that the queen would bring all her obstinacy to bear in order to thwart her eldest son's intention of raising to the throne one of her own ladies-in-waiting.

The poets, and popular tradition too, have delighted to dwell upon Gustav Adolf's youthful love affair. Our only reliable information concerning it is based almost exclusively upon the correspondence between the two young people, and even that has not been preserved for posterity in its entirety. In the course of years, ten of Gustav Adolf's letters and notes to Ebba Brahe have come to light, most of them dated; of Ebba's letters to the king only one genuine example remains. With unaffected naturalness Gustav Adolf lays bare to us his character in these letters: proud, self-confident, impetuous; but at the same time tender, delicate in feeling, imperturbably optimistic under all the harrowing uncertainty of what the future may hold for them. One of the most discerning of our literary critics, Oscar Levertin, has said of his love letters that they are as fascinating from a psychological, as from an esthetic point of view. "It is a noble nature that they reveal to us, a nature which in the utterance of the profoundest emotions can command a style and a range of expression which betray the sensitiveness of the poet." There is no mistaking the genuineness and depth of the passion which Gustav Adolf avowed in these letters to the woman of his heart. This is not the language of a passing infatuation. But, reading between the lines, we can see that his ardent and passionate temperament was no secret to those that knew him.

The love letters to Ebba Brahe also provide a pretty clear picture of the outward course of this youthful episode. The first letter

was written early in the spring of 1613, and at the beginning of
1615 the correspondence was broken off under circumstances
which are better known to us from other sources. But before the
earliest dated letter we may divine a whole chain of events, whose
culmination—the king's demand for the hand of his "well beloved"—seems to be relatively recent. Probably he made some such
declaration at a meeting on the occasion of the celebration of Duke
Johan's marriage in the previous November, for when in March
1613, less than two months after the conclusion of peace with
Denmark, he repeated his request for an answer, it was impossible
that he should have seen her in the meantime. The new factor
in the situation is clearly Magnus Brahe, who had visited his
daughter at Nyköping, and had been informed of the king's suit:
it is immediately after this visit that we learn that she has put the
whole matter into the hands of her father. At this stage, however,
his attitude is still a matter of uncertainty.

From a period of little more than three weeks we have four
of the king's letters dealing with this affair, one of which is to the
Princess Katarina, who had apparently been in his confidence for
some time. The letters reflect his impulsive emotional fluctuations:
his fear that the queen mother may again vent her ill-temper upon
his beloved; his relief at the news that during the last few days
she has proved a little more amiable; indignation because Ebba
is compelled "daily, and more than before" to listen to malicious
lies about the state of his affections; hard-won resignation in expectation of "the day which shall console me." The most important information contained in them, however, is that Gustav
Adolf has made a direct appeal to his mother, but has received
only "the usual dubious answer." Apparently then, this was not
the first time. Kristina elected to try to tire her son out. Ebba
Brahe found this opposition depressing. She implored the king to
think no more of her. He replied that he hoped that he should
never hear or read such words from her again.

Of Count Magnus' reactions nothing is known with certainty.
But it is perhaps permissible to hazard the guess that he played
the part of a prudent politician. It was certainly difficult for him
to oppose either the king or the queen mother; and the prospect
of seeing his daughter queen of the country was at once danger-

ous and alluring. The summer of 1613 brought a decision, or rather, a sort of truce. Kristina had once more been heaping vehement reproaches upon the Lady Ebba. Gustav Adolf, who was still unable to extract anything but evasive answers from his mother, administered comfort to his beloved: she should be plagued no longer for his sake, for he intended now that her father should take her home. Magnus Brahe, however, seems to have kept out of the way, and his daughter remained about the queen's court. Nevertheless, Gustav Adolf was able shortly afterwards to reach a temporary settlement. As intermediary he employed a distant connection of the house of Vasa, Duke Heinrich Julius of Saxe-Lauenburg, who had for some years served as an officer in the Swedish army. Gustav Adolf had no very high opinion of this rather incalculable person, and it was only recently that they had been reconciled after a violent quarrel which had culminated in the king's dealing him a box on the ear, and had led subsequently to a nocturnal duel *à l'arme blanche*. The memory of this episode long survived, and it became the basis for a rumor which gained currency after the battle of Lützen, to the effect that a brother of the duke, after accompanying the king into the battle, had struck him down in the mêlée. The duel, however, had relieved their feelings, and this confidential mission to the queen was clearly intended to be a friendly gesture on the part of the duke. This time Kristina gave a "pretty good" answer. She promised to speak with Ebba, and ask her if she would be willing to wait a year or two longer. If the king changed his mind in the interim—why then, she would have only herself to blame.

Yet Gustav Adolf's happiness at this apparent improvement in the prospect was tempered by a shade of uncertainty. It is fairly clear that Ebba Brahe was a woman of lively and ingenuous disposition, very susceptible to the impression of the moment. Such, at all events, was her character in after years, throughout a life which presented many alternations of sunshine and shadow. Her royal lover, having thus been bidden to wait till he was older, seems to have been principally concerned as to whether she would be able to carry off her interview with the queen successfully, in view of the fact that his mother had so rigorously limited the basis of discussion. He insisted urgently that she must say little in reply, and say it as submissively as possible: "God grant that this time you may answer in a manner pleasing to Her Majesty." At a moment when he felt their sky to be clearing, he permitted himself a mild criticism. However, it seems probable that the Lady Ebba stood the test. If there had been any fresh complications they would have left some trace behind them.

The correspondence shows a long gap after this. It is certain that in these years Gustav Adolf's opportunities for meeting the woman of his choice were few and far between. If the charming letter in which he bids her a long farewell and sends her a forget-me-not belongs to the period of his departure for the eastern front in 1614, then there could hardly be a better proof of the unruffled harmony of their relations at the beginning of this year. This dating is no doubt disputable. But the letter from Narva dated September 20, written shortly after the capture of Gdov, gives further evidence of a calm and easy confidence on the king's part—indeed, one would have said he was certain of victory: to win the favor of his beloved he has overcome his enemies, and hopes soon to be with her again. It can hardly be doubted that at the time of his return from the first Russian campaign he was meditating a decisive settlement with the queen mother. The single letter of Ebba Brahe that has been preserved was in reply to one of his in which he had advised her of his intention to resume negotiations with his mother through the mediation of his sister Katarina; and the idea must have been to induce the queen —she had already given a half-promise—to give a definite consent to his betrothal.

In the meantime, however, the situation had altered considerably. One of the most prominent young nobles in the country, Count Klas Sture, had sued for the hand of Ebba Brahe in due form. Magnus Brahe gave an indecisive answer, and the suitor silently withdrew. And Kristina, on her side, had managed to discover a suitable wife for her son. The initiative had come from the old relatives of the family over in Hesse. In the spring and early summer of 1614 an envoy came to Sweden from Landgraf Moritz (surnamed "the Wise") with instructions of high political import. His first official visit was to the queen mother at Nyköping. By previous arrangement they broached the subject of the desirability of strengthening the dynastic link between the two houses through the marriage of Gustav Adolf to one of the daughters of the Landgraf. The project was part of a plan the immediate object of which was to secure the inclusion of Sweden in the Evangelical Union, the new league of German Protestant princes. It is only too probable that Ebba Brahe—still at the court in Nyköping—knew of this marriage scheme before it reached the ears of the king, who was at that time on his way to the east. From the moment of its proposition she must have seen in the Hessian princess, favored as she was by the queen mother, a rival who would be too strong for her.

There is every reason to suppose that Ebba Brahe, in her intimate correspondence with Gustav Adolf, invariably used the forms of address proper from a subject to her sovereign. The accents of timid humility which distinguish her letter from Nyköping, dated October 19, 1614, are none the less sufficiently striking. The tone is unhappy and evasive. She gives humble thanks for the honor which has been accorded to her, a simple girl, by the king's letters and affectionate consideration; but she avows that it would not be becoming in her to aspire to his royal person. She complains that she is frightened and distressed every day by "frequent cross-examination"—we may be sure that the queen mother did not neglect what she conceived to be her duty. In conclusion she assures him: "I have Your royal Majesty always in my thoughts, nevertheless." There is good reason to suppose that it was to this pathetic epistle that Gustav Adolf was referring when in an undated letter he complained that the tone of her letter showed "a great alteration," which made him uncertain what course he ought to pursue. He appeals "once again" to her promise to give her heart to him, and to none other: he will himself be constant until his "latest breath."

It was at this time, or immediately afterwards, that Ebba Brahe left the queen's court. When at the end of November the king came to Nyköping it is clear that she was already in the safekeeping of her aged kinswoman the queen dowager Katarina at Strömsholm: it was there, certainly, that she spent the New Year (1615). We are perhaps justified in assuming that Count Magnus had intervened to avoid fresh unpleasantnesses. It began to be in-

creasingly obvious that no attacks could shake Kristina's determination. The king, who in matters political felt himself reasonably independent of her opinions, was unwilling in an affair of
this nature to assert his sovereign rights against her authority as
head of the family. The reputation of the Brahe family might be
jeopardized by a fresh struggle of endurance between mother and
son, for the conflict might be prolonged, and its outcome was at
best uncertain. And it was for these reasons that, at the beginning
of January 1615, the Lady Ebba wrote to the king and besought
him to press his suit no further, since the only consequence would
be that she would fall still further into Her Majesty's disfavor. No
doubt she was acting with the approval of her family.

Gustav Adolf's answer is the last letter he is known to have
written to Ebba Brahe, and it is also the longest. There is more
of calm dignity, but more too of deep tenderness, in this letter,
than in any that had preceded it. He has no intention of abandon-
ing their common cause; he hopes rather that his mother's opposition may be "worn down by persistence"—indeed, he has only
lately made renewed representations, though unfortunately they
have not been attended by the effect he had hoped. However,
constancy, which is love's chief glory, may yet achieve much:
though his mother is angry now, time may yet turn her wrath
into a "love all the deeper for being hardly won." If only Ebba
will bide her time, steel her resolution against slanderous tongues,
and put aside all thought of happiness without him, he on his
side "will not be sparing of pains, lacking in constancy, or wanting
in fidelity" in his efforts to persuade the queen mother, on whom
now everything must depend.

Gustav Adolf wrote this letter on January 19, 1615, from the
royal manor of Väsby, near Sala. Magnus Brahe, who had been
his guest for the past week, was staying with him at the time, and
Abraham, brother of the *riksdrots,* who had been summoned specially, was at Väsby too. Apparently there was a family council in
the king's presence. Axel Oxenstierna and Johan Skytte, who had
been sent for in haste, were also consulted. On January 27 the
four lords, together with the king, heard the sermon for the day
from the lips of Johannes Rudbeckius. The preacher dwelt upon
the obedience due from children to parents "in all lawful and

honorable things, even though the way may on occasion seem a hard one." Their deliberations were soon over. A decision was reached whose purport it is not difficult to deduce from what followed.

Every effort was now made to prevail upon Kristina. Gustav Adolf tried fresh lines of attack. Through Axel Oxenstierna he commissioned the queen's own chancellor, Dr. Nils Chesnecopherus, to plead his cause at Nyköping, and to spare no effort on his behalf. Dr. Nils, as the special custodian of the traditions of the age of Karl IX, was considered to have the ear of his mistress in no ordinary degree. Karl Karlsson Gyllenhielm added his own exertions, and finally even Johan Skytte seems to have tried the effect of his diplomatic talents. Kristina displayed more equanimity than had been expected. If her son's suit were to be successful in the end, she remarked, it would be best that she should take the young woman into her service once more. But her opinions remained fixed. No assent to her son's request could be extracted from her. She fully appreciated his strong repugnance to the Hessian project, but now, as before, she refused to take his adolescent sentimentality seriously. "Time will show," she opined, "what will come of it." It was in the course of one of these discussions with Chesnecopherus that she appealed to the opinion of the astrological experts as to the destined time of Gustav Adolf's marriage. He had just completed his twentieth year, so that there were still five whole years to run. But as to Ebba Brahe, it was obvious that Kristina would never yield an inch. "I do not suppose," acknowledged Chesnecopherus to the chancellor, "that there is anyone in the world who can persuade or induce Her Majesty the queen to give her blessing and consent to it." Gyllenhielm, who seems to have received a formal resolution from Kristina to transmit to the king, was of much the same opinion.

The negotiations at the castle of Nyköping, which had been initiated with such decorous circumspection, appear to have been marred on two occasions by violent outbursts of temper. Gustav Adolf, whose anxiety caused him to be kept well informed of what was going forward, asked the chancellor for fuller information as to the "reason for the slaps in the face, and as to how the comedy had ended." Had Kristina then in a heated moment forcibly shut the mouth of one of the king's bedesmen? It certainly looks like it: we can hardly imagine anybody else in this connection interrupting the discussion in such a fashion. That Gustav Adolf now felt that the moment had arrived to give up the struggle may probably be deduced from his bitterly ironical words as to the comedy's being ended. At all events, he felt himself no longer able to continue the contest. We shall probably be correct in assuming that the agreement with the leading members of the house of Brahe had included the king's withdrawal if this last attempt failed.

How Ebba Brahe replied to the king's final letter of consolation, we cannot tell. She soon learned that the queen had beaten off all attacks, and remained impervious to all prayers and representations. Too many persons had been mixed up in the business this time for there to be any chance of keeping the news a secret. Gustav Adolf wrote to Axel Oxenstierna about the slap in the face on March 10. At that time he was staying out at Näsgård in south Dalarna. On March 20 Magnus Brahe received a visitor to his estate at Axholm in Västmanland—a visitor who had come upon a matter of some delicacy. Henrik Horn had arrived under commission from his fellow soldier Jakob de la Gardie, to ask for the hand of the Lady Ebba. He gave it to be understood that Herr Jakob had "a good disposition towards her, and was minded to show her all honor and kindness," which he was desirous of demonstrating by a Christian marriage. Ebba Brahe's new suitor, the famous commander in the Russian campaigns, had been at home on leave since the previous autumn. Henrik Horn, as lord chamberlain and a former comptroller, was intimately acquainted with the king; and both he and de la Gardie were well aware of how the land lay. Presumably de la Gardie had hitherto refrained from proposing himself, out of consideration for the king. Count Magnus at once consulted the queen dowager Katarina at Strömsholm, where Ebba was still residing, and also asked the advice of others of his near relations. In view of Klas Sture's previous offer, of which Magnus Brahe in his confidential letter to the family reminded them with some embarrassment (though he made no allusion to the king), the proposal met with as favorable a reception as could have been expected. De la Gardie, at all events, considered that he had received "a satisfactory answer and assurance," and he pushed on with his policy of writing to the relatives of Count Magnus soliciting their countenance and support.

Such was the state of the case about the middle of April 1615. Three weeks later the king raised Jakob de la Gardie to the rank of count, and conferred an extensive earldom upon him—the first and last he ever created within the boundaries of Sweden. From the same time comes the last piece of evidence that has been preserved to testify to the fact that Gustav Adolf still allowed his thoughts to turn to Ebba Brahe. Lars Sparre, who on several occasions previously had acted as *postillon d'amour*, was in May given a commission, in the king's own hand, to order a diamond brooch to the value of three hundred gulden from one of the leading goldsmiths in Stockholm. He was to inform the king when it was ready. "But if it should happen that the Lady Ebba Magnidotter should come thither in person, then in such a case he is not to write to us, but to deliver the said jewel to the Lady Ebba on our behalf. *Item*, ask her to write to us." If, as seems likely, the diamond brooch was intended as a parting gift consecrated to the memory of the past, it is none the less clear how hard Gustav Adolf found it to tear his youthful love from his heart. He was still sighing for a letter from her, even if it were only a few lines of farewell.

The queen mother felt that she had triumphed. In the course of the summer she wrote to Landgraf Moritz expressing her gratitude to Providence for the turn events had taken. The person who had hitherto been the principal obstacle to her plans had now fortunately been removed (*bei Seite gebracht*), and, as far as she could see, the king thought of her no longer. There seemed to be every reason to hope for the best in regard to the alliance which the landgraf had projected. Axel Oxenstierna was not nearly so sure. He had been deeply involved in the campaign against Kristina at the beginning of the year; but for the moment, at least, he gave his approval to the Hessian scheme, and promised to work for its realization. But, with his knowledge of Gustav Adolf's state of mind, he counselled the greatest caution, for in this case above all others, they must abide the decree of Fate. To the Hessian statesmen who had visited Sweden in the previous

year he explained: "My king excuses himself by reason of the
campaigns which engage his attention, and says that he has not
yet had time to think of getting married." It seemed as though
the king had dismissed all thoughts of matrimony for an indefinite period. There was no lack of fresh offers on the marriage
market, but it irritated him to have them discussed. There were
some who feared at this time that "the pleasure he took in warfare, and his devotion to it" were making the young monarch
unwilling to enter into a life of domesticity. Possibly there was
another and truer explanation. At all events it is certain that the
king's relations to the queen mother were marked during the
following years by undisguised coolness.

In the early summer of 1615, shortly before Gustav Adolf sailed
for Narva, the wedding of Princess Katarina with the Count
Palatine Johann Kasimir was celebrated in Stockholm. The bride-
groom, who belonged to a junior line of the Palatinate house,[3] was
a young prince of good education, with considerable experience
of the world and plenty of self-confidence, but with no political
influence whatever, with no financial resources worth mentioning,
and, what was more, of Calvinistical convictions. It is clear that
Axel Oxenstierna opposed the marriage, and as far as we can
judge many others shared his views. The queen mother was not
enthusiastic, and Gustav Adolf had his doubts. But "Kätchen" had
set her heart on the match—though he was her junior by some
years—and no doubt her brother's love affairs reacted advantageously upon her own: he was scarcely in a position just then to
urge reasons of State against the dictates of affection. In the end,
he became positively eager to bring about the marriage. There
is an old story that shortly before his departure he expressed
a hope that his newly married sister would bear a son who might
one day succeed him on the throne. It seems to have been agreed
from the beginning that the children of the marriage should be
brought up in the Lutheran faith. Some little time afterwards the
rumor went round that the king intended to delegate the duty
of providing for the succession to his brother Karl Filip. Karl

3 Pfalz-Zweibrücken: see genealogical tree, p. 307.

Filip was indeed sent overseas to look for "a virtuous maiden of our own faith," but nothing came of it.

Gustav Adolf's apparent indifference to what was considered one of the most important duties which fall to the lot of a ruler provoked general surprise. Thus one of the princes of Orange asked Johan Skytte when he was on a diplomatic mission in 1617 whether his master would not soon be looking out for a queen. Skytte adroitly replied that the king "had hitherto had other brides to deal with, in particular the Russian fortresses, so that His Majesty had had no leisure to think of matrimony."

[3]

IMMEDIATELY after midsummer 1615 Gustav Adolf left Stockholm for a campaign against Russia which was to prove the most extended expedition he had so far undertaken. It was nearly a year before he saw Sweden again. That he realized how serious an undertaking it was, and how much depended upon it, can best be appreciated from the speech he made to Queen Kristina and Duke Johan upon his departure, in which he vigorously expounded the reasons that had led him once more to assume the command in the east—a step which he had been induced to take, not by any youthful presumption, but by his desire to bring his country out of "the raging, stormy sea of war into the longed-for haven of peace." The speech ended with personal expressions of farewell—extremely short and formal to his mother, but cordial and expansive to his cousin.

In the camp outside Pskov, at the height of the summer, Gustav Adolf contracted an association with a young woman of Dutch nationality, long known to history under the misnomer of Margareta Cabeliau. The part played in Gustav Adolf's life by Margareta Slots—for that was her real name—was limited to the fact that she bore him a son, Gustav Gustavsson of Vasaborg. Her family was of modest station—certainly not noble: one of her nieces who married in Sweden a couple of decades later did indeed bear the aristocratic name of Hamilton, but she was not reckoned as being of noble birth. The earliest report of Margareta Slots, in the narrative of a Dutch embassy, sent from the Russo-Swedish theater of war in the autumn of 1615, mentions her in a way which must imply that she was quite a well known person. At the time when she crossed Gustav Adolf's path she was the wife of another man. Her husband, the skilful sapper-officer Andries Sersanders—himself a Dutchman—had, according to this report, died at Pskov in October of this year, just about the time when the siege was abandoned and the king started for home: the report mentions that the Swedes did not venture to bury him on the spot for fear that after the camp had been abandoned the Russians might revenge themselves by digging up the body and throwing it to the dogs. Curiously enough, we find that Gustav Adolf was still in ignorance of Sersanders's death in the spring of 1616. But this only confirms the conclusion—in itself inherently probable—that the connection with Margareta was a mere transitory episode, and a subject to which the king strongly objected to refer.

Everything that is known of her later life makes it clear that it was not any gifts of head or heart on her part that threw the frustrated young man into her arms, but simply her physical attractions. Thanks to pecuniary assistance from the Privy Purse, she found herself in a position to live quietly in Stockholm, in expectation of her confinement; and after her son was born (May 1616) she enjoyed a very comfortable income. After some years she married again an army engineer, and she was then given the manor of Benhammar in Uppland as a royal donation. She never made any attempt to see the king again, but kept herself modestly in the background; unless we may count as an exception the occasion when she sent him, through a roundabout channel, a lace collar that she had worked. By pure accident Gustav Adolf came across her for a moment early in 1630 in the exchequer, which she was visiting at the time on matters of business. Fru Margareta of Benhammar appears from later documents as a rather troublesome lady, avid for her own advantage, and decidedly litigious; but perhaps after all she was neither better nor worse than many a tight-fisted noble dame among her contemporaries who could boast of a more immaculate past and a more honorable ancestry. She survived till 1669, faithful to the last to her Calvinistic creed, and lies buried in the church at Vada

by the side of her second husband, Jakob Trello. The suggestion
that she was a Cabeliau dates from the eighteenth century.

Among those who accompanied the army to Pskov, and formed
a regular member of the king's *entourage,* was the court chaplain,
Johannes Rudbeckius. He was himself the author of an extremely
competent account of the siege of that strongly fortified town,
illustrated by a sketch of its environs. It was the second time he
had taken part in a campaign in the Russian frontier provinces.
In his farewell sermon of 1620 Rudbeckius allowed his thoughts
to range back over the hardships of his life in the king's service
during these years. "At one time we would be forced to sit our
horses all day in rain and mud; at another we would go sledging
through the snow and the bitter weather, though the weather was
never allowed to interfere with the morning sermon; sometimes
we were at sea in the storm and roaring waters; sometimes on
land, campaigning amid the din of battle. Then the drum would
sound, and the guns go off; and in the middle of a sermon, or
while preparing one, we would hear the alarm and the order to
mount." His duties brought him both fatigue and anxiety. Once
after Gustav Adolf's death, when calling these days to mind, he
confessed: "Often have I wiped away hot tears from my cheeks
because of the difficulties and dangers that beset us."

Many of the sermons that Rudbeckius delivered before Gustav
Adolf have been preserved. For the most part he took his texts
in a regular succession from 1 Samuel, which was admirably
suited to the practical, clinching application beloved of the
preacher. They swarm with contemporary allusions, these sermons; but they are also the expressions of a steadfast faith which
does not shrink from giving utterance to its opinions. No court
preacher could be less reserved than Rudbeckius in his exposition
of "the blessed rule of kings or happy government of peoples."
His whole outlook is theocratic, but he holds that no one form
of government is more acceptable to the Creator than another.
"God does not desire that His holy congregation be bound to
one form of government or one type of constitution; whether
it be a king as sole representative, or whether it be a committee
of magnates, or even a multitude of the common people." In his
interpretation of the Old Testament texts he often shows a

moderation which derives from an inherent respect for equity and law. He is, however, clearly in favor of a polity based on natural law. "There can be no right or law," he says significantly, "that is commanded by God and acceptable to Him, which conflicts with the law of nature."

Yet at the same time Rudbeckius affirms with inflexible rigor the validity of a strict code of ethics imposed by religion upon the rulers of the nations. Their sins are visited, as the Scriptures bear witness, upon their lands and kingdoms (August 1615). And the servants of the Word must learn from the example of the prophet: they must not "permit themselves, through smooth words or other means, to connive at evil, and approve what is done amiss; but they must punish sin with rigor, having therein no respect of persons, for this is a matter proper to their office and calling" (September 1615).

The intimate relation in which Rudbeckius stood to the king makes it probable that he knew soon enough what was happening. At all events it must be considered as out of the question that he was still in ignorance of it after the birth of Gustav Gustavsson. The next sermon he delivered before the king seems moreover to point more clearly to this conclusion than any that had preceded it. It had to do with Saul's intended sentence of death upon his son Jonathan. Rudbeckius cited the popular proverb: "Laws and ordinances are like a spider's web: it catches the little midges, but the big bluebottles fly through it." He held Saul's severity to be easily explicable. For the king of Israel realized that otherwise the people would say to themselves: "If a common soldier had been at fault he would have been condemned to death, but since the culprit was the king's son it was glossed over." The fault of which Gustav Adolf had been guilty could, according to ancient national custom, be punished in certain circumstances with death. A royal ordinance promulgated in the summer of 1615 had allowed the new High Court to commute the punishment for such breaches of the sixth Commandment; but within Duke Johan's duchy of Östergötland the old severe penalties still remained in force.

Gustav Adolf had put himself into a difficult position in regard to his spiritual adviser, and also to all that section of society—

the church—which he represented. It was not until 1617 that a final settlement was reached. The occasion was the proclamation of a general fast day for June 20. Rudbeckius then presented himself to the king and in private addressed to him an earnest warning and exhortation. His speech happens to have been preserved, and it is incontestably a valuable contribution to posterity's knowledge of the forces which contributed to the shaping of Gustav Adolf's character. It gives us a glimpse of the seventeenth century Swedish church in one of its most dominant moods, pitiless in its demand for complete accord between life and doctrine. Rudbeckius observed that while he did not doubt the king's penitence, he feared that he had not fully appreciated how deeply he had offended God by his illicit passion. He had given an evil example to his servants and his subjects, and was even now tempted to connive at sin and immorality, instead of punishing them boldly. He had forgotten the providences that God had manifested to him in his youth; he had put "no small stain" upon the honorable reputation which in many other ways he had acquired. It was not only earnest self-improvement and sincere prayer that he needed now—though indeed they were of the utmost importance: he must also, said Rudbeckius with emphasis, bring himself without delay to enter into "lawful Christian marriage." And he must banish from his presence such persons of light morals as would not shrink from leading him to perdition "provided that their bread was well buttered thereby."

It is arguable that we have here a fair picture of social conditions in an age when the zealots for church discipline did not stickle at any obstacle in their inquisition into private life. But even then such a scene was unusual. The intervention of Rudbeckius takes on a tinge of greatness from his vibrant anxiety lest the king fail in his mission. To that mission were attached duties as husband and father, an obligation to continue the royal line for the future welfare of the fatherland. Hence the typically Lutheran conclusion. The demand that the king shall marry is made in the name of religion.

There can be no doubt that Gustav Adolf responded in the spirit upon which Rudbeckius had counted. For the king very soon appointed him to supervise his son's education—a delicate token of confidence for which no other explanation is possible. And, as we shall see presently, at the time of Rudbeckius' visit Gustav Adolf was in a position to give him reassuring news regarding the "worshipful exhortation" which had formed the last point in his speech—the question of marriage.

Margareta Slots plays so fleeting a part in Gustav Adolf's life that it may well be questioned whether she ever meant anything to him at all. Possibly other women, quite apart from Ebba Brahe, may have made a deeper impression on the young king. Two love poems have been preserved, one in Swedish, the other in German, which have been attributed to Gustav Adolf. They are certainly instinct with passionate emotion. The initial letters of the lines form the name Christina Flemingh. There was in actual fact about this time a young woman by the name of Kristina or Kerstin Fleming, the daughter of a Finnish nobleman. Nothing is known of her earlier history. That Gustav Adolf wrote these full-blooded, erotic stanzas cannot, indeed, be positively proved; but still less can it be disproved. Certainly contemporary writers credited him with their composition.

There is some reason to believe that the poems to Kristina Fleming date from the period of the king's residence in Finland at the beginning of 1616. Zacharias Topelius, the Finnish novelist, based one of his stories on this theme. A somewhat similar *motif,* but in this case a purely imaginary one, is of course the basis of the first part of the same author's *Tales of an Army Surgeon.*

[4]

WHEN Rudbeckius urged Gustav Adolf to choose himself a queen, he was apparently ignorant of the fact that negotiations had for some time been in progress to this end, with one of the leading princely houses of Germany. Admittedly they had hitherto been kept a close secret.

It was to Brandenburg that these approaches had been made, and they demanded especial caution, since, in view of the very delicate position of the house of Hohenzollern in relation of Sweden's arch-enemy, they were particularly liable to meet with a rebuff. The duchy of Prussia (the present East Prussia) was

expected shortly to pass into the hands of the elector of Brandenburg, Johann Sigismund, as heir apparent to the mad Duke
Albrecht Friedrich. But the suzerainty over Prussia belonged to
the king of Poland, as feudal overlord, and a dynastic connection
between the house of Brandenburg and the junior Vasa line
reigning in Sweden—by usurpation, as Sigismund contended—
might consequently provoke the latter to political reprisals of
the most embarrassing nature. On the other hand it might be
argued that such a combination was calculated to give Brandenburg certain advantages in her difficult vassal relationship to
Poland, and, more generally, to act as security against the isolation which sometimes seemed to threaten her. The whole question was a highly involved problem in political mathematics: it
could be viewed from more than one angle, according to the
direction of the swing of the political pendulum in Europe, and
according to the strength of the forces—not always easy to assess—
that swayed decisions in Berlin. But from the beginning it was
clear that a marriage between Gustav Adolf and a princess of
Brandenburg, if it were to be correlated to any common political
programme, would demand a far more adroit statesmanship on
the part of the court of Berlin than Europe had for some time
been accustomed to expect from it.

King Karl had already given incidental consideration to this
combination, among others; but where the idea originated on
this occasion remains obscure. Possibly with the queen mother,
possibly with Landgraf Moritz, who still shared the anxieties
of his kinswoman. These, however, are mere conjectures; and
against them may be set the fact that the projected Hessian match
was still occupying the attention of interested parties when the
Brandenburg scheme first came up for discussion in the summer
of 1615. It was broached in a way that did not commit anybody:
a Swedish resident in Germany—a somewhat superannuated and
officious person of the name of Birckholtz, a Brandenburger by
birth—was made the recipient of a confidential suggestion by
his friends at the elector's court. The suggestion took on the
appearance of being something more than a chance remark, when
it appeared that Johann Sigismund himself had expressed to
Birckholtz his desire to enter into closer and more amicable rela-

tions with the young king of Sweden, whom he had heard to be a "skilful, wise, resolute and valiant gentleman." These communications aroused a certain interest at the Swedish court, though— for reasons already known to us—the matter was not considered to be at all urgent; and in due time Birckholtz received fresh instructions. It is, indeed, doubtful whether he fully grasped the purport of his commission, when he interpreted his task to be that of a matrimonial agent; at all events, he was later ordered to maintain a more prudent reserve upon this topic.

In the main, it was a political *rapprochement* that Gustav Adolf desired from Brandenburg. The settlement with Sigismund, at which he was now aiming after some years of uneasy truces, made an understanding with the North-German electorate appear eminently desirable. In his view, Protestant Europe as a whole was one single community, and to that community he felt himself irrevocably bound: however divergent and indefinite its aims might seem to be, he must, as far as possible, contrive to make them coincide with his own efforts on Sweden's behalf. From the point of view of Swedish interests there was everything to be said for an alliance with Brandenburg—an alliance as close and solid as he was able to make it. The need for support against his Danish neighbor was a further argument on the same side. So the idea of an alliance with the house of Hohenzollern gradually assumed for Gustav Adolf a greater importance as one element in his wider schemes. Towards the end of 1616 he sought the assistance of Landgraf Moritz, who enjoyed some influence through his family connections, as intermediary in this affair. For Gustav Adolf himself it was purely a political question. Maria Eleonora—for from the beginning she had been the only princess under discussion—must at that time have been scarcely more than a name to Gustav Adolf. Still, all reports of her physical and mental qualities gave the most flattering descriptions of the beauty and virtues of the young princess.

Gustav Adolf now proceeded to open negotiations. One step followed hard upon another, as he sought by a variety of methods to realize the object upon which he had determined. He knew already that he had no easy task before him. Perhaps at first he was not altogether sorry; perhaps there were moments when the remoteness and uncertainty of the goal for which he was striving struck chill into his spirit. That Johann Sigismund was personally well inclined towards him sufficiently appeared from Birckholtz's broadly genial reports, in which the worthy elector was sketched with great vividness. He was clearly anxious to form a connection with Sweden, but he pointed out with a sigh that the Prussian question was causing difficulties. Moreover he had unfortunately become infirm of body, and increasingly uncertain of his domestic authority. The Electress Anna, by birth a Prussian duchess, readily made up for the deficiencies of her spouse in this respect. From the beginning she showed a cordial dislike for the Swedish project.

In the course of 1617, the position showed scarcely any improvement. With the support of his father's friend the landgraf, Gustav Adolf proceeded to enquiries which implied a direct offer. Johann Sigismund felt that he could neither reject them, nor answer them with a simple affirmative. He expected much advantage to the common cause from the new alliance, but he was anxious about Prussia, and he entertained the only too comprehensible desire that peace should first be concluded between Sweden and Poland. He took counsel with a selection of his German relations. Their advice proved to be contradictory. Johann Georg of Saxony, whose opinions would naturally count for much, was extremely dubious, in view of Sweden's very difficult position (*"wie gefährlich es itzo umb das Königreich Schweden stehet"*), and also in view of Brandenburg's particular obligations towards Poland. Gustav Adolf's victorious peace with Russia was already six months old at the time when the leader of German Lutheranism was making this estimate of Sweden's position. Before the end of the year, indeed, it might be considered as established that Johann Sigismund was for his part anxious to have the king of Sweden as his son-in-law; but after an apoplectic stroke in the autumn he was a more uncertain factor in the game than ever. It was rumored that his counsellors were united in opposition to the marriage. Johann Kasimir, who was attempting to take soundings on behalf of his brother-in-law, sent back news to Sweden of an almost uniformly disheartening character, although by this time—i.e. the summer of 1618—not only Moritz of Hesse but also

Friedrich of the Palatinate and the diplomatic agents of Holland
were pleading Gustav Adolf's cause in Berlin. Rumor had it also
that several dangerous rivals for the hand of Maria Eleonora
were in the field—young William of Orange, the Prince of Wales,
Wladislaw of Poland, and others besides. Christian IV of Denmark was secretly laying his countermines, and in order to thwart
Gustav Adolf's intentions was trying to induce Duke Adolf
Friedrich of Mecklenburg to become a suitor for the hand of
the Brandenburg princess.

On Midsummer Day 1618 Jakob de la Gardie celebrated in
Stockholm his marriage to Ebba Brahe. Their betrothal had taken
place as recently as the previous November, but this seems to
have been merely a formality, for we have earlier letters from
Count Jakob to his "dearest and best-beloved." The marriage festivities, which were paid for by Katarina Stenbock, drew a numerous and brilliant assembly of guests, among whom the queen
mother Kristina and Duke Karl Filip were most conspicuous.
The king stayed away. He had put out to sea for the trial voyage
of a new warship. Immediately afterwards he undertook an extended cruise, with the intention of making for the German
coast. Thence he proposed to ride in disguise to Berlin, see Maria
Eleonora, and press his suit in person. As far as we can tell, the
moment was anything but favorable. No arrangements had been
made with the elector for such a visit. To judge from the fact that
the queen mother refused to allow one of her gentlemen to accompany him, although the king was anxious to take him, she disapproved of the whole expedition. But Gustav Adolf was thirsting
for action. He seems to have persuaded himself that he could
bring the affair to an issue through his personal appearance in
Berlin. It was his practice to trust to his own efforts on the spot.
At the beginning of September he set sail from Kalmar in the
Sceptre, accompanied by a number of other vessels, under pretext of holding naval manœuvres. He probably made land at
Rügen: at all events it is certain that either now or later he spent
a night in Stralsund. It became known later that the king of
Sweden had been seen in that neighborhood. However, he had
for the moment to abandon the idea of a journey to Berlin. It
appeared that such a journey could serve no useful purpose,

since he was informed by Hans Georg von Arnim, his confidential agent in Berlin, that the elector was no longer occupying his residence on the Spree. The projected visit was deferred till the following year.

Within the electoral family a battle of wills was raging, and it was some time before a decision emerged from the conflict. Johann Sigismund's favorite was still Gustav Adolf, and Maria Eleonora ranged herself on the same side. The electoral prince Georg Wilhelm tried to steer a middle course; he felt himself flattered by the offer of the Prince of Wales, and pushed the claims of his younger sister Katharina as a more suitable wife for the king of Sweden. The advantage of this policy was that it afforded time for reflection; for Maria Eleonora was barely of marriageable age. The Electress Anna, on the other hand, would have nothing to do with any Swedish match, remarking that she would sooner see her daughter in her grave. For Gustav Adolf, who at regular intervals pressed for a decision, and did his best to keep the iron hot, it had become a point of honor to win Maria Eleonora, and none other. In the summer of 1619, however, Gustav Horn was dispatched on an embassy to the old elector, then in residence at Königsberg, and as a result was able to return with the unexpectedly favorable news that there could be no question of any other suitor than the king of Sweden, and that the marriage was to be effected "as soon as possible." But it soon became clear that these promises and policies represented only the personal views of Johann Sigismund.

Gustav Adolf believed the prize to be within his grasp. He began immediate preparations for his wedding. The rooms in the castle at Stockholm were cleaned and painted, the cellars were stocked, the provincial nobility and their wives were invited to come up to the capital. Gustav Horn was sent back immediately to Germany to inform the elector and the electress that the king intended now to pay a personal visit to their court. And with that Gustav Adolf set sail for Kalmar, there to await a reply. By the middle of August Horn was back from Berlin. He brought with him a letter from Johann Sigismund expressing his pleasure at the projected visit. It was accompanied by another letter from the Electress Anna to the queen mother, in which the electress demanded in no uncertain terms that she should prevent her son's journey, as being prejudicial to Brandenburg's interests in view of the state of war existing between Sweden and Poland. Her husband, she wrote, was so enfeebled in will by illness that he could be persuaded to agree to anything, even if it tended to the destruction of his country. It was a rebuff that verged on an insult. What Anna omitted to mention, was the fact that she was hastening to put herself and Maria Eleonora in a place of safety, in case the headstrong suitor was not to be deterred by this broadside. Shortly afterwards they both moved to Brunswick, to stay with the Duchess Anna Sophie, the electress's married daughter.

For Gustav Adolf there was nothing for it but to swallow the insult, break off preparations for the wedding, and postpone the affair once more. He was certainly not inclined to throw up the sponge. When Johann Kasimir, who was dubious of the possibility of success in the struggle with Anna, tried to divert his attention to other German princesses—Katharina of the Palatinate, or the beautiful and amiable Sibylle Magdalene of Baden-Durlach —the king declared that he preferred to suffer a categorical refusal rather than contract a fresh engagement. But everything seemed to be conspiring against him. At the end of the year Johann Sigismund died. With him went the king's best support; and it appeared that the contest must now be a very unequal one, particularly as the question of investiture for Prussia was growing more acute than ever, in view of the death of the last duke in the preceding year, and the change of rulers in Brandenburg.

Nevertheless, Georg Wilhelm did not find it altogether easy to keep on good terms with the dictatorial electress dowager. Anna considered her son's attitude to Poland to be altogether too compliant, and viewed the prospect of a marriage between Maria Eleonora and Wladislaw with repugnance. In March 1620 Arnim paid a visit to Stockholm. Nothing definite is known of its object; but the information he brought with him must have been to the effect that the position was not absolutely hopeless. At the same moment, Johann Kasimir returned to Sweden. Gustav Adolf summoned a council of war. He resolved to hazard a decisive frontal attack on Berlin. If that proved unsuccessful, then he was prepared to reconnoitre the other courts that his brother-in-law had suggested. The plan of campaign was Johann Kasimir's, and Johann Kasimir accompanied the expedition to Germany, when, after sundry false starts, it finally took its departure.

At the end of April the king boarded ship in the greatest secrecy at Älvsnabben.[4] Eight days later he cast anchor off the coast of Rügen, where he and the Palatine were landed, together with a select company of young noblemen, among whom was Johan Banér. The ships' captains were ordered to hold themselves in readiness to meet them on their return, which was not expected to be until the week before midsummer; though the king's suite, which had orders to call him Adolf Karlsson and treat him as a comrade before strangers, considered it relatively improbable that the expedition would get further than Berlin. There were plenty of exciting moments: one of the party, Johan Hand, who recorded his observations and experiences in a diary, remarks that "the whole trip was for all the world like a comedy." Everybody in that merry party knew the purpose of the journey; but matters of importance were discussed only between the king and the Count Palatine, who in public played the part of leader of the expedition.

Gustav Adolf's first visit to Berlin did nothing to clear the air. The absence of Georg Wilhelm—he lived most of the year in Prussia—was the solitary favorable circumstance; but they had already reckoned upon that. The electress dowager, however, maintained an attitude of reserve; she even refused to grant the king an audience for the purpose of private conversation. She allowed him to be presented to herself and her daughter along with the rest of the visiting cavaliers; but she set her face against a personal meeting between Gustav Adolf and Maria Eleonora. Hand's conjecture that the king had "so far progressed in conversation with the lady that he received a kiss from the lips of Her Grace within her chamber" must therefore be dismissed as groundless. All those who were present at the presentation had noticed the unconcealed interest which the lovely princess had manifested in the young stranger. Before her father died, she

---

[4] A naval base in the Stockholm archipelago.

had promised him to give an affirmative answer to the king's suit, and it seems certain that her sister and her sister-in-law—the young electress—were now in favor of the match, and were doing their best to bring it about. The negotiations with Anna, which were conducted by Johann Kasimir, led to no result. It was the opinion at court that she had definitely repulsed his offers. Gustav Adolf now resolved to continue his journey to Heidelberg: "His Majesty was desirous of seeing other ladies, so that if this affair came to nothing he might still be able to come to some arrangement." Arnim, who had served as intermediary in Berlin, was much disturbed at this turn of events, and, simulating a zeal for the faith, tried to discourage a journey "through so many Catholic countries and monkish territories"—but without success.

While the Count Palatine was proceeding on his ride towards the Rhine, with Captain Gars—as Gustav Adolf now called himself[5]—in his train, a *volte-face* was occurring on the Spree. It was occasioned by the Polish marriage project. All unconsciously, Sigismund came at this point to the rescue of his arch-enemy by formally demanding the hand of Maria Eleonora for his son. The electress dowager had heard with growing uneasiness the current rumor that Georg Wilhelm intended to summon his sister to join him in Prussia. In this frame of mind, she was tackled by Maria Eleonora and her confederates—among them Secretary Rasche, who went over into Swedish service immediately afterwards, and became one of Gustav Adolf's most trusted diplomatists. They fancied that they detected signs of weakening. At all events, Gustav Adolf was overtaken at Heidelberg by encouraging messages from Berlin.

If until that moment he had entertained other ideas, he dismissed them immediately from his mind. At Heidelberg he saw the young princess, the sister of the new king of Bohemia; but he did not lay aside his incognito—which, incidentally, he found it sometimes difficult to bear in mind: during a promenade in the castle grounds he managed to attract Katharina's attention by a breach of etiquette, so that she showed her annoyance by exclaiming in French at the Swedish officer's impertinence. Kath-

[5] A name formed of the initial letters of his name and title: Gustavus Adolphus Rex Sueciae.

arina was a well-developed young woman, and the Palatinate agent Rusdorf, with whom Gustav Adolf had a long conversation in the course of a ride down the Neckarthal on the following day (though without revealing his identity) took occasion to point out this favorable circumstance, and expounded to the self-styled Captain Gars the advantages which might follow upon a match between the princess and the king of Sweden. Sweden's cause resembled Bohemia's as one egg resembles another. Among other things Rusdorf expressed his astonishment that the Estates allowed the king to remain unmarried for so long, when the welfare of the kingdom depended upon the succession. "My gracious king," replied Gustav Adolf, "will choose a bride when it suits him to do so, and not according to the wishes and prescription of his Estates." The marriage project, however, seemed to interest Captain Gars far less than the other subjects upon which the Palatinate minister touched in the course of his conversation. And when the party proceeded to Durlach, Gustav Adolf did not trouble to take a look at the much-praised Sibylle Magdalene, and held aloof from the court festivities which had been arranged in honor of Johann Kasimir and his companions. Undoubtedly the strongest impression that he derived from this excursion was of the division and weakness of evangelical Germany, which he had now seen for himself. At the end of May he personally witnessed the crossing of the Rhine by the troops of the League, without opposition from the margrave of Baden, who was encamped with the army of the Union not far off. It was not long before he was on his way back to Berlin.

When at a later date Anna of Brandenburg attempted to explain to her son her remarkable change of front, she laid great weight on her private conversation with the king on Sunday, June 18. With what irresistible persuasiveness he argued, with what confiding modesty he approached his prospective mother-in-law, how he committed his fate into her hands—to all this she bore emphatic witness. There is no doubt that the electress dowager was completely captivated. Probably her earlier brief meeting with him had prepared the way already for this wholly personal capitulation. She did not surrender immediately: she implored the king to spare her afflicted house, and hinted at her knowledge of his exploits in Heidelberg and elsewhere. When he then asked "with great deference" if all hope must be at an end, she replied immediately, No; the question had arisen so suddenly that she could take no decision in the absence of her son. That, however, did not prevent Gustav Adolf from plighting his troth to Maria Eleonora on the next day, with her mother's consent. Only when that had been done did Johann Kasimir, who had been waiting outside the town, put in an appearance. It seems as though the procedure must have been settled before-hand. The king thereupon hurried home to Sweden, to make arrangements for the reception of the princess and to put in hand the preparations for the wedding.

Georg Wilhelm was appalled when he heard what had hap-pened. He had recently informed his mother that out of con-sideration for Poland he had decided to refuse his consent to any family alliance of this sort. He had ordered Maria Eleonora to come to him in Prussia. And now everything seemed to be working in precisely the opposite direction. In this situation the elector plunged into feverish diplomatic activity. He washed his hands of the business before all the world in letters to the various courts of Europe, with loud lamentations at his mother's inde-pendent action; and he dispatched to Poland an embassy charged with the task of proving his complete innocence. Georg Wilhelm hoped to be able to satisfy Sigismund by such assurances, and by a humble explanation that he had no power to stop his sister's marriage with a man of equal rank, provided that it had his mother's consent. Sigismund's answer, however, exceeded his gloomiest anticipations. Sigismund enjoined him to break off this menacing alliance once for all, and demonstrate thereby that he would have nothing to do with that Gustav who, having in-herited his father's perfidy, was now shamelessly usurping his own kingdom of Sweden. What was Georg Wilhelm to do? He ordered the Secret Council in Berlin to protest in his name, if the electress dowager persisted in pushing on the match; and he wrote to Gustav Adolf and informed him that for the present, until Sweden and Poland had settled their differences, he must refuse his consent.

It is extremely unlikely that Georg Wilhelm imagined that this counter-offensive could serve any other purpose than to demonstrate his good will towards his Polish suzerain. At any rate, events moved too quickly for him. The old electress, now Gustav Adolf's most devoted ally, was resolved to strike while the iron was hot. She spirited away her "Mariechen," who had recently shown disturbing feverish symptoms, to Brunswick territory, out of reach of her brother. When Axel Oxenstierna arrived in Berlin early in the autumn at the head of a dignified embassy to complete the necessary formalities, he found that her support made his task a comparatively easy one. With his usual diplomatic ability the Swedish chancellor succeeded in carrying his points at a series of conferences with the electoral council: with imperturbable pertinacity he extracted and dispatched their cautiously worded assent. Their hesitation was obvious, but they made no protest; by the time the counter-order from Georg Wilhelm arrived, Oxenstierna was already in possession of repeated assurances from the other contracting party which put the adoption of a strong line out of the question. The whole arrangement, in fact, depended upon the *patria potestas* of which Anna was the representative. A survey of the position left Oxenstierna with the impression that the elector in spite of everything was "not sorry" to see the marriage arranged. The impression was an accurate one in so far as Georg Wilhelm's main object was to avoid all responsibility. He had, for instance, recently collected opinions from German jurists in support of his contention that he could not as a brother hinder his sister's marriage with the king of Sweden. And he continued to stay in Prussia, though he was well aware of the increased risks which his own absence from the scene of action must involve.

By agreement with the electress dowager, Oxenstierna had proceeded from Berlin to the court of Wolfenbüttel to fetch the princess. Anna, who intended to go with her to Sweden, prepared for departure in a somewhat pugnacious temper; her son had returned no answer to her request for a travelling allowance, but she did not shrink from providing herself with a selection of objects of value from the exchequer by way of compensation, and as pledges for Maria Eleonora's trousseau. In her irritation she

openly threatened him with a demand for reimbursement from
Sweden—which caused Gustav Adolf some embarrassment when
he heard of it. In the middle of September she left Berlin with
her youngest daughter Katharina, and shortly afterwards joined
the chancellor and Maria Eleonora in Mecklenburg. A detachment of the Swedish fleet, under the command of Gyllenhielm,
took them over to Kalmar, where Gustav Adolf was impatiently
awaiting them. The wedding took place in Stockholm on November 25, 1620; three days later Maria Eleonora was crowned queen
in the Great Church. In honor of the ceremony, a "merry comedy"
was performed, upon a subject taken from the history of Olof
Skötkonung[6]—doubtless a good deal less exciting than the drama
of real life which had now, after several acts of suspense, been
so happily ended. And, as things turned out, the astrologers had
been right after all: Gustav Adolf married when he had completed his twenty-fifth year.

[5]

THE capture of Maria Eleonora has been called Gustav Adolf's
"first victory on German soil." Not only that, the whole episode
is as it were a test piece of his statesmanship: tough constancy of
purpose is united to a love of the spontaneous action that attains
its goal by reason of its unexpectedness. The traits which are
apparent here are among the most fundamental to his character.

In one respect, however, the example is not a very happy one.
The expected political fruits of the family alliance with the house
of Brandenburg did not, on the whole, materialize. No new or
closer relationship was formed between the two countries. The
explanation lies partly in the mutual irritation which was the
inevitable result of the methods—rather too reminiscent of abduc-
tion—whereby the much debated marriage was achieved. But
this obstacle could have been surmounted in time. The decisive
factor was the inherent difference between the policies of Sweden
and Brandenburg. Any cooperation with his brother-in-law that
Gustav Adolf did succeed in effecting was almost always obtained
by force. There were times when they seemed to be in directly
opposite camps. It was vain for Gustav Adolf to promise to pro-

---

6 The first Christian king of Sweden, *ca.* 995-1020.

MARIA ELEONORA

Oil Painting by an Unknown Artist

tect the inhabitants of Brandenburg and Prussia "against Poland, or the Devil himself." Georg Wilhelm's attempt to keep on good terms with everybody accorded ill with the king of Sweden's offensive policy, whether that policy was directed to obtaining the final settlement with Sigismund so necessary to Sweden, or to the hurling back of the Catholic reaction in Germany in the interests of Protestantism as a whole. There were indeed moments when the elector and his advisers were prepared to go a long way to realize the latter object, but those moments had passed before the Swedes set foot in Germany. It was only force of circumstances that induced Brandenburg to forego the neutrality to which she had painfully clung for so long, and range herself on the Swedish side against the emperor and his allies.

Within the inner ring of Georg Wilhelm's advisers a conflict of opinions was almost normal; but on the whole the balance may probably have inclined towards those of Swedish sympathies, which certainly had a strong hold upon the people at large. Now and then it was these sympathies which dictated a decision, but more often other forces and other interests prevailed. Sweden's occupation, first of Polish West Prussia (1626) and afterwards of the duchy of Pomerania, which figured prominently in the future hopes of the Hohenzollerns, did not fail to sow the seeds of distrust between the now related dynasties. To remove this feeling through a settlement to the advantage of both, and at the same time to draw closer the bonds beween them, was the task—and it was both a difficult and an urgent task—that Gustav Adolf set himself: it was still unfulfilled when death overtook him.

So the fact that Gustav Adolf, to borrow his own words, "had a Brandenburg lady in his marriage bed" had in the sequel no very important political result. Yet the connection was not entirely without significance. It undoubtedly helped to avert the open breach which on more than one occasion seemed imminent, and at moments of triumph it lent a rather more personal character to the official contracts.

Of domestic happiness Gustav Adolf was vouchsafed but a meagre portion. Maria Eleonora, sentimentally devoted to her husband, was not merely attractive in her external appearance, she was naturally kind-hearted, and she had exceptionally good taste. But her emotional life lacked balance, and anything she undertook on her own initiative was always in need of careful watching. Her jealousy gradually concentrated itself upon Gustav Adolf's obligations as a king, and in this matter she often showed herself unreasonable; though there is something moving in her laments that she never had her hero to herself. She was given to language of unthinking violence, and (if we may trust a later hint of Axel Oxenstierna) she did not spare the person of her royal spouse, even if there were strangers present. Yet he was the only link that bound her to Sweden. She always had difficulty in adapting herself to the people, the countryside, and, not least, the climate. After Gustav Adolf's death, which plunged her into a prolonged crisis of hysteria, she found it more difficult than ever to conceal her dislike of "our rocks and mountains, the freezing air, and all the rest of it."

As the years passed Gustav Adolf came to be better acquainted with the "humor and disposition" of his queen. To the eye of the world, his relations with her were above criticism. But an inner circle knew that his married life was a source of grief and anxiety to him. Shortly before his death he spoke confidentially to his chancellor of his *malum domesticum*; in his view it was an offset to the many sources of happiness that life had brought him. Most of all he was troubled by the thought of the future. When, before his final departure from the country, he spoke of this question on one occasion to members of the Råd, he could not master his deep emotion, and it is said that as he spoke "the tears were rolling down his cheeks." What he desired was that after his death the Råd should provide guardians for his widow, "who, as His late Majesty himself observed, was but a weak woman." Axel Oxenstierna narrates that the king "for a full hour" implored him to take a binding oath on this question. The chancellor at last gave a personal promise, but declined an oath; and in fact the whole business was of extreme delicacy. Gustav Adolf was above all anxious to prevent his wife from having any influence upon the direction of affairs. Four years after the king's death Klas Fleming reminded a meeting of the Råd, as though it were a matter of common knowledge, that Gustav Adolf had often spoken in council of this matter, exhorting them "with the most urgent entreaties"; and the truth of this assertion is fully confirmed by all Gustav Adolf's arrangements for the future.

The grievous disappointment which Gustav Adolf experienced in his married life had, however, its deepest root in the absence of male heirs. His first child, a daughter named Kristina, who was born in the autumn of 1623, died when she was only twelve months old. For several years after this the country waited in vain for good news from the Court. The royal family, which had until lately been relatively numerous, suddenly dwindled away. In 1618 Duke Johan and Maria Elisabeth had died childless; in 1622 Karl Filip died without having contracted any marriage recognized by the law; and the two queens dowager followed each other to the grave within a few years. For some years, indeed, the greatest uncertainty prevailed as to the succession, particularly as it was well known that the king never shrank from exposing himself. This period is marked by the last efforts of Sigismund's secret agitation in Sweden, culminating in the year 1624, and these are undoubtedly to be connected with the insecurity of the dynasty. When in 1622 Gustav Adolf invited Johann Kasimir and Katarina to settle in Sweden, an important contributing cause must have been his desire to keep another possibility open for securing the succession. Such, at all events, was the opinion of the Danish agent in Stockholm. Shortly after the Palatine and his wife had moved to Sweden, their eldest son, Karl Gustav, was born. If Gustav Adolf had met his death in the years immediately following this event, it seems likely that his nephew would have been recognized as his successor, and consequently the Caroline family[7] would have obtained possession of the throne of Sweden far earlier than was actually the case.

However, a new Kristina, the most famous ever to bear the name, saw the light in Stockholm castle at the end of 1626. She herself wrote an account in French of what she had heard of the excitement which preceded her entry into the world, and of the disappointment that followed it. Maria Eleonora was quite certain that it would be a boy; both she and the king had had dreams which seemed to portend a male heir; and the astrologers with

[7] From Johann Kasimir and Katarina descended Karl X Gustav (1654-1660), Karl XI (1660-1697) and Karl XII (1697-1718). See also genealogical tree, p. 307.

whom the queen consulted were of opinion that sure signs pointed that way. When Kristina was born, covered in a caul from head to knees, the attendant women thought at first that she was a boy. "They filled the whole castle with false rejoicings, and for some moments deceived the king himself. Desire and hope combined to mislead them all." There was great dejection when the mistake was discovered. The Countess Palatine, bearing the infant in her arms, undertook to break the news to her brother. The account which Kristina gives of their meeting is a contribution to our knowledge of Gustav Adolf's character which bears the stamp of truth.

"This great prince, however, showed not the least surprise, but took me up and embraced me as tenderly as if his hopes had suffered no disappointment. To the princess he said: 'Let us thank God, sister. I hope that this daughter will take the place of a son, and I pray God, who gave her to me, to have her ever in his keeping.' The princess, thinking to please him, attempted to console him with the fact that he was still young, and the queen also, and that she might soon give him another child. But the king answered again: 'Sister, I am content. God preserve her'; whereupon he dismissed me with his blessing, and seemed so satisfied that all were amazed at it. He commanded the hymn 'O God, we praise Thee' to be sung, and the rejoicings usual at the birth of a male heir to the throne to take place. The king smilingly said of me: 'She is going to be clever, for she has taken us all in.'"

Kristina narrates that she had heard that at the time of her birth her father was seriously ill. The statement can be confirmed. Per Brahe, who as a gentleman of the bedchamber kept the king company while he was waiting, has noted in his diary that he was at that time laboring under a severe shaking-sickness, or ague, which he had contracted during his campaign in Prussia. By sheer will power he shook off the attack: "The king fenced with me double[8] in the dining-hall for some days, and so exerted himself that the shivering left him."

The right of the little princess to the throne was, by the terms of the Succession Agreement, incontestable; though it was a

[8] i.e. with a sword in each hand.

notion sufficiently foreign to traditional Swedish ideas. There is a story that even after Kristina's birth the king continued to discuss the rights of young Karl Gustav with his closest advisers; and as it is a tradition that goes back to first-hand authorities it is perhaps worth relating.

It was at Dirschau in Prussia, towards the end of August 1627. Gustav Adolf lay very sick of a dangerous musket-ball wound in his shoulder; not far away lay the Polish camp, at which Sigismund and Wladislaw had recently arrived on a tour of inspection. The high admiral, Karl Karlsson Gyllenhielm, who had been ordered to leave the fleet and wait upon the king, found him stretched on his bed. While he was speaking with him, Axel Oxenstierna came in with news. Among other things, he had intercepted a Polish "discourse" alleged to have been pronounced at table by King Sigismund. If anything were to happen to Gustav Adolf, to whom would the crown of Sweden fall, in view of the fact that he refused to bestow it on Sigismund? Sigismund had essayed to answer that question: "Perhaps he would give it to his nephew." And Gyllenhielm, who is the narrator of this scene, graphically continues: "Thereupon, after considering a little, looking from me to the chancellor and back again, His Majesty made answer to the chancellor: 'Yes, I don't know where you will find a better.' Immediately afterwards the chancellor changed the subject, and nothing more [was said] of it."

Gyllenhielm's account is in his own hand; it is addressed to Queen Kristina, and it was written some time in the latter half of the decade 1640-1650. Probably the queen would never have seen it if the old admiral had not been guilty of a serious lapse of memory. For although he could recall these circumstances to mind with such particularity that the occasion can be dated to within a week, he labored under the misapprehension that Kristina had not been born at the time the conversation took place. The queen was not the only person to whom he confided his reminiscences. The same setting, the same reflection on the part of Sigismund, and nearly the same answer by Gustav Adolf—"Who else?"—were incorporated into the report of the trial of the Messenii for high treason in 1651, on which occasion Gyllenhielm (by this time dead) was cited as the source of the story.

Axel Oxenstierna's view of Gustav Adolf's attitude towards his Palatine relations at this time was rather different. He too has a story of a conversation at the time of the king's illness at Dirschau in 1627; but it was a private conversation between the king and himself. Gustav Adolf had one day earnestly entreated Oxenstierna to tell him without equivocation whom he thought the Estates would take as king after his death. The chancellor, who at first sought to parry the question, was at last constrained to answer, and named Johann Kasimir, or, in the event of his dying before the king, his son Karl Gustav. Thereupon the king prayed to God to turn the chancellor and the Estates from such courses. "You may be certain of this, that if you crown either of them your king one day, you will regret it the next!" For the accuracy of this report we have the witness of the secretary who in 1649 called upon Oxenstierna at the queen's orders, to obtain his signature to the instrument dealing with Karl Gustav's succession, and made notes of his conversation immediately afterwards. And if the source may possibly be a little tainted, there are other *dicta* of Oxenstierna preserved in the reports of council meetings, which at least go to show that his views differed from Gyllenhielm's. "The late king never entertained any such idea," he said on one occasion, with obvious reference to this controversy.

How far the versions of the admiral and the chancellor are in the last resort reconcilable cannot be discussed here. There is indeed no reason why the king should not have expressed himself more freely to the latter than to both of them together. In any case it may be held to be proved that as late as 1627 Kristina's succession was considered as to some extent uncertain, in spite of the Succession Agreement. This conclusion is further strengthened by a remarkable circumstance. Kristina was born on December 7, 1626. In the course of 1627 two meetings of the Riksdag were held, one at the beginning, and one at the end of the year. At the latter, arrangements were made to confirm the Succession Agreement in the female line by a new resolution of the Estates. The reason given was that "many simple persons among people of all degree" had not grasped the provision as to the right of hereditary princesses to the crown. It was something fundamentally new and strange to the traditional ideas of the Swedish people.

Gustav Adolf's thoughts often dwelt uneasily on the future that awaited his wife and little Kristina. To Axel Oxenstierna he confessed: "If anything happens to me, my family will merit your pity, not for my sake only, but for many other reasons. They are womenfolk, the mother lacking in common sense, the daughter a minor—hopeless, if they rule, and dangerous, if others come to rule over them." (December 1630.) It has always been a matter of astonishment that he should have for so long postponed his ratification of the Form of Government, which arranged for the organization of the administration after his death—for so long, indeed, that in the end it never received his final approval and signature. One important reason, though possibly not the only one, at once leaps to the mind: there can be no doubt, that consideration for Maria Eleonora's feelings held him back. The welfare of the State, with which he never compromised, ruled her out from any influence upon the direction of affairs. To state this openly would probably have involved Gustav Adolf in an awkward personal crisis in his relations with his wife.

With regard to Kristina, Gustav Adolf in the last years of his life kept steadily before him the idea of a new family alliance with the house of Brandenburg. At all events he was anxious to test the strength and practicability of such a scheme—the proposal was that the heiress to Sweden should marry the electoral prince Friedrich Wilhelm, later known as the Great Elector—with reference to the possibility which it might offer for smoothing out the conflicting interests of the two powers. In an indefinite future lay the dream of a great Swedish-German State under a common ruler. The marriage project survived Gustav Adolf, but the wider scheme of which it was a part was buried with him.

THE MAN AND THE MONARCH

THE MAN AND THE MONARCH

[1]

AMONG the historical anecdotes which have passed into the popular consciousness is the story of the exchange of pleasantries between Gustav Adolf and Axel Oxenstierna as to the ardor of the one and the phlegm of the other.[1] It is entirely credible, for the chancellor himself in his old age told it to a foreign diplomat—Cromwell's ambassador Whitelocke; though it had not then the epigrammatic form of the less authentic version which usually appears in our text-books. It seems, for instance, that in reality Oxenstierna made no allusion in his reply to the danger that the king might "burn himself out"; he merely permitted himself the observation that his master's affairs would scarcely have gone so well, if the hot blood of the king had not been tempered by the cold douches administered by his chancellor. And he was able to add, when telling the story to the Englishman, that the king had laughed heartily at this answer, and had begged him to speak his mind freely upon all occasions.

This dialogue, however characteristic of Gustav Adolf's relations with his famous chancellor, may easily be given too narrow an interpretation, which would be quite misleading; for in Gustav Adolf himself there was something of this mingling of "humors," and it was sufficiently marked to put its imprint upon his whole personality. No doubt the most fundamental, and therefore the most easily perceptible trait in his nature was his impulsiveness; and this trait provides the clue to the lively tempo of his ordinary life, as it certainly does to his mental processes. The inner fire was never quenched; at any moment its blaze might irradiate his being anew. But side by side with this ardor, which provided, over and over again, the human motive force behind those deeds which speak so eloquently of the strength of his will, there lay, buried deep in his soul, an inexhaustible treasury of qualities less

---

[1] On one occasion the king, indignant at the scruples of his chancellor, is said to have let fly at him with the words: "If my ardor didn't put some life into your phlegm, we should never get anything done at all." To which the chancellor replied: "If my phlegm didn't temper your Majesty's ardor you would have burnt yourself out long ago."

characteristic of his temperament than of his actions, though they permeate these latter so markedly that they must be assumed to have been innate hereditary qualities rather than the result of systematic schooling and self-induced habit. These qualities may be summed up for the sake of brevity in the single word circumspection, provided that the term is not taken in too restricted a sense. It implies the sober foresight of his calculations, the systematical planning of his undertakings, his predilection for a nice weighing of counsels, his ability to hold off or stop short when necessary. These characteristics—for that term may fairly be applied to them—had no doubt been moulded by Gustav Adolf's upbringing (we are already familiar with the main principles that inspired it), and still more by his long and fruitful collaboration with Axel Oxenstierna, that distinguished exponent of the art of imperturbable composure. In short, they cannot be dissociated from the picture of Gustav Adolf that has come down to us. And it is worth while adding that this same self-mastery—vigilant and often slow in decision—was perhaps most clearly evident in that field of activity where the king was most independent of his chancellor—the field of battle.

Yet, if we isolate these aspects of Gustav Adolf's character and subject them to individual scrutiny, the resemblance to the original diminishes at once. It is the combination of qualities that is decisive. The contradictory tendencies of his nature, of which one of his historians speaks, are really a fundamental and indivisible feature of it. Side by side with his calculating caution there lay within him a *penchant*, profound and unmistakable, for the bold stroke; side by side with his methodical circumspection, an urge to rush in and stir things up by his own personal exertions—an urge to which there are witnesses from every day and every hour of his life. With his anxious cogitation went decisions often hasty, sometimes premature; with his patience, occasional precipitation. The discords inherent in his temperament were never fully resolved, but the spiritual riches they brought him were of a fortunate quality that transcended the common measure of humanity.

Enthusiasm was with him a normal condition. When he conversed, he soon talked himself into a heat, accompanying his words with emphatic gestures, and throwing his head back in that favorite attitude which a sculptor has immortalized in bronze. He had a trick of striking himself on the breast in token of his sincerity, and by way of lending emphasis to his words. It is thus that an enemy—Prince Kristoffer Radziwill—described him, after a personal meeting during the Livland campaign of 1622. Later in life he became more deliberate in his movements—partly, at all events, as a consequence of the famous "Dirschau bullets,"[2] which made his right shoulder and arm somewhat stiff. But his blazing spirit remained unchanged. As a negotiator he was dangerous because he so seldom lost the spirit of attack. Hercule de Charnacé had immediate experience of it when in the autumn of 1629 he began his long negotiations for a Franco-Swedish alliance against the emperor. The king plunged at once into the subject by observing that Cardinal Richelieu was used to say of the Venetians that they were people who preferred to stay in port and send others to take their place in the storm: was it an arrangement of this sort that was now in contemplation? He was famous for his desire to convince his adversary at any price, and also for the shattering candor with which he expressed himself. He could command either bitter irony or dignified appeal as effective rhetorical weapons. His orders were, as a rule, extremely peremptory. Even the first years of his reign can show a long list of examples of personal orders and reproofs which for bluntness and peremptoriness of tone can bear comparison with those of his father or his grandfather: "As you desire to avoid our wrath and displeasure. . . ." He loved clear and rapid explanations, but on the other hand was perfectly able to talk round and round the point, if that were necessary. No stickler for ceremony himself, he was yet appreciative of its value in certain cases. He was to an exceptional degree what is called a man of action; but he took unusual care to choose the precise moment to act.

When he was in an equable mood, he developed a personal amiability which had few rivals. We have innumerable proofs of it. He had the art of lightening labor with a jest, and the art also of throwing off care and joining in the gaiety of others.

[2] See below, p. 125.

"Always *allegro* and *courageux,* as though he had not a care
in the world," as a witness from Frankfurt-am-Main described
him in 1631. Not one of the pictures of Gustav Adolf that has
been preserved—and they are of very varying merit—gives any
idea of the vivacity and mobility of his facial expression. "He
says everything with a smile on his lips," writes one observer;
"he cannot speak ten or twelve words without laughing," says
another, with reference to a somewhat later occasion. He had the
knack of getting on well with high or low, clerk or layman. "It
is impossible not to admire how gracious, courtly, and friendly
this king is, so that any man at the mere sight of him must feel
his heart warming towards him," says our observer from Frankfurt, a young man in the service of one of the town councillors.
"He can talk so affably with the smallest child, and even with
peasants, that no description can do justice to it." The judgment
comes indeed from a time when the king's fortunes stood at their
zenith, and when his outward demeanor was a matter of some
importance to the Protestant propagandists, who had as a matter
of fact several possible strings to their bow. But Gustav Adolf
really did tally with the description: his attitude to all and sundry
was invariably free from artificiality or constraint, and abundantly
human. He had no difficulty in finding things to talk about.
When he liked, he could fascinate from the first moment of
meeting. Johannes Botvidi, whose funeral sermon upon the king
strikes an unmistakably personal note, does not forget to call
to mind how "he accommodated himself to the age and condition
of each, as time and occasion might demand; conversing with
spirit, and answering with graciousness." This was a trait which
early attracted general attention. "He is not vindictive," ran the
judgment of a Dutchman written in 1616, "but a most gracious
monarch, sagacious, bold, and wary, and in particular most
lovable and friendly in his dealings with every man."

Gustav Adolf had the faculty of condescending without seem-
ing to do so, and without loss of dignity. Men knew that the
charm radiated by the infectious liveliness of his manners was
the product of a warm heart. And this sunny side grew still more
attractive with the passage of time, since no one could be in-

sensible of the imperious spirit which increasingly permeated his whole personality.

[2]

BUT it was easy—far too easy—to put him out of temper.

He had naturally a strong choleric vein, and his anger often boiled over. Frequently he forgot himself, though it was usually in speech rather than in action. He was himself fully conscious of this weakness, and strove to overcome it, though never with complete success. Now and then his face would redden for a moment—a sign that he was fighting down his anger. Sir Henry Vane, who had come into violent collision with Gustav Adolf in the summer of 1632 during the negotiations regarding the conditions for a restoration of the Palatinate to its exiled sovereigns, wrote shortly afterwards: "It is usual for this king to feel remorse after the blow has been struck. He has often remarked to me after the incident in Munich that he regretted his behavior, and that he would willingly give all he had to be master of his passions, but he has something which rises in his brain when he is excited, and makes him forget what he is doing or saying. He is quite conscious of it as soon as he has recovered his good humor, and then he realizes what unhappiness it has caused. But none the less he cannot control it, although he has often desired to do so, and he hopes therefore that God and the whole world may pardon him." The excellent character sketch of Gustav Adolf which was incorporated into *Le Soldat Suédois*, a work published shortly after his death, the author of which was almost certainly the diplomat and publicist Rasche, gives a milder version of the king's self-reproaches. "He used to say," it runs, "that since he was constantly forced to endure humors of all sorts—the inertia of some, the drunkenness of others—he felt that he ought to be able to count on some small indulgence to his temper, by way of compensation."

A number of cases are known to us in which this hereditary trait came uppermost. Gustav Adolf's wrath, which usually mounted rapidly, found its normal outlet in mouth-filling utterance. Sometimes he would proceed to threats, and then it was safest to bow before the storm; but it was never a very enviable situation, least of all for such as were suspected of not having a clear conscience. A deputation from the nobility of Estland, for instance, which arrived at Stockholm in the spring of 1629 to present a variety of complaints, had bitter experience of this. One of them has described how they stood "a good while, blushing or pallid, yea, trembling before His Majesty, while His Majesty held such sharp and violent language to us, and charged us, as representatives of our countrymen, with such deeds, such improprieties and such sins, that the very dogs (as the phrase is) would have refused a crust from us." On this occasion the king had been roused to indignation beforehand, by what he considered the egotism and imprudent zeal of the Baltic nobility, and as the audience proceeded his indignation turned to fury: he displayed (in the words of the narrative) "a blazing wrath; he consigned us and our province to perdition in the presence of the whole Råd." An interview with some deputies from Reval in 1626 came to an equally violent conclusion. The question at issue was the introduction of the so-called "Little Toll," which had been imposed some years earlier in Sweden, but to which the town was unwilling to submit. At last the king wrathfully threatened that in the last resort he would "write such proclamations on the walls of their houses with his cannon-balls that the citizens would never believe their eyes." They must have realized that it was only a figure of speech, but they found, to their infinite chagrin, that they had no alternative but to give way.

The milder and more frequent manifestations of Gustav Adolf's vehemence were the results of that impatience—natural to his active temperament—which made him the moving spirit in great and small undertakings alike. He, who was always weighing difficulties, could give way to fiery indignation when he saw his path barred by objections which seemed to him irrelevant. It was, moreover, his firm conviction that righteous wrath would always prevail. And when in addition he felt his honor to be called in question, his passion brought strong language to his lips. Read, for instance, his indictment of the German officers at Nürnberg, in June 1632: "You—princes, counts, gentlemen, nobles! It is you who have been guilty of infidelity and impiety towards your fatherland—that fatherland which you are yourselves despoiling, harrying, reducing to a desert. You—captains, officers—high and low alike—it is precisely *you* who steal and plunder, without a single exception. . . . God my Creator is my witness that my blood turns to gall within me when I set eyes on one of you. . . . I had rather ride without a shirt to my back than be clothed at your expense. All that God put into my hands I gave you. Not a pigsty, in all reverence be it spoken, have I had in my possession, but I have shared it with you. . . . You take it upon yourselves to rebel: well and good! Then I, with my Swedes and my Finns, will first have such a bout with you as will make the fur fly to some purpose. . . . It sickens me to be amongst you; it enrages me that I must have dealings with so perverted a people." The king was more transported by passion than the spectators had ever seen him. The cause of this outbreak was the growing laxity in the discipline of the German soldiery. The speech, which as a matter of fact ended more indulgently than it began, had, according to an eyewitness, an overwhelming, indeed stunning, effect. When the king had finished he caught sight of two stolen cows outside a corporal's tent. After verifying the facts, he took the offender by the ear and hauled him off to the executioner: "Come along, my son, it is better that I punish you than that God punish you—and not you only, but all the rest of us on your account."

It is hardly surprising that his interviews with representatives of foreign powers should now and then have taken a rather stormy course. The episode with Sir Henry Vane to which reference was made above was but one instance out of many. The arts of dissimulation were not for Gustav Adolf. In verbal negotiations he preferred to go straight to the point, and he allowed his antipathies to appear without apparent scruple and sometimes in very trenchant fashion. On one occasion in the spring of 1627, when he received in audience the envoys of Georg Wilhelm of Brandenburg, who had been sent to avert the infringement of their country's neutrality, the king expressed himself with the greatest acerbity in regard to one of the elector's councillors, the Catholic Count Schwarzenberg, who was always—and with good reason—considered to be hostile to Sweden. He advised the disconcerted Brandenburgers to follow the famous Bohemian example, and throw him out of the window: "You should play *defenestration* with the count, and break his neck for him." The remark, which was at once reported to Berlin, and thence to Warsaw, was no doubt made in hot blood. Yet more than once he expressed himself hardly less frankly, if not quite so forcibly, when he had obviously chosen his words deliberately. In the course of a single conversation, moreover—there are reports extant of several of Gustav Adolf's audiences—he would be amiable one moment and angry the next, and then he would growl away with a malicious twinkle lurking in the corner of his eye. This was his tactic in the negotiations with the envoys of Riga, when he was besieging that city in 1621. He told them, *inter alia*, that it was his intention to take up his quarters inside the town, for he found camp life too uncomfortable. Charnacé, in his dispatches to Paris, describes how the king, in the course of the tedious negotiations of 1630, several times became "outrageously" violent; though he adds that fortunately the storm regularly "blew itself out, leaving a dead calm behind it."

Passionate natures are apt to suffer periods of reaction and enfeebled will power. Gustav Adolf was not of that type. He had his hours of discouragement and depression, but the ability to stick to a resolution was one of his strongest assets. And on the whole his nervous crises did more to forward his work than to impede it. This element in his character was indeed the natural concomitant of his resilience and energy. He possessed, says *Le Soldat Suédois*, "the temper usual in fiery spirits who warm to their work." Quite apart from the crises, the mental temperature remained at a constant high level, and was thus less liable to capricious variations than might normally have been expected.

It goes without saying that Gustav Adolf also came into collision now and then with his own family, and with the narrow circle of his collaborators. During the Stockholm Riksdag of 1617 he had a severe struggle with the queen mother and Duke Johan over the extent of the rights which the hereditary princes were to enjoy within the limits of their duchies. The form of knight service due from their nobles was a particularly contentious point. The king's brother, Karl Filip, who had a temper not unlike Gustav Adolf's, made the most obstinate efforts to induce him to accept a deed signed by his mother, embodying what she conceived to be a satisfactory settlement. Gustav Adolf refused, but Karl Filip persisted. At last Gustav Adolf lost all patience: there was a fire crackling upon the open hearth, and in a fury he hurled the document into it. The incident could hardly be ignored; and it was in fact reported in the official minutes of the Riksdag.

In the council chamber too, where under the king's guidance harmonious collaboration was the general rule, there were times when his dissatisfaction expressed itself with characteristic vigor, to the accompaniment of words of cold displeasure. "The king angry," notes Abraham Brahe of the meeting of April 23, 1629. On the previous day he had been unwilling to shake Count Abraham's hand; and he stayed away from the two following meetings, although the Råd sat waiting for him. So much ill-temper within a short period was, however, exceptional. Evidently, the king's equanimity was especially sorely tried this spring. We remember how trenchantly he took the Estonian nobles to task. This was, moreover, a time of great tension, very trying for one whose craving for action was not always equalled by his patience. The decision had been taken for war with the emperor.

[3]

THE oft-told story of Gustav Adolf's magnanimity to Colonel Seaton—how he offered him satisfaction, pistol in hand—must no doubt be rejected as apocryphal in origin and improbable in fact; but even when this has been discounted there remain numerous and well attested proofs that Gustav Adolf was not the man to bear a grudge.

He was quick to recover his equanimity, and as a rule he was prompt to make amends when he felt that he had been guilty of losing his self-control. To sweep away injustice was for him an imperious necessity; and it was his invariable policy to compose differences wherever that was possible without sacrifice of principle. The best witness to this is not so much the amicable settlement of his private quarrels as the great work of internal conciliation which was carried out in his reign. The majority of those nobles who had gone into exile for their fidelity to Sigis-

mund were gradually reclaimed for their fatherland, and the sons
of those lords whose heads had fallen on the scaffold were bound
to the new dynasty by the twin ties of administrative responsibility
and personal devotion—and all this without the smallest devia-
tion from the historic doctrines inherited from Karl IX.

On the other hand there are not lacking proofs of the fact that
Gustav Adolf could be inexorable on occasion. He had in general
a marked predilection for making an example of an offender; and
in this he had the support of contemporary opinion. In particular,
where it was a question of prevention by the threat of punishment, he had an obvious taste for Draconian formulae. Unjust
judges were threatened with being nailed to the gallows, corrupt
bailiffs were promised a hempen collar, and so on. He is said once
to have permitted a duel on condition that only one party survived, and that the survivor was afterwards to be shot. All of
which was very much in the manner of his father. But he added
a note of implacability which reminds us once more of the
inherent contradictions of his character.

Posterity has certainly attached more importance to the unhappy
fate which overtook the learned Messenius than his contemporaries ever did. Humanly speaking, it was a grievous loss to
Swedish culture when in 1616 Messenius was exiled for life to
the desolate wilds of the remotest corner of Österbotten. Within
a few years Messenius had by his own exertions achieved more
for Swedish historical criticism than the whole generation that
had preceded him. The sentence pronounced upon him was in
strict accordance with the letter of the law, since in defiance of the
stringent prohibition of the Estates he had entered into relations
with the Swedish exiles in Poland; but in view of the fact that
no proof was forthcoming of any treasonable intention, the punishment certainly seems to have been extraordinarily severe. At
the time when sentence was pronounced, Sweden was in a state
of great nervous excitement, in consequence of all sorts of rumors
of plots against the safety of the realm. The unhappy savant's
plea for mercy therefore left the king unmoved: in this case he
showed himself absolutely pitiless. He had a profound suspicion
of Messenius. He saw in Messenius's proceedings a gross breach
of trust, a sign of ineradicable bad faith. He was not mistaken;

Messenius was in fact a man of divided allegiance. His heart was in another age and another faith.

Especial notoriety attaches to Gustav Adolf's disgracing of Erik Brorsson Rålamb. Rålamb had only recently been appointed one of the king's chamberlains. At a dinner given at Höchst on November 18, 1631, he was ordered to serve the king and his distinguished guests. Such a service was no part of his normal duties; he therefore refused to obey. His refusal is susceptible of various explanations: "haughty insubordination and malevolence" according to the king; a swollen hand and consequent diffidence, according to the letter which Rålamb wrote to his stepmother in Sweden. It is not possible to come to any certain conclusion; in a subsequent petition Erik admitted his "sudden lapse and lack of consideration," but denied absolutely any "unfaithfulness or disobedience." Yet is it possible that Gustav Adolf's view was the right one. At all events, Rålamb withdrew and sent a gentleman of the chamber to perform the duty in his place. When the meal was over—not without the usual toasts in the meantime—Gustav Adolf's pent-up anger burst its banks.

Brushing aside all excuses, he ordered the young man to be arrested. Rålamb implored his pardon, but received such a blow on the head from the flat of the king's sword that the blade broke in two. Rålamb's statement, that he thereupon took the opportunity to abscond, is plainly untrue. Indeed, on the following day the king wrote to the Råd that he was about to send the youth home to Stockholm to stand his trial for impertinence. It was not until more than a week later that Gustav Adolf could inform the Råd of a "fresh affront" from Rålamb; the young man had fled—perhaps to the enemy. It was now, and not in his earlier communication, that he gave the famous order that the culprit's father was to be suspended from his official functions, and the royal estates which had been conferred upon him to be sequestered until he had handed over his son to receive his due punishment at the hands of the Råd, "so that other parents may learn thereby how they ought to breed up their sons to better docility, obedience, reverence, and respect towards their sovereign."

A long time elapsed, however, before this letter was actually sent off. It was not until four months later that it reached the

Råd, who by that time had in their possession messages from the king of much more recent date. The explanation must be that Gustav Adolf upon more mature consideration found it fairer to wait, in case the fugitive should return to stand his trial. But as nothing was heard of him, the letter was at last dispatched. Naturally it produced a most disagreeable impression upon the lords of the council. The father of the vanished youth, Bror Andersson Rålamb, was an old and trusty servant of the State; he had at this time risen to be president of the recently created supreme court at Åbo. It seemed to the Råd unthinkable that he could have had any part in his son's "monstrous insolence," particularly as he was known to have employed a good part of his fortune in an attempt to interest his son in the pursuit of learning, by sending him on study tours overseas. They therefore asked that the king should spare him the ignominy of dismissal from office. The appeal left Gustav Adolf unmoved. He reaffirmed his order in a new letter from the camp at Nürnberg at the end of June 1632. He considered that he had the more reason to be annoyed, since he had shown signal favor to Erik Rålamb in making him his chamberlain, although on his father's side he came of mere peasant stock. And the order was carried out.

In this last letter, however, the king had already admitted that the case might perhaps merit "further reflection." And it is certain that before his death he had so far yielded as to declare that "he would no longer continue in his displeasure against the son, and especially against the father," as Axel Oxenstierna later expressed it. Erik Rålamb, who had at last reappeared in Stockholm—at all events he was there shortly after Gustav Adolf's death—was informed of this concession; and he wrote to the chancellor, asking him to testify in the presence of the Råd, that the king had in the end "abated his wrath and begun to incline his heart to mercy." There could be no question, however, of anything but a verbal pardon: the king never found time to promulgate any new order concerning the case, although it seems that he contemplated doing so. It was for this reason that Bror Andersson had to wait until 1634 before receiving a new appointment as *landshövding*. The old man was all but broken. The affair, he told Oxenstierna, had played such havoc with his health "that neither my head nor my hands can well perform their office." How far Erik Brorsson suffered any further punishment seems to be quite uncertain; it was at all events limited to arrest for a comparatively brief period. It may perhaps be assumed that he had presented himself before the Råd at Stockholm in the autumn of 1632, and that this fact, having been brought to the king's notice, helped to induce Gustav Adolf to change his opinion.

Not the least remarkable feature of the case is the part played by Axel Oxenstierna in arranging a settlement. His own version is that it was the humane intercession of the queen that softened the king. To judge from the fact that Maria Eleonora, immediately after her return from Germany, showed her displeasure at the fact that Erik Rålamb was still suffered to remain in the kingdom, her intervention was purely formal. The chancellor, who after Gustav Adolf's death took a fatherly interest in Erik Rålamb, was undoubtedly the person who made the most important efforts to plead his cause with the king as opportunity offered. It can be inferred that he disliked and deplored Gustav Adolf's method of procedure. An old friend of Bror Andersson, he came to think highly of his son, attached him to his service in Germany, and allowed him to accompany the great embassy to France in the spring of 1635. When it returned from Paris, Erik Rålamb had to be left behind sick; and in Paris, a few days later, he died, in the care of no less a person than Hugo Grotius. That he was a man of learning and talent may be considered certain. Possibly as a youth he was a little lacking in balance; for it is said that during a previous stay in Paris he had run into debt "to an extraordinary extent," and that in Amsterdam he had involved himself in "needless brawls."

After the incident at Höchst, Gustav Adolf had nourished suspicions that "there may be more in this than meets the eye." Earlier writers who have dealt with the affair have put the question as to whether Erik Rålamb may not perhaps have held opinions hostile to the monarchy. We know nothing of any such opinions. But a younger brother of his, Klas Rålamb, was in the next generation to stand out as the most energetic, and undoubtedly also the most talented champion of the aristocratic opposition.

[4]

"His Majesty was of lofty stature, of finely proportioned build, with a fair complexion, long face, blond hair, and pointed beard of an almost golden hue." Such was Gustav Adolf at twenty-one, as described by a foreigner—a Dutchman—who saw him in his capital. Descriptions of his external appearance are otherwise extremely rare for the period before he took the center of the European stage; and it is unfortunate that there should also be very few portraits dating from this time. An engraving of 1616 gives decided confirmation to the impression that he had a rather elongated face; it brings out also the large eyes and the hooked nose—we remember how his people nicknamed him Gösta Hooknose—while the mouth is small, as though it were pursed up, and is as yet shaded only by a sparse moustache. A picture of the king in his coronation robes gives the same impression of youthfulness, though the expression is now tinged with more of firmness and maturity: the typical Vasa features are appearing with striking distinctness. Complexion, color of eyes and hair, all emphasize that here is the Northern type in all its purity. The hair was described in 1620 as "pale gold"; to judge from the print of 1616 Gustav Adolf let it grow longer as a youth than in later years, though he always brushed it straight back from the forehead. The breadth of the shoulders spoke of physical strength. One bodily defect, though it was not of a really serious sort, was a great handicap to him on the battlefield—his short-sightedness.

Most of the portraits of the king, whether they are verbal descriptions or pictures, date from his years in Germany. "He is an exceptionally handsome man, very full-featured, with a reddish pointed beard, short hair, and middling stature," says one of his many admirers. The general impression was that his appearance was commanding, indeed majestic, and the South Germans in particular seem to have delighted in the sight of him. Increasing corpulence and a greater heaviness of the features towards the end of his life were scarcely blemishes upon his appearance according to the taste and style of the time; it is even difficult to resist the feeling that several of his portrait-painters revelled in these particular details. In the camp, indeed, the king's girth was the subject of many a good jest among the soldiers; and if the jest reached the king's ears, he did not take it amiss. It was a touch of irony at his own expense when he went to a masquerade at Mainz in 1632 dressed as—a stableboy. By the middle of his reign his tendency to run to fat was already very noticeable—and was, moreover, well known abroad—and it increased pretty steadily, especially in the last years of his life, in spite of an anything but sedentary existence.

Gustav Adolf affected a simple style of living, at least for ordinary occasions, and when there was work to be done. It was a habit which dated from his childhood, when he had evidently not been too well provided for, if we may judge from the fact that on one occasion Johan Skytte made him a present of a pair of silk stockings. For his own part he entirely renounced all superficial pomp, "seldom wearing a ring on his finger, a chain over his coat, or a feather in his hat." (Botvidi.) The Germans were struck by the fact that he was usually to be seen without any jewels or ornaments; he reminded them, according to one account, more of a count or a rich merchant than of a prince. On campaign this simplicity was carried to extreme limits. Whilst the Polish generals lived in Turkish tents furnished with velvet cushions, the "duke of Södermanland" contented himself with such rude accommodation that his enemies made merry over his "sackcloth." He realized, moreover, the educative value of example. When the duke of Pomerania invited him to take up his quarters in the castle of Stettin, he preferred to spend the night aboard ship, remarking that "If the king lies on a sailor's bed, the soldier will be content with a bundle of straw."

His everyday fare was simple too. He did not care to sit long at table, and ate whatever was provided with relish; and we have the chance information that the elegance of his table manners aroused admiration. In the heats of summer, in particular, he suffered much from thirst; and he loved to slake it with great draughts of cold water—a habit which was certainly not without its dangers. It brought on an illness during the Danish campaign of 1612. At meals, too, he drank water for choice. The priest who pronounced his funeral oration is loud in his praises of the king's sobriety. Standards were very different in those days, but it is noteworthy that his daughter Kristina, who was very strait-laced upon this point, and often severe in her judgments, concurs with only very slight reservations. "He was not over-fond of wine," she writes; "he did drink—a common fault in the North—but never in such quantity as to prevent him from caring for his honor, or attending to his duty. It was a matter, not of inclination, but of reasons of State."

On ceremonial occasions, on the other hand, Gustav delighted in the pride of pageantry. "When he must needs appear in his royal state, he assumed such dignity that all who saw him were filled with pleasure and gladness thereat." He never grudged expenditure upon ceremonial. His coronation, though it was long deferred—mainly from considerations of economy—was marked by the pomp demanded by Continental custom; and according to a tradition later current in the Råd, the people, burdened as they were at that time by the Älvsborg Ransom, expressed their disapproval. At moments when it was necessary that he should appear clad in the authority of a conqueror, he assumed a habit proper to the occasion. At his entry into Frankfurt (November 1631) he was mounted on a black Spanish charger, and was arrayed in a scarlet coat embroidered with silver—the noble "Polish coat" which he wears in the picture at Skokloster. But his personal expenses were always kept within pretty strait limits. The proportion of the country's budget appropriated to the Court is well known to have been a mere fraction of that allotted to the Court of Kristina.

It is impossible to resist the temptation to insert here the lively and striking character sketch of the king given by Count Gualdo Priorato in his work on the campaigns of these years. A soldier and a historian, Gualdo Priorato had served as an officer in Wallenstein's army and had subsequently studied Swedish tactics under Gustav Horn and Bernhard of Weimar. The directness and precision of this literary portrait are evidence of the fact that the king had already become part of a living military tradition.

"Gustav was of tall stature, upright and well proportioned, stout, but not excessively so, with something so majestic in his bearing, and something so tender in his gaze, that there was not a man who saw him who was not filled with reverence, wonder,

GUSTAV ADOLF IN A "POLISH COAT"

Oil Painting by M. Merian

and love. He had a high forehead, a pink and white complexion, regular features, beard and hair of pale gold, and large, short-sighted eyes. He was still in his thirty-eighth year, and continual military service, dating from his youthful campaigns under the king his father, had inured him to hard labor. He had a fondness for the profession of arms, even from his childhood, and it was soon apparent that he thirsted for glory, and would one day make a great reputation for himself. He was prudent in action, eloquent in speech, and positively fascinating in the graciousness of his manners; his undertakings were designed upon the grandest scale; he was fertile in resource, unshaken in adversity, valiant in battle, dauntless in danger, vigilant when vigilance was necessary. In short, there was nothing that he was not; nothing that he did not do; nothing that he did not do well. There has never been a commander who served with more zeal, and with more love of service. Moreover, the man who served him well was never forgotten; a brave action remained written on his memory in ineffaceable characters. In conversation he was gay, affable, easy of access, taking pleasure in encouraging such as spoke to him by asking each one kindly who he was, and what he desired. The gentlemen of his court went freely into his chamber. Any officer, without distinction of rank, was admitted at his table. Gustav used to say that good cheer is a torment to the indiscreet and a hook for securing the well disposed: meaning thereby that it is at table that a man learns best how to estimate character, and there too that he forms his best friendships. He disliked pomp, and was too great to have need of flatterers: anything that smacked of affectation was repugnant to him. If anyone in ignorance of his character approached him with exaggerated humility, he would say, 'My friend, keep all that for the queen's ladies. I am here to command and to fight, not to play the dancing master!' "

The hospitable spirit of seventeenth century Scandinavia found in Gustav Adolf a worthy representative. At such times he loved to throw himself into the business of entertaining: whether the occasion were a sad or a merry one was, by contemporary standards, a matter of minor importance—as for instance, at the funeral feast for Abraham Brahe, which took place in the spring of 1630 at Rydboholm Castle in the Roslagen, the old family seat of the Vasas. "This was the last fête that the king attended here in Sweden," says the dead man's son, Per Brahe, "and he made himself very merry with my brothers and some of the other officers." We meet this phraseology over and over again: His Majesty showed himself very merry. But it was not only at the table that he enjoyed himself. In spite of his bulk Gustav Adolf was a skilful and enthusiastic dancer. During those months in west and south Germany when, in the intervals of his activity, he had better opportunities than at other times for the diversions proper to his rank, he frequently ordered balls to be given, sometimes of a hastily improvised nature. It happened at Frankfurt on one of these occasions that when the dance had been in progress for some time, the king decided that there was a shortage of ladies; whereupon reinforcements were hastily procured from the town. At Nürnberg, where he expressed a wish to be allowed to see the daughters of the leading burghers in the "antique" festival costumes of the district, he had to break off the dance upon the arrival of a courier with a report: he read it through in haste, but plainly found it to his satisfaction, for we are told that when the dance was resumed he appeared even gayer than before, and "über alle Massen tapfer gesprungen."

From a similar function at Augsburg one tangible memorial has been preserved, in the shape of a lace collar, once the property of Gustav Adolf. According to a family tradition apparently written down at an early date, it was then presented by him to a young lady of that city, Jungfrau Anna Maria Bresler. She is said to have been the fairest woman at the ball held on May 30, 1632, and the king danced with her again and again. While he was "graciously caressing" the young beauty, she in her embarrassment accidentally tore some holes in his collar; and he thereupon presented it to her, together with some jewellery, as a memento of the occasion. The little episode may perhaps be taken as a confirmation—a very innocent one, certainly—of Kristina's character sketch of her father, where she accounts it as one of his faults (besides his hasty temper) that "he was too fond of the ladies."

[5]

THE temperamental restlessness which was so characteristic of Gustav Adolf appeared most strongly in his incessant activity. "His late Majesty often went sweating to bed," to use Axel Oxenstierna's blunt words. It was with a clear conscience that the king could claim, towards the end of his life (December 1630), that he had sought no higher goal upon earth than to do his duty in a manner fitting to the station into which it had pleased God to call him. And though this ideal of duty, if only because of the conception of kingship traditional to Vasa Sweden, was notably free from the narrowness inherent in the limitations of royalty, it was no less so in virtue of the interpretation which Gustav Adolf put upon it in thought and action. He was, as it were, in a state of perpetual motion, for one enterprise or another was invariably engaging his attention.

A habit of trusting to his own exertions in all matters which might affect his work was early developed in Gustav Adolf, not without some help from external circumstances. It was a habit which often stood him in good stead. "Lars Nilsson and Peder Ersson are both ill, so I am secretary and chamberlain in one— I only need to be batman too, and I shall be a complete staff," he writes with some humor in an oft-quoted letter to the chancellor during the Polish campaign of 1625. In his everyday enterprises and occupations he was notably independent of the help of subordinates. He could, at need, dispense altogether with one or other of them, though naturally there were limits to what he could undertake himself. Even in the matter of administrative competence, his relations to Axel Oxenstierna are no exception to this rule. The members of the embassy from the States-General which visited Sweden in 1616 observed with astonishment that in the course of the negotiations he seemed to be in no need of the assistance of a chancellor. This was no illusion; though no doubt Axel Oxenstierna's absence was always felt to be an inconvenience. After 1626, however, when Oxenstierna had his sphere of activity transferred to the newly conquered Prussian provinces, Gustav Adolf may almost be said to have been his own chancellor, as long as he remained in Sweden, though he did indeed keep in constant touch with his absent minister. This can be inferred from the fact that a strikingly large number of acts of State dating from these years, and in particular a series of Riksdag papers of great importance, all betray his own hand, or give evidence of having been dictated by him; although according to the usual—but not invariable—practice of earlier years they would have been drawn up by the chancellor.

Yet, however handy with his pen, however skilled in the use of words—and of this much could be said—Gustav Adolf was first and foremost a man of action. This fact could hardly be better expressed than in a sentence which he himself once wrote: "And so, what I mean to do, I will give proof of rather by deeds than upon paper." In this case he was referring to the greatest of all his decisions—his decision to intervene in the German war. But it was the same with him whatever the issue. The itch for action took a complete hold of him, driving him on. A multiplicity of tasks clamored for his attention, others were forced upon him by circumstance, yet he was always looking for fresh work to do. Enterprise was the very breath of life to him; his motto— and it was a practical one—was to work while it was day, nor seek to cast aside the burden. "As soon as his meal was over, he went to his business, supervising the affairs of army and navy, chancery and exchequer." (Botvidi.) In short, he had (to employ Oxenstierna's phrase) "a passion for enquiring into everything." And, as is so often the case, the little things, the episodes accidentally preserved in remembrance, illustrate this fact as well as any. Let us take a look at some of them; in each case the scene is set in Sweden itself.

Norrmalm, now in the heart of Stockholm, was in 1616 still open country, and here one spring day Gustav Adolf was to be seen conducting firing tests with a new cannon—it was a new type, built to his specifications—in the presence of the ambassadors of Holland, who were at that time the personal guests of the king and the official guests of the State. The first shot hit the center of the target, which was a great block of stone on one of the neighboring slopes. The king fired again, and this time the shot whistled over the target, and the gun-barrel burst. The king thereupon confessed that he had loaded the gun with a double charge for the second shot, with a view to testing the strength of the metal. The Dutchmen report that though the weapon weighed only twenty-two pounds it could hurl cannon-balls of as much as twenty pounds in weight. And the king had told them that he was hoping to be able to reduce the weight of the gun still further.

At Älvsnabben, four years later, we see Gustav Adolf, in his "simple grey travelling suit," stepping aboard the *Sceptre*, as he sets out, incognito, in search of a bride. He was scarcely aboard, Erik Hand informs us, before he "began to issue commands, and enquire how well off the ship might be for this or that, what provisions and what ammunition she carried, whether the gun-ports were properly closed, whether the ship had been thoroughly cleaned, whether they carried a spare compass, if the ship were well caulked, if they had wood ready sawn to repair any holes that might unexpectedly be caused by gunfire, if anyone was ill aboard, whether they carried a topgallant-sail, whether they had soap or fat for greasing spars and bearings—exactly as though he were an East India captain. Most of all I admired the way in which His Majesty knew the name of every object, loose or fast, tackle or gear, mainsail or jib. Afterwards we weighed anchor; the wind was fair, but not strong enough, so His Majesty entered a boat and rowed round the ship, and at once shot a duck. But the wind beginning to freshen, His Majesty came on board again."

A third scene takes us to Kalmar in the summer of 1623, immediately after Gustav Adolf's return from the short naval demonstration in Danzig roads. The situation was still considered to be threatening, for Sigismund was suspected of planning an attack against Sweden itself, and the important fortress of Kalmar was therefore put into a state of preparedness. The king employed his short stay in inspecting the defense works, mustering the burghers, and drilling the new Småland levies, some squadrons of whom were stationed in one of the new bastions, while others were drawn up outside. "Those who were inside he instructed in the method of fighting behind fortifications, and the use of musket and sword, and so forth. Those who were outside he taught how to attack and storm a redoubt." On the following day he sailed north to Nyköping, accompanied among others by Bengt Oxenstierna ("Bengt the Traveller") well known as "a most sapient gentleman." Some soldiers, who were taken with them to attend the king on board, received a personal exhortation from him touching their good behavior on the return journey. "And Olof, skipper of the *Malmen*, recounted that among other things that the king spoke of on the journey was this, that he had still one task unperformed in this kingdom which he would dearly love to finish in his life-time, namely, that churches, schools, and hospitals should have adequate provision made for them."

It is to the pastor of the Öland parish of Kastlösa, who made a note of them in one of the parish books, that we owe the preservation of these glimpses of the king. We note in particular how frank and easy in address the king could be when dealing with his subjects.

Axel Oxenstierna in after years made a practice of appealing to the authority of the late king upon all sorts of occasions, and in 1649 at a meeting of the Råd in the presence of Queen Kristina, he testified to the fact that her father had had "an extraordinary aptitude for all sorts of business, and not merely military matters." Such words imply something more than the homage of pious remembrance. They imply a state of affairs which can be amply confirmed, and which renders superfluous any allowance for the stylistic conventions of the panegyric. Gustav Adolf had mastered—though no doubt in varying degree—all the diverse questions upon which, as a ruling prince, it was necessary for him to frame a policy. In a purely technical point of view they were certainly simple as compared with those of a modern State; much of the old patriarchal system of government still survived, and such a system permitted personal supervision and personal intervention. But under Gustav Adolf, and indeed as the result of his efforts, this same system began to give place to another, characterized by an increasing complexity of organization in every field. In short, two eras meet in his person.

Travelling took up no small proportion of Gustav Adolf's life. Ruler of one of the most extensive, but also one of the most sparsely populated countries in Europe, he managed to see most of the more important portions of it not once but many times. His annals present the appearance of a long list of miles covered; and the places from which his letters are dated vary almost from day to day.

It is, for instance, characteristic that he should have visited the Kopparberg on fully a dozen occasions; incidentally, as we shall see, he had a good many scores to settle with the Dalesmen. His winter trip round the Gulf of Bothnia in 1602, to which allusion has already been made, was followed by several later journeys in both directions, some of them remarkable for the speed with which they were accomplished. An order dating from February 1614 to the lord lieutenant at Uleåborg, commanding him to furnish accommodation and fresh horses for the king's journey, adds: "We aim to cover ten miles[3] each day, and ten miles each night likewise, for time seems to be getting short." Two bailiffs from Lapland were ordered to meet him at Umeå with stores of Lapp fur coats, snow boots, snowshoes, and gloves, as protection against the arctic winter. And similarly upon other occasions.

During the campaign of 1611-1612 Gustav Adolf had managed to develop an extraordinary ability to move rapidly from place to place. As one author strikingly puts it: "If at this time we try to ascertain his whereabouts, we find him almost everywhere, now in one place, now in another. He appears everywhere as a dominating, unifying force. He practises the art of being in several places at once." He had plenty of scope for practising it later on, even in time of peace. "When he was at home in Sweden he travelled round the country, hearing the complaints of his subjects, inspecting mines and dockyards, scrutinizing accounts and correspondence, revising judgments." This statement, by a contemporary eulogist, is indeed the literal truth. These journeys, which for the most part were made on horseback, were not always without their adventures, some of which might easily have had serious consequences. One January day in 1619 the king rode his horse into a crevasse in the ice on Bråviken. The horse was never seen again.

We have seen how completely at home the king felt on shipboard. Probably no king of Sweden, in all the long era of sailing

[3] The Swedish mile = 10 kilometers.

ships, ever acquired a more intimate knowledge of the Baltic. These naval expeditions or crossings of transports were usually attended by considerable hardship, and on occasion they might involve deadly peril. In August 1621 the king writes to his chancellor from the neighborhood of Riga: "We kept the sea for three days, in rain, wind, and foul black weather, which caused our ships, especially the cavalry transports, to make water, and carried away their masts and sails. In what condition the horses were, you may well imagine. The men's food was so wetted by salt water, and by beer leaking from the casks, that it was not much improved thereby. . . . My own galley stranded at Pernau, her consort at Salis. Some ships lost their boats, which is the most apparent damage the storm has done to us, but the worst is to our cavalry horses, who are so exhausted by the sea and the sands (where we now are) that we shall soon be without cavalry." Of his own sufferings the king, as usual, did not deign to say a word.

Johannes Botvidi, whose great funeral oration of 1634 has been cited more than once, counts it among the dead king's titles to fame—no doubt with the deliberate intention of drawing a contrast with other contemporary rulers—that "he refrained from hunting and jousting, which do not accord with the dignity of a sovereign." The pursuit of the chase and the accomplishments of horsemanship were, on the whole, confined to his early youth. Such pastimes apart, he found as time went on other and diverse outlets for his lusty vigor. And if that vigor failed him, and aches and pains appeared, he could upon occasion succeed in regaining health and strength by a mere act of will. Thus, when in December 1626 he fought with Per Brahe in the castle hall, a sword in either hand—such at any rate is Brahe's account of it— he shook off an ague contracted in the course of his last campaign.

[6]

IN the great speech on the conclusion of peace with Russia which Gustav Adolf delivered before the coronation Riksdag in 1617, he turned, as he drew to a conclusion, to his faithful soldiers. He thanked them for so dauntlessly risking life and health, and for so cheerfully bearing the hardships of the long marches. "The perils of skirmish and storm have been to you as it were child's play;

dust and sweat, rain and sleet, you have counted it a pleasure to endure. The cold of winter, which has been fatal to not a few of you, you have suffered perforce many times with patience; you have battled almost without respite against hunger, yea, against Nature herself; but your sufferings have served merely to add to the brightness of your glory."

Gustav Adolf knew the craft of war to the bottom. To every side, every branch of it, he gave his earnest attention. "He was not content to be commander-in-chief," says *Le Soldat Suédois,* "he must needs be captain, subaltern, engineer, gunner, and private—in short, everything." This is but one witness among many. We recognize immediately that this is typical of the man: it is not in his soldiering alone that he displays these traits, though here perhaps they emerge with especial clarity. This is no place to deal with his qualities as a military organizer and as a commander; but one deeply ingrained quality, revealed in all its strength only in war time, cannot be passed over if we are to endeavor to plumb his real character—namely, his impetuous courage, his contempt for death in the most literal sense of the phrase.

There are not lacking indications that the king's contemporaries suspected him of a hankering after the performance of great feats of arms. More than once we find him, verbally and in writing, rebutting any such interpretation of his motives. He pointed out with some force that he had only too many opportunities to "satisfy his curiosity" in this respect. His motives were of quite another order, dictated by urgent political necessity, or conditioned by a prescience which simply anticipated the moment when such a necessity would arise. The fact that his wars, which he considered to be purely defensive, were begun and carried on for the most part in the form of an offensive, might none the less prompt a possible question as to where the line between offensive and defensive was to be drawn; and this was a problem which occupied critics of his achievement, of both camps and many nationalities, long after Gustav Adolf was dead. Gustav Adolf himself was fully conscious that the problem existed. Johan Bure has noted in his diary that one autumn day in 1622 his master put the question to him how far a Christian might "without sin" wage war—

not merely a defensive, but also, explicitly, an offensive war. The diary has no further information upon the subject. Whether Gustav Adolf, one of the great commanders of the age, had in fact an absolute abhorrence of war or not, remains in a purely historical point of view a question of minor importance. At all events he consistently condemned war as a dreadful visitation. Remarks which he let fall on various occasions, and which may be assumed to reflect his private, unfeigned, and impartial opinion, are unanimous upon this point. Thus he writes to his sister the Countess Palatine during the Livland campaign: "I should think it is no great profit to your Grace to listen to tales of the miseries of war." In his *History* he speaks of the "frenzy of soldiers in a conquered country." In fact, he could find no words strong enough to apply to war: it was "not a river, nor a lake, but a whole ocean of all sorts of evil." When in a German town he saw twelve captured cannon ornamented with casts of the apostles, and bearing each an apostle's name, he expressed himself with some bitterness upon the *evangelium* which they preached to the children of men.

Yet his contemporaries had some grounds, more or less valid, for imputing to him a thirst for warfare. He was continually campaigning; he obviously thrived on a soldier's life; he was a master of the military art. Good fortune attended his arms. And in the presence of danger he displayed a smiling intrepidity which seemed too genuine for it to be possible to doubt that he felt himself in his proper element. There were not a few who condemned it as foolhardiness, or lust for adventure.

Gustav Adolf's first serious adventure in war, the unfortunate skirmish at Vittsjö in the winter of 1612, is among the best known, though hardly the most typical, of these episodes. The ice gave way under his horse as he was fleeing across the Pickelsjö, and he was lucky to escape drowning. The young king considered his rescue as the direct intervention of Providence. He imposed a fast upon himself on the anniversary of the event, and seems to have observed it as long as he lived, and he honorably fulfilled his promise to Tomas Larsson—the cavalryman who had helped Per Banér to drag him out of the water, under a hail of bullets—that he would see to it that he should not want for bread, either for himself or his descendants. It had been a narrow escape, but it could hardly be attributed to the king's contempt for danger.

One thing, however, which was justly censured in him, and which later became a subject of criticism even in his own camp, was his obvious disinclination to "separate the duties of a commander from those of a carabineer"—his constant, almost irrepressible tendency to get into the front line. He loved to take part in "reconnaissances and skirmishes," and on the whole he persisted in this habit up to his death. The author of the character sketch in *Le Soldat Suédois* even goes so far as to say that he never missed a risky enterprise. It is narrated that at the siege of Pskov in 1615 the king preferred to have his quarters in "the foremost approach trenches." It was the same at the siege of Riga, where he was to be found in the miners' tunnels whilst attacks were in progress against the enemy fortifications. During the bombardment of this town, which was one of the strongest fortresses in the north of Europe, the king is reported to have been three times in grave danger of his life. On one occasion a cannon-ball fell precisely on the spot where he had been standing a moment before; on another his clothes were splashed with blood from a man who had been hit; on a third, a ball from a "heavy gun" passed right between the king and a squadron leader with whom he was conversing, so that a slice of his cloak was cut away, and "His Majesty was very nearly knocked over." It was no wonder if his entourage grew uneasy. It was not merely that the king did not hesitate to expose himself to danger; he even seemed deliberately to seek it. Many contemporary letter writers are agreed on this point; Per Banér, who had rescued him at Vittsjö, explicitly affirms it.

Events of this sort, as they became generally known, could not fail to make a strong impression, and to suggest supernatural explanations. In connection with the siege of Riga a report took shape and passed into general circulation which bears all the hallmarks of a legend: the cannon-ball had entered the king's tent in a direct line for his head, but it had swerved to one side—clearly a miracle from Heaven! There are a number of similar cases from the following years. In the autumn of 1625, as the king was riding along the river Düna, his horse was brought down by a falconet shot from the other bank. Gustav Adolf himself was unhurt. "I have indeed to thank God," he wrote to Johann Kasimir, "who has so graciously put me in mind of my mortality, but has withal been unwilling to give me over into the hands of mine enemies, to be a mock and a scorn unto them."

The less pious gradually became convinced that—like Tilly—he was "proof" against steel by the protection of some secret powers. A similar superstition, deeply rooted in the imagination of the age—that of the luck-bringing amulet, the "king's ring"—is the thread upon which is strung the most widely read historical romance in the Swedish language—the first part of *Tales of an Army Surgeon* by Topelius. Gustav Adolf is known to have tried to suppress superstitions of this sort; his Articles of War contain provision for the punishment of "weapon-turners"—i.e. those who claimed the power to ensure invulnerability through magic arts. Even the more respectable science of astrology turned its expert attention to this question. One of the best known practitioners of the art, for instance, believed that he had discovered, in the summer of 1627, that the king of Sweden would suffer no injury to his body as long as he lived. The reports of this discovery are to be read in a hand-written "Intelligence" from Hamburg, in which town the sage in question at that time carried on his practice.

In spite of this discovery, this same summer of 1627 brought disturbing reminders that Gustav Adolf was in fact exposed to the same dangers in the field as the rest of humanity. On May 23, while rowing down the Vistula at night, he was hit in the thigh by a bullet, as he was standing up to direct the boat—less than a stone's throw from the enemy, as Per Brahe, who was with him on this dangerous expedition, informs us. The fire of the Poles was so hot, that nine shots passed through the boat between Brahe and Gustav Adolf. The attempt to carry one of the enemy's earthworks near the river by surprise was a complete failure, a fact which gave the king more concern than his wound. "Yet have we cause to thank God," runs his comment in a letter dictated a few days later, "that we have sustained no hurt in life or health, but hope within a few days at most to direct operations as usual." More serious was the bullet wound in the region of the neck, which he sustained on the evening of August 8 during a mounted reconnaissance near Dirschau, and of which he bore a souvenir for the rest of his life in the form of the bullet itself, which it proved impossible to extract. The king at first believed that the carotid artery had been severed, and began to prepare himself for death. He lay dangerously ill for some time afterwards; and at first his life seemed to hang in the balance. The Råd at home conjured him to reserve his royal person for more important tasks in future; and there was some feeling that his habit of continually exposing himself to danger might be derogatory to the dignity of the crown. The question of the succession, too, came under discussion at the same time.[4]

In due time Gustav Adolf was on his legs again, but he was never quite the same man as before. The bullet—a lead ball—had caught him "two fingers away from the throat." His right arm continued to be somewhat stiff, and some of his fingers refused their office, which hampered him, especially when writing. Thenceforward he commonly wore a thick buff jacket instead of armor, for armor pressed on his tender shoulder. During the interview with Christian IV at Ulvsbäck parsonage in the winter of 1629, Gustav Adolf made his neighbor of Denmark feel for himself where the bullet lay, declaring that he was ready to "house" other three in his body, and if necessary to lay down his life, in the good cause. As a rule, however, he did not like to hear anyone talk of the dangers he ran in battle. He considered it unseemly that such details should become common knowledge, from fear—whether real or assumed—of becoming the object of the "mock and scorn" of his enemies. The accidents at Höfft and Dirschau, however, had made too great a sensation to be hushed up. And Gustav Adolf himself had ordered that the clothes he wore on both these occasions should be preserved in the armory of Stockholm "for a perpetual memorial." They are to be seen there to this day.

It is possible that the king tried thereafter to be more prudent. His dangerous experience in the sharp rearguard action at Stuhm, when in the summer of 1629 he came into contact with the

[4] See above, p. 92.

Imperialists for the first time, does not seem to have been the result of his rashness, though it is probable that, once under fire, Gustav Adolf made no effort to withdraw. When the attack suddenly developed he was "unarmed and dismounted." Naturally he leapt hastily into the saddle, and, as the account runs, "fought on horseback amid the enemy for a full hour." Arnim, the commander of the Imperial auxiliary force, was able to send the king's hat, which had been captured in the mêlée, to Wallenstein as a trophy. It is very characteristic of Gustav Adolf that in the detailed description of the engagement which he sent to his brother-in-law the Count Palatine there is no mention of the fact that he had himself been in danger. As to this, however, we have reliable information. On the day of the battle (June 17) Secretary Grubbe writes to the chancellor: "His Majesty said himself that he was three times their prisoner." And he adds: "By all accounts, it was Wrangel in person who rescued the king." The Wrangel here referred to is the squadron leader Hans Wrangel; but according to a contemporary and usually well informed chronicler, the king's rescuer was Captain Kalenbach, who was later to fall on the battlefield of Breitenfeld. It is possible that we have here to do with different phases of the same engagement. One early version, which can be traced back to a book which appeared in 1664, gives Erik Soop the honor of having delivered the king from his captors at the battle of Stuhm. This, however, is incorrect, for Soop can be proved to have been in Sweden at the time. But the curious fact remains that upon Soop's sarcophagus, which was erected, at his widow's expense, as early as 1637, and now lies in Skara cathedral, there is a representation of a completely identical scene. We see Soop charging on horseback, pistol in hand, against a group of enemy cavalry, one of whom rushes to meet him, while the other three pursue their course, driving before them a dismounted, unarmed, and bareheaded cavalier— apparently their prisoner. And this prisoner bears the features of Gustav Adolf. His hat lies on the ground. Clearly some other incident is indicated; but the puzzle is to know which. It is no easy task to come to a decision. But the question is interesting, for it strengthens the impression that our knowledge of Gustav

Adolf's experiences in the field is very far from complete, even
in regard to particulars of importance.

Soop had fought with great distinction at Dirschau in the summer of 1627. At the end of that year he was rewarded by Gustav
Adolf with the honor of knighthood. Now there had been a number of engagements near Dirschau. The king himself mentions
"a little skirmish at the end of July," when two companies of
hussars and four companies of Cossacks had been routed by a
small troop of Swedish cavalry. He personally took part in the
fighting on that day, and according to one account a Cossack
hewed off the blade of his sword during the mêlée. It is not in-
credible that the king on this occasion was in danger of being
taken prisoner. There is a signed battle picture by a Dutch master,
de Jongh, dating from 1633, which is strongly reminiscent of the
bas-relief at Skara. The composition as to the figures is very
largely identical. In the foreground Gustav Adolf is to be seen
running, surrounded by enemy cavalry, while to one side a
cavalier is leading away his chestnut horse. The incident—for
clearly the same occasion is intended in both cases—must have
excited general remark, though it is difficult at this late date to
determine the exact circumstances.

Nevertheless, such data as we have may be considered sufficient. The campaign in Germany brought with it fresh presenti
ments, fresh presages of disaster. At Ingolstadt in the spring of
1632 the king's horse was killed under him, and his companion,
a young margrave, knocked to pieces by a cannon-ball. Axel
Oxenstierna discerned the special providence of God in an occurrence of this sort. Yet it is certain that he, and others with him,
found it impossible to shake off an uneasy sense of foreboding.
Gustav Adolf seemed to them to trust God's providence a little
too far. When on one occasion in the course of his German campaigns, someone warned him against exposing himself, he is
said to have replied: "You are a doubting Thomas; I shall die
when God wills it." Numerous remarks of this sort are traditionally ascribed to him. Probably not all of them are authentic. But,
whether the tone be grave or gay, they have all a remarkable
similarity. And their significance cannot be mistaken.

Much, no doubt, may be set down to his own lively spirit, ever spurring him on to action, intervention, or example. Yet this tendency, however strongly emphasized, cannot provide a wholly satisfactory basis of explanation, in view of his deeply reflective nature. As a strategist, Gustav Adolf was, for a great part of his career, calculating, prudent, circumspect, anxious to feel the ground firm under his feet, economical of blood and material resources. Yet when his own life was at stake he must be pronounced prodigal. We are here presented, without doubt, with one of the most revealing contradictions in his character. He was, on religious grounds, a fatalist—one who laid his whole destiny, without a tremor, in the hands of the Almighty.

In one of his writings he speaks of "the fear of death, which is the greatest fear of all." For himself, he seems to have treated the question of life or death with absolute indifference, almost with frivolity. After the incident at Ingolstadt he remarked gaily, "Now they will have to shoot thousands of times before they hit me again." But according to several witnesses he was haunted by a feeling that he would "die on the battlefield." It is said that he wished for a quick end, when his race should be run. And he did not consider himself irreplaceable: his own death would not be the end of his country, of that he was certain; his cause would find a new champion when he was gone. The only thing to trouble him was the thought of the uncertain fate that awaited his family.

Many a word, and many an epithet, was pressed into service by contemporaries in an effort to describe what manner of man the king of Sweden was. But the word they used most often was— *heroic*.

[7]

It was an age strong in faith, but strong also in superstition. At almost every turn in its history, we find our feet tripping over a tangle of superstitious credulity. Not enough has been made of the fact that in this matter Gustav Adolf, though inevitably a child of his age, was more emancipated than the majority of his contemporaries.

As far as we know, there is not an atom of proof that he ever took any interest in astrology, though it was a recognized science,

encouraged by kings and princes, and honored of the learned.
He started, indeed, as all his contemporaries did, from the assumption that sorcery and magic were realities, and on occasion
he denounced them as manifestations of a perverted and evil
spirit; an example of this has been given above. Still less was he
any exception to the belief, common to all countries and all
classes, in the importance of such portents as might be gathered
from the heavens. Thus a proclamation for a day of intercession,
promulgated upon the occasion of the king's visit to the Kopparberg at the end of 1618—the first year of the Thirty Years' War—
recalls how of late there has been visible "a fearful and wondrous
great comet, which is always the presage of national misfortune."
On the other hand he had an evident distrust of popular credulity
in all its various manifestations. In the spring of 1614 the country
was alarmed by tales of dreadful phantoms at Kalmar, and at
various places in Småland. Without absolutely denying that there
might on occasion be some such "well merited punishment for
sin," the king plainly rejected the whole story. "It is, however,
impossible to know," he wrote to Oxenstierna, "what to believe
of such signs and *prodigia*; but it may be doubted whether it
be not the work of some turbulent and evil persons, who by such
portentis presume to terrify the simple and the credulous." In a
later letter dealing with the same matter, he expresses himself
still more decidedly. On the whole, he was temperamentally un-
sympathetic to superstitious beliefs—wherein he differed much
from Christian IV.

Of Gustav Adolf's dreams we have several accounts. They show
him possessed of an imagination busy with the labors of the mor-
row, and pursuing its activities even in the subconscious. "The
king dreamed that he had Sigismund prisoner" notes Bure on
May 31, 1623—shortly before the swift expedition to Danzig.
Kristina has told us that before her birth her father dreamed of a
son. Contemporary tradition, which is certainly not always reliable, but is still deserving of some consideration, narrates how
in a dream before the battle of Breitenfeld he struggled hand
to hand with Tilly, and how at Nürnberg he dreamed that he
fought Wallenstein on horseback. All these dreams seem to point
forward to the accomplishment of the action he has in mind. In

so far as they have any value as shedding light on the king's personality, they bear witness to the balance and harmony of his volitions: there is high nervous tension, but no infirmity of purpose.

The world in which his imagination moved was thus in harmony with his naturally active temperament.

Gustav Adolf's philosophy of life may be said to have centered in his belief in honor; honor in the widest sense of the word, honor conceived of in the first place as synonymous with duty done. His passion for honor, moreover, accorded so well with his character that it appears as something more than an acquired taste. Honor was in fact an imperious instinct in his very blood, an instinct which afforded his temperament its natural outlet.

He early began to extol the glories of honor, and he harped incessantly upon the subject. One of the first conspicuous expressions of this is a passage in the resolution of the Riksdag in 1612, which is a document very much in his spirit. As their forefathers (it runs) had won eternal fame by their valiant and knightly defense against the Danes, and thereby, unlike the Norwegians, preserved their immemorial liberty, "so in like manner will we tread in the footsteps of our fathers." The accent was new and strange, but the substance was a program for the future. Some years later the Dutch delegates heard the young king discuss his conception of his duty. He held that his duty was to endeavor to attain to true and undying honor, and this he hoped to do by leaving behind him a kingdom enriched and at peace. At the same time he was singing the praise of honor in the following verses written in a leisure moment at Kymmenegård in Finland, on January 16, 1616. The virtue to which he here pays homage is above all manly virtue, the Roman *virtus*, whose meaning and aim is honor. He is speaking of the constant mind, undaunted in a changing world:

> *Thou, who this race of life wilt run*
>   *Through darkness constant to the end,*
> *Whatever be thy station here,*
>   *Virtue will stand thy truest friend.*

Who cleaveth to her valiantly
  Him leads she with protecting hand
To honor in the world's despite—
  What better meed canst thou demand?

Yet must thou steel thy purpose so
  That no dismay thy heart appall,
And stoutly stand by Virtue's side
  While empires rock and kingdoms fall.

But when thy term is overpast
  Right gloriously rewardeth she;
Then shall the hero-destined crown
  Be thine for all eternity.

Such a passion embraces as its own the path of labor and duty. It is thus that on the occasion of his coronation in 1617 Gustav Adolf says: "Moreover I pray God in His Divine Majesty to grant me a good understanding of the laws of God and man, that I may so rule that after my death my voice also may be heard among you, and that my deeds and reputation may by you be honored, and kept in your hearts with praise, commendation and remembrance." This solemn promise he believed himself to have kept. In the same letter to the chancellor in which he expresses anxiety for his wife and daughter, he speaks of himself as "one who now these twenty years, with great labor, but, I thank God, with great honor, has reigned over our country." This is no vanity; it is profound self-knowledge.

When this belief in himself showed itself in the presence of strangers, it was usually because the prestige of Sweden seemed to be involved. In this cause Gustav Adolf was prepared to go to considerable lengths, and on occasion he did not shrink from drawing the long bow. Thus he would even refuse to admit the poverty of contemporary Sweden as compared with other countries. Rusdorf, as he rode with the *soi-disant* Swedish officer on that summer day in 1620, was incautious enough to broach this subject. "What's that?" cried Captain "Gars," "my mighty sovereign short of money? Do you not know, then, that Sweden is

richer in copper and silver mines than any other area in all
Europe, and has besides innumerable opportunities, both by land
and sea, to procure financial resources? How much copper, gold,
and silver does not my most puissant master cause to be coined
every day! How numerous are his mints! And, finally, how
much money does he not derive from taxes and tolls! Has he not
but recently paid the king of Denmark a million rix-dollars in
ready money, to ransom Älvsborg?" But the truth was that
Gustav Adolf did suffer from lack of capital, and that he did
experience difficulty in financing his undertakings. And he was
no stranger to the art of "crumbling things up small, as one
would for hens, that the people may swallow them"—to borrow
a phrase he used during the campaign of 1625.

Just as he was insistent to maintain his country's prestige
abroad as a general principle, so he was in particular painfully
anxious to inculcate respect for her material resources. As he
feasted with the princes and generals of Germany he would grow
emphatic on this point, taking care not to forget Lapland with
its Lapps and its reindeer. And if his behavior easily took on a
jingoistic tinge, it was at bottom only the expression of that faith
in the future of Sweden which he had avowed so often. In his
view it implied no perversion of the truth. Gustav Adolf many
a time spoke his mind to his people about their various deficiencies, and his language on these occasions was equally unmeasured.
What he really meant was, in a word, that Sweden was a land
of enormous possibilities. And he felt, in no small degree, that
those possibilities had been his discovery.

But Sweden was to him also the land of proud forbears who
had never bowed their necks to a foreign yoke. In his eyes it
stood in a unique position among the countries of the world. "All
kingdoms of any consequence since the birth of Christ have at
some time or other been subjected, made dependent provinces,
or at the least have submitted to and recognized the supremacy
of the Roman or German emperors; this Sweden has never done,
for which reason it is right and proper that it should enjoy precedence and preeminence over all other kingdoms." This comes
from Gustav Adolf's sketch for his own *History,* written probably
while he was convalescing from the wound received at Dirschau,

in the autumn of 1627. He professed this historical conviction in all good faith; but no doubt he was not uninfluenced by the fact that it fitted in so well with his own sentiments. It satisfied his craving for independence; it put Sweden as it were on a par with the Empire, which was already emerging as the arch-enemy of his country. And the old Roman Empire itself, whose mantle was admitted to have fallen ultimately upon the German emperor—had not *this* Empire once been brought to the ground by those Goths who were featured so prominently in Sweden's earliest annals, as narrated by nationalist historians? Although in his unfinished *History* Gustav Adolf makes no allusion to it, there is ample evidence to prove that he adhered to this popular belief with fervent conviction. In another of his works, the *Ordinance for the Military,* he avows it in express terms. "The name of Goth, which beyond all question has its origin in Sweden, has become terrible to the whole world." And were not these ancient Goths his own predecessors?

He had been brought up in a view of history which unhesitatingly incorporated the Goths into Swedish annals; more than that, he had identified himself with a conception of his country's past which in fact had no room for any unknown "pre-history." The historical theory which Johannes Magnus had developed to its imaginative conclusion in his great work *Historia de omnibus Gothorum Sueonumque regibus,* was Gustav Adolf's theory also, as it had been the theory of his father and his uncle. His daughter Kristina gives us a good idea of it, when in the introduction to her autobiography she puts the number of the "internal" kings of Sweden at 150 "including myself," and the number of "external" kings at 87. "Those kings are called 'external,' " she explains, "who left the country to conquer foreign lands." In this long chain of rulers, some peaceful, some warlike, and all known by their names, Gustav Adolf could therefore think of himself as an individual link. His study in Stockholm castle was decked with "tapestries" representing "the histories of the Goths," and when he went to Finland in 1614 he ordered them to be taken down and packed up, so that they might accompany him. At the tournament which he ordered for his coronation in 1617 he himself appeared in the guise of the legendary King Berik. The

Gothic spirit swept through the whole of Swedish life in this period like some unseen current; and even in the enemy's camp men fell gradually into the habit of alluding to these "latter-day Goths and Langobards."

This view of history, with all its literary romanticism, certainly acted as a stimulus. Yet there can be no doubt that Gustav Adolf's conception of the past, and in particular of the history of his own people, derived its inspiration from other sources. Johannes Magnus here counted for less than Johannes Rudbeckius or Johannes Botvidi. The influence which these court preachers exercised upon the development of his ideas may easily have been exaggerated; but this much at least is certain, that upon all essentials he was completely of one mind with them. The character of Rudbeckius has been analyzed already when dealing with one of the critical moments of Gustav Adolf's early life. His successor, Botvidi, was a man of the same stamp and of similar convictions, though he was more discreet and politic in his methods. At the king's instigation, he, among others, in 1621 delivered a series of sermons in commemoration of the Reformation, and also of Gustav Vasa's liberation of Sweden from the Danish yoke. They give very much the same impression as the sermons of Rudbeckius. These homilies—and others too, for contemporary literature is rich in sermons—may in many respects be described as applied history, instruction in the interpretation of history based on the Bible story. Their choice of words, their terminology, powerfully reinforce the examples they adduce. The centuries seem to roll back, and it is as if we moved in the world of Old Testament Israel, with its nobles and people, its stewards, its councillors, its captains of cities—much as they are depicted in some of the old Dalecarlian paintings in familiar Swedish garb. The history of classical antiquity, too, is pressed into service in the same way. It is an interpretation of the human story in the light of religion and morality, and its alpha and omega is the certainty of the inadequacy of human wisdom and earthly institutions.

Gustav Adolf was scarcely thinking of the lists of Gothic kings when he introduced into his historical sketch a discussion which provides us with a summary of his view of human development.

Harassed as he is by the consciousness of the weight of his own imperfections, he has a deep and earnest trust in God, he is sustained by a faith in a higher purpose behind the events of this world of troubles, and he has, implicitly, a thoroughly theological explanation of the course of human affairs. Some of these passages, moreover, show him at the height of his literary powers. "This have the heathen witnessed; but we Christians should read history with more profit than they, for we know that it is God's hand upholds the government. And therefore will we give heed to His marvellous works, how that sometimes by His instruments, sometimes without human aid, He helps those whom He will deliver from oppression, building up anew their city which had been like to fall into servitude and bondage, and bringing them to prosperity again. And again, how by reason of their wickedness He overturns such as the world deems safe and strong; takes from valiant nations their courage and their manhood; gives to dread warriors the heart of a woman; removes judgment and wisdom from the learned and understanding, and to the wisest counsel gives a laughable or tragical conclusion; how, on the other hand, counsel foolish in the world's eye may bring a bounteous harvest, and in virtue of its issue (which is the crown or condemnation of all counsel) is later adjudged to have been wise; whereby He teaches us not to presume upon success, or to despair in failure, but to trust in God, and repent us of our wickednesses, which are the cause of this world's wondrous changes of fortune."

It was in this light, moreover, that Gustav Adolf tried to see his own work. Axel Oxenstierna told the Råd in 1641 that the king had admitted to him, in a confidential conversation shortly before his death, "that no sooner had God given His Majesty any great success in war than it had been balanced by some reverse, whereby His Majesty had learnt to know himself better." He counted it as one of the greatest gains that life had brought him, that success had never been able to extinguish his sense of his own limitations. It was upon this occasion that the chancellor uttered the words which have so often been quoted as a description of the religious side of Gustav Adolf's character: "As long as he lived he was in all his works and ways a God-fearing man."

A significant trait in Gustav Adolf, at the time when he stood at the summit of his fortunes, was his secret dread of the temptation to spiritual pride, a dread of what the Ancients called *hubris*. After the battle of Breitenfeld, he confessed to his German pastor, the court preacher Johann Fabricius, "I am much disquieted in spirit; I commend myself and my victory to God's mercy." The same cleric heard his confession some days before the battle of Lützen: "Doctor, I fear that God will punish me, since the people exalt me so high, and would make a god of me." After the king's death, these words quickly became famous; and they are to be found quoted—with insignificant discrepancies which do not affect their general sense—in a whole series of German panegyrics from the following years. The idea that they might be published, or used for purposes of propaganda, never occurred to him.

Gustav Adolf was decidedly less of a theologian than his father. Unlike him, he did not believe himself capable of divining the meaning of the Scriptures by his own unaided efforts, nor did he ever lay claim to independent authority in matters spiritual. Like every man of education in that age, however, he was well acquainted with such questions, and quite prepared to speculate about them; but for guidance he preferred to entrust himself to those upon whose knowledge and judgment he felt he could rely. The story is told of him that when he was on campaign, he would now and then in the evening summon the preachers in the camp to discuss with him for an hour or two some Biblical text which had aroused his interest. His whole attitude to religion bore witness to the strong attraction which it exercised over him, and to the positive spirit in which he regarded it. His faith in God was obvious, absolute, and free from doubt; his whole conception of life was based, with only trifling modifications, upon the Old Testament; his view of fundamental doctrinal questions, that of the Gospels themselves. He belonged, moreover, to a century in which religious habits had sunk so deep into men's minds that even the indifferent habitually employed the language of piety, and hymns were sung even on the alehouse bench.

Although the effects of such an environment must no doubt be taken into account, it is not easy to dismiss Gustav Adolf's piety as the common veneer of the age, or as conscious affectation. It is too nearly kin to his sanguine, optimistic spirit. He performed, eyewitnesses tell us, all such pious exercises as he attended with joyous devotion—and there is no reason to suppose that he did not derive spiritual refreshment and new courage from them. Not a day passed without hymn-singing and prayers; on practically every other weekday there were sermons, either in his own home, or in the house of a friend. In war time it might happen that the king himself threw the drum-strap over his shoulder, and emerged from his tent to call his soldiers together for service. During the German campaigns, prayers were held at every Swedish and Finnish regiment every afternoon at four o'clock. "It seemed odd to us at first," writes a chronicler from Augsburg. Gustav Adolf believed firmly in the efficacy of earnest prayer. There is good reason to suppose that such a belief was a vital personal necessity to him, a method of emancipating his thoughts, and defeating doubt—doubt as to his ultimate goal, and doubt as to the road that led to it. A German historian, who saw in Gustav Adolf simply and solely the protagonist of a deliberate policy of Baltic expansion, attempted with misguided zeal to prove that the king's prayer upon his landing in Pomerania in 1630 was never in fact uttered. It would be difficult to imagine an occupation more barren of historical importance.

Apart from the commentary on a text at Matins and Evensong on Sundays, Gustav Adolf as a rule heard two sermons in the course of the week, on Wednesdays and Fridays. Botvidi remarks that the king was an attentive listener, and made a mental note of the content and disposition of the discourse. Evidence of the truth of this report is to be found in memoranda made by Gustav Adolf of his second visit to Berlin in 1620, which prove to be mainly a *précis* of a sermon delivered in the Castle church upon the subject of Dives and Lazarus. This, incidentally, is the only surviving example of his notes which is at once autobiographical and in the king's own handwriting.

As the representative of a mode of life based upon the classic doctrines of Protestantism, Gustav Adolf carries conviction. It is no surprise to us to learn that he is reputed to have taken part in hymn-singing in a high voice audible above all the congregation.

Johan Bure notes in his diary for January 1626 a dream in which he imagined he saw the Swedish army drawn up in battle-array against the Danes. "The king and all his host sang 'The Lord is my trust.'" So strongly did the rhythms of the hymn book stamp themselves on men's minds, so completely did they fill brain and eye and ear. In one aspect they induced an easy sense of fellowship; in another, a strict and inflexible discipline. Absentees from public prayers were threatened by proclamation with fine and punishment.

It sometimes seems as though many of our own contemporaries found it more difficult to appreciate the cheerful piety of Gustav Adolf than the gloomy devotion of Cromwell—as though the warrior and statesman who puts God in his heart were quite inconceivable without a seasoning of acrid melancholy. The mere attempt to describe the religious feeling which provided a ground-bass to Gustav Adolf's personality may seem to some to smack of apologetics. It is possible on the one hand to dismiss it as a mere characteristic of the age; or on the other to accord it a significance far above all earthly things. In this matter the historic Gustav Adolf cannot be misunderstood. This is the man as he really was. Of a nature which was by no means simple in the ordinary sense, he lived and died in a faith which was single and entire. The political realist, whose proceedings might upon occasion appear unscrupulous; the diplomat, who did not at need despise the finer arts of dissimulation: the popular leader who could employ the means of the agitator—he was these too. But a cynic he never was. His heart was warm, and in his eye dwelt serenity.

[8]

IN ANY attempt at a character-sketch of Gustav Adolf, some mention must be made of his activities as orator, author, and patron of culture.

His tutors had made it a capital object to accustom him to fluent and effective speaking, and early in his career he was given opportunities to apply this talent. Even in the last two Riksdags of Karl IX the Estates learned to listen to his speeches with attention. The gift of words was innate in him; in this respect he resembled the earlier Vasas. Facility in finding perspicuous, comprehensive, and subtle expression for what was in his mind was plainly a part of his heritage. With effortless ease he spoke in language that was readily understandable by the people. He often seasoned his speeches, and still oftener his conversation, with proverbial expressions or allusions to folk-tales. Nor did he shrink from a certain raciness of expression, though here he observed more moderation than his father. He differed from his father, too, in that he frequently displayed a predilection for the high style in his choice of words and the rhythms of his sentences— an effect, no doubt, of his youthful assiduity in the practice of Latin rhetoric; but also (if we have understood him aright) a trait which fits in very well with the rest of his character.

For more important occasions he worked out his speeches beforehand, at least during the earlier part of his reign. Johan Skytte mentions, in connection with the Riksdag of Örebro in 1617, that the king consulted him several times, and carefully discussed with him the speech he had prepared. The great importance he attached to a lucid and well ordered exposition is proved by the many autograph drafts of his Riksdag speeches. The earliest of them, intended for the Nyköping Riksdag at the end of 1611, is marked already by that earnest and emphatic tone which may be considered characteristic for his dealings with the representatives of the nation. The young king, in dismissing the Estates, invoked the example of his ancestors, and promised his auditors "to work together with them in defense of the Christian faith, the liberty of the fatherland, and the welfare of them all; and for that cause to hazard his life."

In spite of his grounding in rhetoric, and of the impassioned note which he so often struck, his speeches were clearly not intended to be mere oratorical exhibitions. They served the purely practical purpose of explaining, as comprehensively as possible, the king's policy; they were intended to reveal the righteousness of his actions and the necessity of his proposals. Now and then they expanded into broad historical retrospects: his great speech of welcome to the Estates of Finland at the so-called Landtag at Helsingfors in 1616 was of this type. Brevity was not one of his qualities—he could speak for hours at a stretch—but what he

said had always a precise meaning and a definite purpose. It was
only natural that well turned phrases and considerations of stylistic excellence were in these circumstances relegated to second
place; in particular he sometimes forgot to observe the rules of
syntax—a failing which was general in the language of contemporary chanceries—and he made many concessions to his age's
evil habit of importing Germanisms. But he had, to an unusual
degree, the mastery of his own language; he had a natural command of its resources; and he had the knack of infusing freshness and force into whatever he had to say. He was undoubtedly
the greatest Swedish orator of his time. Oxenstierna was in this
matter no match for his master, though his own style of speaking
was naturally dignified, and became richer and more sonorous
with the years.

A number of Gustav Adolf's speeches have been preserved
through early transcripts of his autograph manuscripts. The origi-
nals were lost in the great fire which destroyed the old castle at
Stockholm in 1697. Others have been preserved in the minutes
of the Riksdag, and similar official sources, whether in a sum-
marized form, or as literal transcriptions, or as a combination of
the two; this last is the case with the justly famous farewell speech
to the Estates in the spring of 1630, which is inserted into the
minutes of the deputation of the Nobility attending the Secret
Committee. It occasionally happened also that a more or less ex-
temporary speech of the king's was noted down immediately afterwards by someone who had heard it; it was in this way, for instance, that posterity secured a report of his outburst at Nürnberg
against his staff officers, from which extracts have been quoted
above. Many of his speeches, however—apparently the great majority—have been lost, and there is no reason to doubt that among
them there may have been masterpieces fully worthy of comparison with the best of those that have come down to us. Of
such as have been preserved, about half were delivered at the
Riksdag sessions held in 1617. These all seem to have been written
out by the king himself, as summaries of what he intended to say
in the Riksdag chamber. Clearly he relied more and more in later
years upon his gift for free improvisation.

The bulk of such of Gustav Adolf's oratory as is known to us, therefore, dates from a time when he was still a young man. And yet, apart from his farewell speech before his departure for Germany, he never seems to have reached a higher level of eloquence than in this year, when peace with Russia was concluded, the religious settlement laid down anew, and the coronation celebrated at Uppsala. For freshness and vivacity, for directness and clarity, parts of these speeches stand almost unrivalled. In essence they are all more or less speeches for the defense, and together they form a sort of summing up of this tense opening period of the reign. The arch-enemy Sigismund still presumes to affirm that Gustav Adolf has made himself master of the throne by violence and constraint. "Who was I," retorts Gustav Adolf, "when I came to the throne, that I should be able to constrain anybody?" After six testing years as "elected" king, he had stood ready to receive the royal unction. And he boldly develops his theme: "Was I not a youngster of seventeen, with no such authority as might enable me to constrain anyone? Duke Johan was much older; he had been in possession of his land and title for some years; he had many subordinate to his authority, and bound to him by duty and service; so that if his Grace's benevolence had not made him complaisant, if he had not bound himself to unswerving adherence to the promises he had made beforehand, how would it have been possible to prevail against him, especially since it would have been necessary to compel and constrain all the Estates of the kingdom against their lawful will? What power have I used for such compulsion? What armed forces have I relied upon, to impose my will upon a whole nation? What foreign help and assistance have I employed in such a work? In truth, I have never, under God, trusted to any other power than that which comes from the fidelity of the Swedish people."

As an author, Gustav Adolf is remarkable for much the same qualities as those which distinguish his oratory, except perhaps when he is dealing with purely technical military matters. The most considerable and the most carefully finished of Gustav Adolf's writings is his *Ordinance for the Military*. Only the first section, indeed, dealing with regulations for the national levy, was ever completed; but even in this fragmentary state the treatise possesses great interest. Above all it reveals how deliberately and purposefully the king sought to implant his reforms of army organization firmly in the national consciousness. The army drawn direct from the people, and raised in provincial regiments, which became a reality in this reign, was itself a creation of the old Swedish juridical spirit. Nowhere does Gustav Adolf approximate so closely to judicial language as in this sketch for the *Ordinance for the Military*. Sheriffs and lord lieutenants stand as twin pillars of that system of recruiting a popular army which the treatise sought to develop, a system worked out to the last detail with a view to the prevention of arbitrariness and injustice. It was here that Gustav Adolf let fall those winged words about "foreign rulers who overturned Swedish customs and upset the good old order." Side by side with the *Ordinance for the Military,* which must have been written in 1619 or 1620, stands the king's sketch of the famous *Articles of War,* drawn up on July 15, 1621, on the occasion of the army's embarkation for Riga. Mention may also be made of the short fragment entitled *The Duties of the Swedish Soldier,* from which we can gather the qualities which Gustav Adolf demanded from a commander-in-chief. They are "virtue, knowledge, prudence, authority, success." He had a pretty broad idea of what was implied by "this word virtue": "uprightness of life, zeal in enterprise, diligence in service, valor in danger, hardiness in action, and swiftness in execution." It is, as near as makes no matter, a self-portrait.

Except for the short speech in memory of his brother Karl Filip, all Gustav Adolf's writings are in a more or less fragmentary condition. He took up the pen now and then in his spare moments, but his other preoccupations never gave him leisure to work out his ideas. Naturally this does not apply to the voluminous official documents for which he was responsible, nor to his numerous letters. Among the former are a number of important acts of the Riksdag which are known to have been drawn up by his hand: the Riksdag resolution of Örebro (1617), the propositions at the two Riksdag sessions of 1627, the decision of the Secret Committee of January 1628, and the proposition to the representatives of the staple towns in regard to ship-money in June 1629. On internal evidence, too, the noble and eloquent

message to the Riksdag which met in the summer of the same
year must be attributed to the king, for its tone and phraseology
is throughout strikingly reminiscent of his style.

It is particularly lamentable that Gustav Adolf's intention to
write his own history never came to fulfilment. He did begin
upon the introduction, but it remained a mere fragment, for it
broke off at the meeting of the Arboga Riksdag in 1597. Reference has already been made to this notable work in so far as it
sheds light upon the nature of the king's views of history. As
we saw, its composition may probably be assigned to the autumn
of 1627. Bure has noted that on November 28 of that year he
was with the king in the conservatory at the castle from twelve
to one o'clock, and that the king read "his chronicle" to him. They
were on too intimate a footing, and saw each other too frequently,
for it to be conceivable that the work had long been written at
the time when Gustav Adolf submitted it to the judgment of his
old tutor. The date is of significance, for it makes it plain that
Gustav Adolf all his life retained undiminished that feeling
of complete solidarity with his father's work which he had acquired in early youth.

It is at least possible that he broke off his narrative because he
shrank from reviving memories of the great crisis which had
terminated in the judicial murders at Linköping. He certainly
had this in mind when in his introduction he spoke of "the
wounds but newly healed" and expressed a doubt whether they
ought "as it were to be broken open afresh." It may moreover
be considered as certain that the events of the turn of the century
were not regarded in precisely the same light by the king and
by his aristocratic collaborators. The portion of the work that
he did complete shows already that he took his father's part ener-
getically and unreservedly. It shows too that in the main he inherited his father's view of the chief events and actors of the
preceding century. The purely human judgment of Erik XIV
here expressed must thus appear very natural in a son of Karl IX.
Of his royal grandfather Gustav I he speaks with veneration
and warm admiration. In him he sees the founder of modern
Sweden. "This King Gustav," he says, "was the instrument by
which God raised again our fatherland to prosperity. By his

wisdom he gave peace and good government to the land. God sent him His light, and taught him to know His statutes; in his time was the pure word of God taught among us, and man-made precepts done away with." Perhaps a still stronger proof of Gustav Adolf's admiration for his grandfather is the circumstance that in 1621 he instituted in his honor the first centenary known to have been celebrated in Sweden. In his eulogy of Karl Filip, which must have been delivered at his brother's funeral at Strängnäs in the autumn of 1623, he expressed before the assembled people the hope that the gap left by the dead man might be filled "in such fashion that upon the royal throne and seat of my fatherland there may sit no less a man than King Gustav was, who a hundred years ago sealed again our covenant with God's word."

Such was the strength of his belief in the future of his dynasty. We may judge, therefore, how keenly he felt the disappointment when his marriage failed to bring him a son.

Gustav Adolf's letters reflect the rich diversity of his nature, and also, very clearly, his methodical habits. Their number can never be precisely determined, since he usually dictated them extempore, and since no doubt many letters written in this way went off without his appending his signature. A not inconsiderable number of them, especially in his later years, are written in German. Gustav Adolf was a considerable author in that language; but his writing, though original and personal, is more remarkable for the pithiness and concentration of its thought than for the exactness of its style. On his literary productions in German the judgment of an Austrian historian may be cited. "Of the prolixity by which learned and unlearned in Germany at that time won an unenviable distinction, there is no trace in his autograph letters. He was often compelled to contend, under the forms of intimacy, for vital interests, and with highly placed personages. So lucid and unambiguous is his style, so direct and to the point, that these letters might serve as models of their kind."

Gustav Adolf has long been credited with the authorship of the famous fighting hymn, *Versage nicht, du Häuflein klein*. According to an old story the king is said to have dictated the substance of it in prose to his court chaplain Fabricius before the battle of Lützen, and Fabricius thereupon hastily cast it into metrical form. All the evidence however shows that the hymn, or "war song," was written shortly after the battle of Breitenfeld by an evangelical pastor from Thuringia, and that he took his inspiration from the Swedish device "God with us." It is plainly for this reason that it soon came to be called "His Majesty of Sweden's song." Indeed, the high-flown allusions to Gustav Adolf as a new Gideon make it impossible for any reasonable person to contend that he was the author. But in the two earliest printed editions, one of which is possibly only a few weeks later than the king's death, there is the most unequivocal indication that he sang this hymn before his last battle. Sometimes it is described as his "swan song," and this name has a good tradition behind it, for it derives from the very earliest printed edition.

In the course of discussions as to the origin of the hymn—its original three verses were soon increased by innumerable new ones, which is good proof of the song's popularity—the argument has been adduced from the German side that there is no other evidence that Gustav Adolf had a poetic turn. Even if his early poems dedicated to that shadowy figure, Christina Fleming, are to be considered as of dubious authenticity, there still remains the verses written in January 1616 in praise of Virtue, of which some stanzas have been given above. Of the two closely linked love songs, one, we remember, was in German, and it is incontestably the better poem of the two. The fact that the paternity of this ardent pair of poems (the interpretation of which remains indeed a baffling problem) is attributed to Gustav Adolf with much better reason than the famous war hymn, may be considered a warning against the constant temptation to stereotype, as it were, his historical figure.

There was an artistic vein in Gustav Adolf. A glance at his speeches or his prose writings reveals this clearly. To this quality he added an appreciative eye for the beautiful in nature and in art. He must for instance have been one of the first to realize and pay tribute to the loveliness of Stockholm. As Rusdorf and the king rode together in 1620, Rusdorf began to tell him of the fertility of the Palatinate. The king, of whose identity his companion was ignorant, took this as a friendly challenge, and grew expansive in praise of the natural beauty of Stockholm's environs. It is doubly characteristic of him that he should have put out a printed proclamation decreeing the death penalty—for his patience was exhausted—for hunting the swans who gave life and splendor to the waters surrounding the capital. His solicitude sought to preserve the old oaks in the neighborhood of the city. His imagination was of the visual order. The sight of Munich prompted a comparison which has accidentally been preserved: he likened it to a "golden saddle on a lean old hack." That he formed his own judgment as to the finest artistic monuments of the past in his own country is clear from the very remarkable words put into his mouth by seventeenth century tradition. "King Gustav Adolf used to say: 'There are in Sweden three masterpieces excelling all others: 1, the St. George in Stockholm Great Church; 2, the reredos at Linköping; and 3, the Salvator at Vadstena.' "[5] He might have made a worse choice. He was fond of music, too, and is said to have played passably upon the lute.

The patronage he dispensed was, however, strongly flavored by his zealous care for the advantage of the State. Posterity has no single picture of the first artistic excellence by which to remember the king who presented the Gustavian hereditary estates to the University of Uppsala. For this Gustav Adolf must himself bear the blame. As a great builder, he takes his place by the side of Johan III. It is only in relatively recent times that due attention has been paid to the stimulating effect of his personal initiative and organizing ability in this field. This too was in the interests of the country and the service of the State, though it is possible that considerations of what his eulogist of 1634 calls his "royal state" may have counted for something too. Sometimes he got no further than laying the foundation stone. This is even more true of learning and literature; Gustav Adolf's Sweden was on the whole a good deal nearer the stage of laying down the keel than that of christening the ship. The harvest was to be reaped in a later age; but as a rule the impulse had been given, and the lines of future development had been mapped out.

[5] Presumably a triumphal crucifix dating *c.* 1440, formerly the property of the abbey of Vadstena; the work of a Lübeck master.

Sometimes, indeed, it is not easy to decide how much of the work completed or begun in the course of the reign was the king's own work, and how much the work of his collaborators; but it can hardly be denied that the whole movement, so clearly visible, powerfully assisted the progressive elements in the intellectual, as in the material sphere, and that it stands in intimate relation to the king's personal interests and inclinations. A foreigner calls the young Gustav Adolf in 1612 "a lover of all arts and sciences." A very striking expression of his spirit is the severe reprimand which he administered in the following year to the University of Uppsala, which at that time had fallen somewhat into decay. He told the professors that there was such disorder there that if he had not learned from his own experience what advantages were to be gained from learned studies, he would have had small cause to interest himself in that institution. Of his zeal for the study of the monuments of his country's civilization, for which the preceding age had cared little, the best evidence is his collaboration with Johan Bure, whom he strongly urged to compile a Swedish grammar and a Swedish dictionary, and in whose study of the traditions of the North, whether preserved in writing or in stone, he never ceased to take an interest. The instructions he drew up for Bure, as antiquary of the realm, before his departure for Germany, are really remarkable for their knowledge and foresight, and undoubtedly correspond to his private convictions and personal wishes.

His technical interests, too, of which he gave ample evidence in his military and civil activities, are no doubt equally to be considered as a natural expression of his talents and genius. His encouragement of Swedish cartography is worthy of remembrance. His gift to Anders Bure of over a thousand copies of the Church Bible of 1618 furnished Bure with the means of finishing his great map of the North. This appeared in 1626, and for its date it can only be described as a superb production.

[9]

It is said that Tilly once remarked that the odds must necessarily be against him in a struggle with a man who was commander-in-chief, statesman, and sovereign all in one. The authenticity of the remark is, indeed, not clearly established; possibly the words were put into the old soldier's mouth by a later age. However that may be, they succeed in conveying a very just judgment of Gustav Adolf.

Previous kings of the Vasa dynasty, though they had been richly endowed with talent of one sort or another, had not been remarkable for military gifts of any very high order. Gustav Adolf's uncle Erik XIV had shown a lively and in some respects far-sighted interest in military affairs; but his restless nature had dissipated his energies, and it is indeed no accident that it has been left for our own age to estimate the fascinating experiments in this sphere which are now associated with his reign. Gustav Adolf's father, Karl IX, had not lacked strength of purpose, but he lacked any deeper insight into military science. When his son ascended the throne, the Swedish army had not yet wiped out the shameful defeat of Kirkholm (1605), where a three-to-one superiority over the Poles had not availed to avert defeat. During the War of Kalmar, the Swedes never considered themselves to be in a position to meet the main army of the enemy in a pitched battle. The military forces of the country were in full decay.

Gustav Adolf had deliberately been brought up as a soldier— though certainly not as a soldier only. This branch of his training was no mere luxury; it was an absolute necessity, an imperious duty. As to that there was general agreement. Rudbeckius—whose views had in other respects a strong flavoring of practical paci- fism—insisted in his sermons upon the importance of bringing up the king's sons to the command of the country's forces. It was the spirit of the age. In the years that followed, Gustav Adolf's education in the military art was continued, until in the end he was able to rely securely upon his own judgment. Opportunities for practical experience, indeed, presented themselves in abundant measure during the relatively frequent campaigns. At the same time his taste for military problems found satisfaction in continued study of the scientific side of war. He had a high opinion of the value of military theory, and enjoined his officers not to neglect "study," in foolish reliance upon their own experience. It was thus that he evolved his own system, based upon—but not slavishly copying—the Dutch tactics introduced by his master Maurice of Orange, which had proved their effectiveness in the great struggle with the veteran armies of Spain. "Maurice," says an author of expert authority, "was the inaugurator of a new tendency in Continental tactics. Gustav Adolf developed that tendency, combined it with the best features of the Spanish school, and by leading the new method to definitive triumph laid the basis for a general European system of fighting—formation in line."

To this new creation he added another, which gave it strength to decide the issue against the most formidable opponent that the age could produce. A Swedish army organization embracing the entire nation was brought into being, dispensing both with the conscripted national militia which in the traditional view had hitherto been accepted as the true method of utilizing the strength of the nation, and also in the main with the hired mercenaries who constituted almost without exception the backbone of foreign armies. This new, purely national system, with its provincial regiments, was gradually evolved after the conclusion of the Russian war, and was powerfully developed in the earlier half of the sixteen-twenties, until, at the moment when the main theater of the war with Sigismund was transferred to Prussia, it was in all essentials complete. It was an organization which very largely embodied the king's own personal ideas. Many of his sayings bear witness to the deep interest he took in the national army, and to the profound confidence he reposed—largely because of its morale—in its efficiency, its valor, and the soundness of its temper. The reform of the army must undoubtedly be accounted one of the most profoundly influential achievements of the reign, and as evidence of the king's creative ability it has a claim to be mentioned here, in spite of the fact that this chapter is concerned less with his work than with his personality.

For Gustav Adolf, war and diplomacy went hand in hand. The one reinforced the other. This, in itself, could scarcely be called unusual; but we find, in Gustav Adolf's career, so close a correlation between military demonstrations and diplomatic negotiations that it stands out almost as a salient characteristic. This union of military with political action is, in particular, more clearly and convincingly apparent in him than in most others who worked under much the same conditions—he presents, in this respect, a strong contrast with Karl XII. In his diplomacy, which was as active in peace as in war, and which became increasingly complex with the passing of the years, Gustav Adolf displays, perhaps better than anywhere else, his inherent ability to survey with unremitting attention a wide political scene. There was hardly a detail which he did not grasp sooner or later. His intelligence service was developed by him to a pitch previously quite unknown in the North. Already before his expedition to Germany his diplomatic feelers had reached Venice and Constantinople. His foreign policy was profuse in suggestions and exhortations, and not all of these were equally seriously intended. Some were thrown out for what they were worth, to keep the diplomatic ball in play; for the king was no stranger to the art of improvisation, and he dealt largely in alternatives. He drew heavily upon the expedients and resources of diplomacy, but he was far from using them at hazard. He kept his end well in view throughout. His initiative had one constant, common root: the welfare of Sweden and of the Protestant cause. Of this we shall have something to say later on.

A comparison between Gustav Adolf as a general and as a diplomat is not without interest. He has been called the first man in modern times to reduce war to a system, and to secure brilliant results by a strict application of that system. Before he sought a decision in a pitched battle, he set himself to minimize the risks by the slow occupation of the enemy's country, and by the securing of his own lines of communication to the rear. Only then did he strike his blow. This prudence gave to his earlier campaigns at times an appearance of hesitancy. During his later years in Germany he increasingly discarded precautions, and concentrated boldly on beating and, if possible, annihilating the enemy. His diplomacy, on the other hand, gave freer rein to his impatient temper. It was undoubtedly more impulsive than his strategy. There was less danger: diplomatic reconnaissances do not presuppose an army ready to strike. Still Gustav Adolf's diplomacy, though it had the necessary quality of subtlety, betrayed also a weakness for violent frontal attacks of a kind that were, on the whole, foreign to his military strategy. Not seldom they had the desired effect, and when they missed their mark there was generally no great harm done, since his attitude from the beginning had been too clearly defined to be misunderstood. He could, however, on occasion allow himself to be committed to promises or engagements which he had not the means to fulfil. The chain of events which led to the catastrophe at Magdeburg is a glaring example. The promises of others he assessed in a dispassionate and critical spirit.

Once again we are reminded of Tilly's verdict—if indeed it was really his. Yet the old general had already by his victory over Christian IV proved himself a match for one royal commander.

When Gustav Adolf fell at Lützen, it was not only the soldier and the statesman that died with him: the king, ruling by Divine Right, had been taken away. It was only then that men realized the irresistible, unifying force which this divine commission had implied. The king was irreplaceable. Not even a man of the stature of Axel Oxenstierna, successfully summoning to his aid his vast ability, experience, and strength of mind—assisted, too, as he was by veterans of proved capacity—could fill the vacant place. In order to hold the army together in the weeks immediately after Lützen an attempt was made to arrange for the body of the king to accompany the Swedish forces.

THE SWEDISH ESTATES

THE SWEDISH ESTATES

[1]

A T THE beginning of the seventeenth century Swedish society
fell into a number of well defined orders. The division into
four Estates, which was to be fundamental to its political
organization for many years to come, may be considered to have
been definitely established in the reign of Karl IX, though the
aspect it was ultimately to assume had not as yet been clearly
realized.

The Riksdag had by this time become the principal means for
securing cooperation between the government, on the one hand,
and the various classes of society, or Estates, on the other. The
violent internal disorders of the last decade of the sixteenth century
had greatly increased its importance in the life of the nation, and
the almost uninterrupted succession of crises which filled the next
ten years had given a stability to its functions, and to a certain
extent to its procedure, which had been unknown in earlier years.
This was very largely the consequence of the constant endeavor
of Karl IX to enlist the support of the Estates for his undertakings, to assure himself of the assent of the representatives of the
people, to bind them to his cause: a device which resulted in a
certain amount of friction, but which in essentials led to the goal
at which the king was aiming. That goal, in accordance with
older Swedish political ideas, was perfect unanimity in national
decisions. In all questions of major importance this unanimity
was in fact secured, though on many occasions it involved a more
or less forced acquiescence in the policies for which the ruthless and
imperious monarch was contending. If new and more extended
spheres of action fell to the lot of the Riksdag, that was to be
attributed less to their own desires than to the wishes of the king,
who in this matter was more concerned with the practical needs
of the moment than influenced by any theoretical views as to the
Riksdag's functions and competence. There was nothing of the
doctrinaire about Karl. Nor was he much concerned to cast about
for models to imitate; though it has been established that the
English Parliament had attracted his attention.

The position of the Swedish Riksdag was not as yet established by law. The Riksdag alone did not form the "Estates" of the nation. Other assemblies, or "gatherings"—Karl made numerous experiments with them—could equally represent the Estates, though their right to do so varied with their composition. The whole mass of the population, of whatever station, the land-owning population of every district, could in the last resort be considered as the Estates of the kingdom, and in virtue of a conception which still survived, and was very generally held, the national representative body—undefined as it still was—had no right to take definitive decisions. This point of view emerged most clearly when there was any question of revising the law. Karl IX's attempt to build up a new national code had to be abandoned when the Riksdag declared itself incompetent to arrive at a conclusion, and referred the decision to the "Estates" of the provinces.

On the whole, it was only natural for contemporaries to regard the deputies of the Estates who came to the Riksdag, or to other similar meetings—the *herredagsmän*—as directly limited by the assent and approval of their "brothers" at home. To this extent the deputies were not really representatives of the people in the modern sense; for their view of their duty was strongly colored by ideas which we associate with an imperative mandate. All sorts of complications and difficulties resulted from this fact, especially when the granting of taxes came under discussion. To suppress or weaken the direct dependence of the deputies upon their constituents in the country, which often put obstacles in the way of a decision, became, therefore, a most desirable object for the royal power. On the other hand it was not in the king's interest to cut himself off from the possibility of dealing, on occasion, directly with the people in each province, either through the lord lieutenants, sheriffs, or by other means; and hence of circumventing the Riksdag (or some assembly corresponding to it) by securing the assent of the nation to the measures in contemplation. It therefore sometimes happened that the Estates, instead of allowing separate negotiations of this sort, preferred to come to a decision, as nearly unanimous as possible, in the Riksdag. It was precisely in this matter of the granting of taxes, a matter traditionally conceived (at all events in principle) as an inviolable right of the nation as a whole, that these two tendencies came into clearest conflict. However, mainly as a result of Karl IX's active collaboration with the authority of the Estates in all its manifestations, both king and Estates came to consider the Riksdag as at least the most important forum for fiscal legislation. An idea began to gain ground—less readily, it is true, in some sections of society than in others—that taxes and impositions ought legally to be granted by the Riksdag. In comparison with the views and customs of former times, this was an alteration of profound significance.

Participation in the work of the Riksdag, indirectly by means of a vote, or directly by attendance at its deliberations, appeared to the deputies far less as a privilege than as an obligation, and a burden. The Riksdag's lack of regular forms is apparent above all in the fact that it was summoned only when need arose. In this matter the decision lay in the hands of the government. A summons to a Riksdag was, as a rule, an omen of financial stringency or difficulties of one sort or another at home or abroad. Karl IX was considered to have indulged in Riksdag meetings too freely: "God in Heaven preserve us Swedes from so many diets!" as a political pamphleteer wrote, shortly after the king's death. Gustav Adolf was compelled to promise in his Charter of 1611 not to "oppress the Estates with many diets," and, in general, not to summon them but upon real necessity, and with the approval of the Råd.

With this stipulation the king did his best to comply throughout his reign. Nevertheless he based his achievements, even more than his father had done, upon cooperation with the Estates of the nation. "He came to his kingdom," says Botvidi in his funeral sermon, "with empty hands, as we also very well know; yet he deprived no man by force of that which was his own, but rather in free assemblies made known to his peasants what the necessities of the State demanded, so that they might consider these things, and give lawful aid in the defense of the Crown."

The Charter of 1611 was the point of departure. Its important sixth clause bound the king in the first place not to introduce any new law nor alter and abolish the old without the assent of Råd and Estates. This was precisely the line adopted by Swedish constitutional theory from time immemorial. More debatable was the condition that no ordinances envisaging a general imposition, of whatever nature, were to be promulgated by the king unless he had submitted the question to the Råd, and had secured "the consent of those concerned": whether through the Riksdag or by other means was not specified. There follows the provision already referred to, which aimed at reducing the number of Riksdag meetings, and which in this connection accorded to the Råd a certain power of control. Finally Gustav Adolf bound himself not to declare war or conclude peace, truce, or alliance, without the knowledge and consent of Råd and Estates. This was a very considerable limitation of the king's traditional control of foreign policy. And it is no accident that Axel Oxenstierna, who was mainly responsible for the Charter of 1611, was later driven to the opinion that this provision in particular put an unduly severe curb upon the actions and discretion of the government: he confessed as much in the course of the Riksdag debates upon Karl X Gustav's Charter of 1654.

A glance at the provisions cited above makes it immediately apparent that the Riksdag is nowhere expressly mentioned. This is true of the whole document. The first constitutional law accepted by all the Estates in which the word *Riksdag* is used is the Form of Government of 1634, which was drawn up by Axel Oxenstierna, and, according to him, had been approved in all essentials by Gustav Adolf. It is, however, plain that in various contexts in the Charter of 1611 where mention is made of the Estates the reference is really to the Riksdag—but not to the Riksdag only. We have already noticed the significance to be attached to the word *Estates*. Here the term is to be applied in its more general sense; though it it well to bear in mind that in the previous decade the Riksdag had made notable advances as the main organ for cooperation between king and people. With regard to taxation (and incidentally also with regard to the raising of troops) the Charter makes no mention even of the Estates; it speaks quite generally of the consent of "those concerned." The method of obtaining this consent, whether through Riksdag, other assembly, or direct negotiations in the provinces, is thus left completely open. The same formula is used in those Representations in the name of the Råd and Estates which formed the basis upon which the Charter was drawn up.

It was felt that the time was not ripe for laying down fixed rules in these matters, and still less for proclaiming the exclusive right of the Riksdag to grant taxes. Nevertheless, this conception was gradually making headway: at the Nyköping Riksdag, for instance, the Estate of Burghers demanded that no other taxes should be imposed than those which had been granted at a "general Riksdag."

[2]

IF NOW we try to compare the constitutional guarantees which these regulations were intended to provide with their practical application upon relevant occasions in the years that followed, we shall find that upon the whole they agree very well. It would be possible to point to modifications in several respects; but these modifications are not very conspicuous, and they are all explicable by reference to the circumstances and ideas of the age.

This is true not least of the exercise of the right to tax. There can be no doubt that the procedure employed in this matter was sometimes such that the consent of the people was rather assumed in advance than definitely ascertained. It was so in the case of the Älvsborg Ransom. The unusually heavy exaction which was considered necessary for this purpose—though it turned out in fact to be inadequate—was granted in 1613 at a meeting which was representative only of the three upper Estates. The reservation of the rights of the absentees, introduced into the resolution at the request of the Clergy, carried in fact very little weight with the government when it came to bargaining with the individual provinces. It was held that necessity knows no law. There was no intention of allowing the vital strip of coast on the North Sea, now by the Treaty of Knäred in pawn to Denmark, to fall permanently into the hands of that power; and besides, the peasantry never had much liking for the long journey to and from a Riksdag. A Riksdag had been sitting very recently (November 1612); another was shortly to be summoned (January 1614). So that it was only here and there that the levy met with opposition, and even this was soon silenced. The Älvsborg Ransom bur-

dened everyone, without exception, from the queens dowager to
the farm-hand and the servant-girl, in proportion to their capacity
to pay. It must be considered to be an important precedent, in
view of the class-consciousness of the age, that the nobles, who
were legally exempt from taxation, should have had to pay on
the same basis and at the same rate as the rest. When the privileged classes set an example, it was felt that the unprivileged
could hardly hang back.

A more notable case is presented by the introduction of the
stock-tax in 1620. This fiscal innovation followed immediately
after the last payment of the Älvsborg Ransom, and was succeeded by a number of others which were passed and put into
operation in the early sixteen-twenties. The grant, which incidentally was renewed time and again and, as usual, gradually
came to be considered as an ordinary tax, had its origin in 1620
at a national assembly, to which, however, the peasants received
no summons. The intention of the government was to levy a tax
on the produce of the soil, graduated according to the individual's
private means, and hence at once more equitable in its incidence
and more advantageous to the Crown than earlier methods of
taxation. The Nobility granted the tax as regarded their own
privileged peasantry on the usual basis—i.e. half the amount ex-
acted from Crown peasants or free peasants, and this probably
had its effect on the absent Estate of Peasants. The stock-tax was
thereupon collected in the provinces in much the same way as
the Älvsborg Ransom. There is no record of any protests; but
in the sixteen-thirties it became clear that in certain districts, at
all events, the peasants had not forgotten the circumstances of the
tax's imposition. In general it may be said of these frequently
recurring negotiations with the individual districts that the local
meetings hardly felt themselves entirely at liberty to accept or
reject the proposals of the government, when those proposals
were accompanied by the public reading of official proclamations,
usually giving pressing and explicit reasons for the exaction. There
are, however, examples of the peasants' refusing their consent:
they did so in 1627-1628 in several large areas of west and southwest Sweden. The king put the blame on his agents. His theory

was that the peasantry would be willing enough if they were approached in the right way.

Usually, however, the decisions upon fiscal questions were taken in the Riksdag, and with the cooperation of all the Estates. If Riksdag meetings did not come too often, the peasants had no objection. The journey to a diet, and its attendant expenses and inconveniences, were admitted as a distasteful duty. It was not until the last few years of the reign, when one Committee meeting succeeded another—there were four in the years 1630-1632 and the peasants were not summoned to any of them—that there were signs of a change in public opinion. The common man was ill-satisfied to be excluded from these proceedings, and voiced his complaint through the Estate of the Clergy. More than ever before a summons to the Riksdag appeared as a valuable privilege.

It is usual to attribute to Gustav Adolf a certain inclination towards meetings of the higher Estates, or a Committee of them; but in so far as this is supposed to have involved any idea of superseding the general Riksdag it is a contention which can hardly be substantiated. Before 1630 there were only two meetings (those of 1613 and 1620 already mentioned) which had the clear character of Committee meetings, and against these are to be set not less than eleven Riksdags of the ordinary type, and one (the "Committee Riksdag" of 1625) of a more unusual sort. The famous Landtag at Helsingfors in 1616, which all the Estates of Finland attended under the presidency of the king himself, had the character of a sort of provincial Riksdag. Some smaller meetings from the sixteen-twenties, to which lord lieutenants and bishops were summoned, together sometimes with a number of nobles summoned by special writ, must really be considered as meetings of an afforced Råd, and appear in the majority of cases to stand in close connection with actual meetings of the Riksdag, for which they were deliberate preparation. To these must be added, as regards the period when the king was in Sweden, the Committee meeting of the spring of 1630, especially celebrated for his farewell speech. But we know that on this occasion he would have preferred a full audience of all the Estates. Again, the meetings which took place during the German war, and which undeniably appear to be a step in a retrograde direction, may largely be explained by the deeply rooted reluctance to call a general Riksdag in the absence of the reigning monarch. The fact that the Riksdag of 1629 was presided over by the Råd and not by the king in person was entirely due to unforeseen circumstances—the invasion of Prussia by the Imperialists—which compelled him to quit the country in haste.

It is natural that our interpretation or, perhaps, our appreciation of Gustav Adolf's collaboration with the Swedish people must be determined in no small measure by the extent to which its "immemorial right to tax itself"—a right oftener ignored in practice than some are disposed to admit—can be shown to have been respected in his reign. Modern historians who, for one reason or another, have felt themselves called upon to conduct an inquiry into his acts as a king, have sometimes levelled criticisms at him on this account. Obviously, it is impossible to apply modern standards in this case. An impartial judgment is to be attained only by a comparison with the epochs which preceded and followed him. A modern investigator of radical views who has studied the problem from this point of view thus sums up his conclusions: "It is only in Gustav Adolf's reign that there is evidence to any marked degree of tendencies in the direction of a respect for the people's right to tax itself."

For centuries the Estates had exercised no control over the appropriation of incoming revenues, except in so far as they were generally designated by the government for specific purposes. But the ideas of Gustav Adolf went further than this in the direction of constitutionalism. "And that the Estates may know what use is made of their sweat and blood," runs the report of a speech which he delivered at the Riksdag of 1624, "His Majesty graciously offered to allow the leading men among them to see a draft of the kingdom's income and expenditure, as was done in the case of His Majesty's Råd and some of the bishops and lord lieutenants, at the recent meeting at Strängnäs; presuming, however, that in any case no honorable man could truthfully accuse His Majesty of applying the country's revenue to pleasure, pomp, or other vanities (as indeed is often the case with kings and potentates) but solely to the wants and necessities of the kingdom." In view of the general tendencies of the century this was a remarkable policy. How far it was carried out is not clear.

The age had no clear realization of the true significance of legislation and the legislative power. Its chief concern was that the old and venerable law should not be changed save for the most urgent reasons. The outcome of the attempt of Karl IX to replace the 250-year-old *Landslag* by a new code had revealed how deeply rooted this idea was. We saw just now that when the subject was raised in the Riksdag that body denied its competence to make a law binding on the whole people. The antique forms of provincial legislation were still lurking in the background. The project of a real revision of the law had therefore to be dropped in Gustav Adolf's time. A comprehensive reform of judicial procedure, long desired in vain, took its place. At the Riksdag of Nyköping in 1611 the Estates had presented memorials regarding the deficiencies of the judiciary, and their seriousness could not be glossed over. Grave abuses existed which demanded the prompt intervention of the monarchy for their correction.

The scheme of judicial procedure which was introduced and carried at the Örebro Riksdag of 1614 involved one radical alteration, inasmuch as it transferred the judicial powers of the monarchy to a new High Court. Was not this "new law"? The *Landslag* knew nothing of such permanent courts of appeal; its appellate system was of a wholly different order. The Clergy, in particular, were dubious, and cited the king's promise in the Charter not to alter the law by the unilateral exercise of his authority. For their part, they explained, they were not empowered to accept any departure from the law and the laudable ordinances of past ages; they would have preferred to see the question studied "with the greatest care and attention" before it was put into legislative form. A symptom, this, of the ingrained doubt as to the right of the Riksdag to legislate in conjunction with the king. In a famous speech Gustav Adolf utterly refuted this point of view, maintaining most emphatically the full competence of the king and the Estates to determine this question between them. If this power were to be denied, it would in the last resort be impossible for any government to maintain itself, "seeing that

customs change, and laws which are beneficial in one age may
with new times and persons become injurious and bad in another." If the Clergy believed that they were not entrusted by
their Estate with any authority, of what use were their commissions as deputies? After the king had made some alterations in
the interests of clarity, and in deference to the criticism of the
non-noble orders (who objected to the provisions concerning the
use of the Appeal Court as a *forum privilegii* for the nobility)
the spirituality gave way, and the scheme was unanimously
adopted.

The reform of judicial procedure is without doubt one of the
most important events of Gustav Adolf's reign. The original
design—to make the new High Court the court of highest instance—was abandoned in principle as early as 1615, when the
"Code of Judicial Procedure" was promulgated, for this permitted
a "humble appeal" from the High Court to the king. The character of the High Court as a court of mediate instance was emphasized still further later on through the creation of other High
Courts at Åbo and Dorpat. "How the aforesaid courts have served
and benefited them," says Johannes Botvidi, "all the inhabitants
of the country will testify, high and low, rich and poor, one with
another."

In Gustav Adolf's dealings with the Estates of the kingdom
foreign policy took a leading place. This was one consequence
of the Charter he had given in 1611; but it was also his method
of ensuring that the national propaganda which was indispensable
to his fundamentally defensive statesmanship should make its full
effect. At first, perhaps, he felt that these methods had been forced
upon him, but he soon grew accustomed to them, and he handled
them with complete mastery. A survey of Sweden's relations with
foreign powers, particularly with her neighbors, was the usual
framework for his verbal and written messages to the Riksdag.
Such a survey would also contain the "fundamentals of the postu-
late"—i.e. the motives underlying the government's demands for
men and money, which usually took the form of a question rather
than of precise proposals. These speeches were innocent of reti-
cences or ambiguities, as they certainly were of detachment or

impartiality; their purpose was rather to give expression to strong convictions, and to voice a resolute acceptance of his own duty.

The German war was the only war that Gustav Adolf began on his own initiative, and he resolved upon it only after repeated consultations with the Estates. As Gyllenhielm told the Råd in 1632, it was with their unanimous consent that the king had gone forth to succor the Protestant cause. Gyllenhielm was quite right. In the same way, though with less thoroughness, Gustav Adolf prepared the way for the more important of his campaigns against Russia and Poland. The Riksdag of 1621 was summoned to be informed of the first great expedition to Livland, and to give its assent to that expedition. By these measures it was hoped to avoid "recrimination and ill-will." Sometimes the place of the Riksdag was taken by what were traditionally called "the leading Estates" —a somewhat vague term. This was the case when in the spring of 1626 the resolution was taken to transfer the seat of the war with Poland to Prussia. The presence of foreign agents made this a matter of great delicacy, and the king contented himself with laying his plans before a group of high confidential servants in Church and State who duly gave in their adherence. The innumerable crises in Sweden's relations with Denmark were sometimes discussed in a similar fashion. Within the Riksdag itself the king created an organ—as yet occasional only—for the treating of matters of foreign policy: this was an augmented Secret Committee, which at the end of 1627 was constituted from all four Estates for the purpose of debating his memoranda and his plans. The plans on this occasion had reference to developments in North Germany, which had recently taken a still more threatening turn by reason of the advance of the Imperialists to the Baltic coast. This committee, which was furnished by the Riksdag with authority to take decisions on its behalf, is the origin of that Secret Committee which was to become so important in the future.

The candor with which the king felt himself able to conduct his proceedings with the Estates is particularly evident in his great message to the Riksdag of 1629, which surveyed the menace of the growing power of the Empire, the threat to the Baltic, and the general crisis in the Protestant world. This document, which was undoubtedly written to his dictation, is, for all its striking simplicity, a brilliant piece of political rhetoric, and it lays bare to the members of the Riksdag with an almost reckless frankness the whole game of war and diplomacy. But it was only when his line of action lay clear before him in his own mind that he spoke so plainly, and with such absence of reserve. In this case he seemed already to have burned his boats; the question, as it was put in his message to the Riksdag, was not so much a choice between peace and war, as whether to await the enemy at home or meet him upon foreign soil.

For purely practical reasons a full and literal compliance with the Charter of 1611 proved to be impossible in matters concerning the conclusion of peace, the arrangement of truces, or the contracting of alliances. As a rule the participation of the Estates was confined to receiving information and to sanctioning what had been done. It proved more easy to keep in touch with the Estates in connection with the conclusion of a truce with Poland, because the negotiations with this obstinate enemy remained stationary at much the same point for long periods at a time. The projected conditions for a friendly settlement with the emperor were laid before the Riksdag and approved by it; but the negotiations for alliances, which became so complicated and extensive, especially during Gustav Adolf's years in Germany, fell outside its sphere of action. By then circumstances had developed in a manner which no one had foreseen at the time of the king's accession.

It was in fact alien to the ideas of the age to interfere positively in the monarchy's management of foreign policy. The Estates contented themselves with giving their adherence and expressing their confidence, though always in language which betrayed their lively consciousness of the blessings of peace and their hopes that it might be preserved or restored as the case might be. We even find the same note in their acquiescence in the resolution of 1629 to interfere in the German war. Custom demanded that the Estates in these matters should rely on the king's enlightened judgment and his zeal for the true welfare of his kingdom. The Riksdag's ability to take up an independent attitude was thereby no doubt limited; so that the real bone of contention, in so far as friction was unavoidable, was always how far they were prepared to go in granting supplies.

Yet this is undoubtedly an inadequate explanation of the success with which Gustav Adolf invariably managed to win over the Riksdag, or the other meetings of the Estates, to endorse the aims of his foreign policy. Events at the close of Karl IX's reign had shown that the Estates, despite their habitual respect for the monarchy, would on occasion venture upon an opinion of their own even in questions solely concerning foreign affairs; but Gustav Adolf's Riksdags can show scarcely any incidents of this nature, unless we count the opposition which broke out now and again to the king's personal participation in campaigns on the other side of the Baltic. There is plenty of evidence of an opposition movement among the people outside the Riksdag; on several occasions, indeed, Gustav Adolf, in his speeches and messages to the Riksdag, openly alludes to recalcitrant and discontented spirits. But whenever it was a question of obtaining the Riksdag's support for enterprises outside the boundaries of the kingdom, he had that body well in hand. The explanation must be sought in the first place in the fact that to his growing authority he united a gift of vivid persuasion and vigorous eloquence, and an ability to influence men privately before the debates. The success which, with but few exceptions, attended his undertakings stood him in good stead as a credit upon which he could draw at need. Men came to understand that the government rightly interpreted the signs of the times. A profound national sentiment made the learning of the lesson easier. As we saw in another connection, the average man believed himself to have grasped the fact that if a settlement with any of the enemies of the country were really necessary, it could most advantageously be reached upon enemy soil.

What then was to be done? On that point the popular mind was, perhaps, something dubious and uncertain. But no one was prepared, in the full daylight of responsibility, seriously to back his opinion against the king's. Of him they were sure.

[3]

DURING the first period of Gustav Adolf's reign there continued to be a complete absence of any fixed rules for the Riksdag's procedure. Its forms of business were on the whole undefined, and in some respects primitive. Some advances had been made under Karl IX. The normal way of reaching a decision came to be by written interchange of views between king and Estates, and the elements of a committee system had made their appearance; but procedure varied in different cases, and the general meetings, when the king was present in the assembly chamber—they had formerly been held in the open air, either in the courtyard of the castle, or in the market place of the town where the diet was meeting—were especially conspicuous for a lack of form and order.

The two first Riksdag meetings after Gustav Adolf was declared of age—that at Stockholm in 1613, and that at Örebro in 1614— seem by all accounts to have followed the same course. The method of written proceedings and the exchange of question and answer was adhered to perhaps more consistently than before. Gustav Adolf, however, found that this ceremonious method of doing business did not suit him. A new system, intended to bring king and Estates into closer contact with one another during critical discussions, took shape in the Riksdag Ordinance of 1617. This Ordinance was essentially a form of procedure for the general assemblies of the Estates, and it defined in particular the respective places of the different orders. A fixed ceremonial was laid down, which had the additional advantage of excluding improper persons from the meetings.

At the close of the reign of Karl IX, for instance, the fact had emerged that Danish merchants had smuggled themselves into the chamber among the deputies, in order to listen to the discussions. We are told, too, that during the meetings immediately preceding this Ordinance the emissaries or spies of Sigismund had wormed their way in among the Peasants, and had actually managed to get themselves entrusted with the task of drawing up their replies. A stop was now put to such abuses.

The Riksdag Ordinance, which had been drawn up by Axel Oxenstierna, saw the light at an extremely critical moment. The Riksdag at Örebro in 1617 was in fact marked by an internal tension more acute than in any other assembly in Gustav Adolf's reign. The relations between the monarchy and the hereditary princes represented by Duke Johan and Kristina the queen mother (as guardian of Karl Filip) were at this time clouded by un-

resolved controversies and open distrust. Gustav Adolf's prime
object at this Riksdag was to strike a blow at Sigismund's propaganda—which had been steadily increasing in audacity, and had
even attempted to seduce Duke Johan, as the king well knew—by
drastic legislation against every sort of connection with the camp
of the deposed sovereign. In this Gustav Adolf was able to carry
his point. The famous Örebro Statute, accepted by the Estates
in February 1617, put high treason and conversion to Catholicism
on the same legal footing. At the same time Duke Johan, who was
in attendance at the Riksdag, was reduced to submission.

In brief outline, the Riksdag Ordinance envisaged the following method of reaching a decision of the Estates. After the opening of the diet by the king, and the deposition of his proposal
at a general meeting in the Riksdag chamber, the four Estates
were to separate to their specially appointed places of meeting
to debate their answers. These were to be drawn up in writing—
the Peasants receiving the help of sworn clerks—and were pre-
sumed to be ready within the course of a few days. The hereditary princes, who in the eyes of contemporaries were an integral
part of the Riksdag, were also to draw up their reply in the same
way. The handing over of these replies was to take place at
another *plenum* in the Riksdag chamber, at which both the
hereditary princes and the Estates—the latter by their appointed
delegates—were verbally to explain to the king the attitude which
they had adopted. If the king had any objection to make, he
then incorporated it into his answer which was given either orally
or in writing, according to the importance of the issue. If the replies were not in agreement among themselves, a discussion followed in which every Estate through its spokesman attempted
to justify its opinion. The object was to determine in this way
which Estate had "the best grounds" for its answer. If it proved
impossible to obtain unanimity, then the king was to settle the
issue by "adopting whichever view is best."

There are two points worthy of note here: the public debate
before the throne, and the king's position as arbiter. It was the
former of these that mainly interested contemporaries. A discussion of this nature under the immediate surveillance of the king
was something new and strange. The Estates therefore drew back,

as though they felt that they were venturing upon dangerous ground. The lower orders requested that henceforward, as in the past, they might be allowed to express themselves in writing, if necessity should arise. The king felt himself unable to refuse this request. When the draft of the Riksdag Ordinance was approved, it was with a clear reservation regarding the scheme for verbal discussions. On the other hand, no objection was taken to the point about the king's liberty in certain cases to choose between the answers. It was plain that no one supposed that the provision could imply any attempt to extend the prerogative of the Crown. It was recognized that in doubtful cases the monarch had the right to decide which order or orders must give way so that a unanimous decision might be obtained. And the implicit assumption—very typical of the whole outlook of the age—was that every effort must be made to obtain unanimity. But, since the Crown alone had the right of initiation, it undoubtedly thereby acquired a possible means of coercion.

The Riksdag Ordinance of 1617 was never promulgated as a statute, although it was subsequently adopted and observed. Gustav Adolf conformed to it with certain modifications at his later Riksdag meetings. We know of occasions when the king obviously made use of his right to elicit a positive decision at a time when the Estates were divided—e.g. at the coronation Riksdag later in 1617, in regard to the obstinately contested question of the Trade Ordinance which aroused particular opposition among the Burghers, and was not really very acceptable to the Nobility. The fact that there was scarcely one of the Estates that wished a decision to be taken at that time did not restrain the king from promulgating the Ordinance as a measure sanctioned by the approval of the Riksdag. The queen mother, with whom his relations continued to be strained, criticized the measure with much acerbity. The question had, however, earlier been the subject of lengthy discussions, and the Burgesses were in some respects undeniably contending for the arbitrary interests of their class. In the same way the king dealt with the Clergy in 1622, when at the Riksdag of that year they decisively rejected the "General Customs," a tax based on Dutch models, and levied upon all "consumable and utility goods" brought to market in the towns. The Estate was forced to withdraw and amend its answer. The king broke down what at first was apparently a general opposition by inducing the nobles to accede to the demand in return for various ameliorations in regard to their privileges. This "Little Toll," which initiated the system of customs barriers at town gates, had a subsequent existence of close on two hundred years.

Verbal negotiations in the Riksdag chamber also occurred upon occasion, in spite of the cold reception which had been accorded to this particular point in the draft of the Riksdag Ordinance. There are examples of such debates in 1624 and 1625; but they took place with the chancellor, not the king, in the chair. At both these Riksdags tempers grew pretty warm. In 1624 the Peasants, represented by their appointed delegates, put up a most stubborn resistance, declaring that it was impossible for them to increase their offer. Oxenstierna, representing the king (who undoubtedly stayed away deliberately), was quite prepared to admit the difficulties of the lower orders, but pointed to the overriding consideration of the danger from abroad. It would be better, he contended, "to pay out a part of what God had given them into the hands of the bailiff or some other of the king's agents, than to have a foreign army invading and harrying the country, and killing the population in all directions." A breach with Denmark was at that time a serious possibility, though eventually the danger passed away. The government got its way in the end: a doubling of the stock-tax and increased contributions under other heads. The following year, when the Estates were summoned in fewer numbers than usual (though the Peasants did attend, so that it was not a mere Committee meeting) it was a question of approving a new form of impost—the mill-dues. The revenue to be derived from these was intended to form a fund for the maintenance of a standing army. The project was finally carried, but not without some lively opposition, and not until the king had put forward a proposal which was even less to the taste of the Estates—that they should themselves tax their richer members with a view to raising a reasonable total. Of all the new taxes, however, it was the mill-dues that secured least popular acquiescence.[1]

The most careful and methodical preparations were made for meetings of the Riksdag. First the king discussed the situation with the Råd. During the whole of Gustav Adolf's reign matters which were to be laid before the Riksdag underwent a careful preliminary examination in the council chamber. Only when the king had the support of his councillors, and after they had put their signatures to a formal resolution of the Råd—often after a more or less lengthy period for consideration—could there be any question of the matter's proceeding any further. One of the questions customarily decided after preliminary discussion by a vote of the Råd was whether or not the Riksdag need be summoned at all. It sometimes happened, therefore, that the lords of the council found it unnecessary to call a Riksdag, although the king had proposed to do so.

The circle of Råd members was occasionally extended, especially during the early sixteen-twenties, to include outstanding representatives of the higher branches of the local civil service such as governors and bishops, and also selected representatives of the first Estate. We have already encountered these meetings of the afforced Råd, which as a rule were summoned in connection with a forthcoming Riksdag. Their significance lay, among other things, in the fact that they gave the government an opportunity to influence opinion beforehand throughout a rather more extended sphere. It was moreover the plain duty of the Råd to attempt to predispose their "brothers" of the Nobility in favor of such demands as might be in contemplation. The Riksdags which coincide with the crises in the military fortunes of German Protestantism (1627, 1629) are especially noteworthy for such attempts to influence the nobles through the Råd. If the nobles were gained, then, in the king's opinion, the battle was as good as won. Gustav Adolf considered that the Peasants, who in spite of all differences had many interests in common with the Nobility, especially in questions of taxation, would not hold out for long once the Nobility had been induced to surrender. And sur-

[1] The reason for this was that they prohibited the use of hand-mills, which were the normal method of grinding corn among large sections of the population.

render it must, to a degree hitherto unheard of. In actual fact, the plea of State necessity compelled, during these years, a veritable abrogation of noble privileges which left little of the established economic advantages of the order untouched.

At the opening and dissolution of the Riksdag it was usual for the king to make a speech welcoming or dismissing the Estates. Gustav Adolf made good use of these opportunities. His speeches of greeting or farewell were never mere formalities, but were designed as propaganda for the State and the State's religion. Moreover, he frequently intervened with a speech while the Riksdag was still in session. If the occasion demanded, he would sometimes speak impromptu, as in the Riksdag chamber in 1624, when he criticized "verbally and extempore" the view of the Clergy upon the scheme for a unified form of church government to comprise both priests and laymen—the "general consistory" so long debated, though never realized.

The forms of procedure in use in the Riksdag tended on the whole to draw the ruler and the representatives of the people into closer touch with one another in a way to which later ages afford no parallel. Kristina and Karl X Gustav maintained the tradition, though in an attenuated form; Karl XI, on the other hand, hedged his throne with a barrier of taciturnity. In Gustav Adolf's time the general meetings in the Riksdag chamber were fairly numerous; thus no less than six were held in 1624. After his death they became less usual. Axel Oxenstierna attempted in this and other respects to infuse new life into the forms of 1617, but in the end abandoned the attempt. Other forms of procedure were in course of rapid development, and of these the characteristic feature was the increasingly independent activity of the Estates. It was these methods, which already tended towards a government by committees, that came into conflict with the Carolinian autocracy; and it was the last vestiges of them that were taken over by the Age of Freedom.[2]

Thus Gustav Adolf's Riksdag Ordinance, in common with all his methods of government, contrives to avoid the stamp of

---

[2] The period between 1719 and 1772 when the Riksdag was the supreme political force in the country.

arbitrary rule, but remains the clear reflection of his personality and his needs. There was no room for a system which did not assist the collaboration of king and Estates. He had no thought of drawing a hard and fast line between their different spheres of action when the advantage or necessities of his kingdom were in question. In his own words, king and Estates "together represented the sovereign monarchy." He had a profound contempt for the government of the many. A people which was not firmly led by its ruler was in his eyes fast hastening to decay; but he considered it to be equally impossible to govern a people against its own will, and in conflict with its innate instincts. The problem was, how to awaken, when necessary, the slumbering consciousness of the nation to a realization of its true interests, and this was not to be done by smooth speeches. "The people are so foolish that they believe that he who goes oftenest whining to them means best by them." He attached great importance to persuasion; but he knew perfectly well when to apply pressure. He avowed, however, that he recognized in the voice of the people the voice of God: *vox populi, vox Dei.* "The humor of the Estates is in the hands of God," he remarked to the Råd in 1629, when, uncertain of the issue of the critical Riksdag that was approaching, he prepared to take his hasty departure to Prussia. If their answers were satisfactory, well and good; if their answers were not so satisfactory, he was prepared to see in that circumstance an omen of approaching misfortune. *Nota est futurae malae criseos,* as the Latin of the Råd minutes has it.

Perhaps it is not altogether easy to crystallize Gustav Adolf's views into constitutional formulae. Certainly they contained a strong undercurrent of constitutionalism; but they had also elements of an absolutist spirit akin to his father's. His conception of the liberties of the Estates could not be uninfluenced by the degree to which they made common cause with himself. In his public career he identified himself with the office he held—the office of king. Hence his claim to lead his people, and to secure by paternal supervision the subordination of administrative forms to the service of the monarchy.

[4]

THE hereditary princes stood in close relationship to the Råd and the Estates. They formed in themselves the "Order of Princes." They were, with the king, co-heirs to the kingdom. The Charter of 1611, moreover, in its constitutional provisions had given a particular preeminence to Duke Johan of Östergötland (p. 48). We have already seen, however, that Queen Kristina, although not expressly named in this connection, came in her capacity of guardian for Duke Karl Filip to represent the power of the princes at least as much as Johan. They both attended Riksdag meetings, though Kristina never appeared publicly in the Riksdag chamber. It was she and Johan who were the first to sign the resolutions of the Riksdag, and from 1614 their names and titles appeared in the preamble. The king sent them separate proposals in regard to the business under discussion, and they each returned a separate answer. In the intervals between the Riksdag meetings they kept up an almost incessant correspondence with the king upon questions in which the kingdom proper and their own duchies were equally concerned. Our picture of the social structure of Sweden in the first half of Gustav Adolf's reign will not fully correspond with the facts if these important aspects are neglected.

When Gustav Vasa provided his younger sons with dukedoms, he took a step in full consonance with the ideas of his time. The result, however, was dissension and danger. The unity of the kingdom suffered prejudice through the rights and pretensions of the territorial power of the princes. Karl IX, in his capacity of duke, had defended these pretensions with the greatest obstinacy; but once in possession of the throne he acted upon very different principles. His widow, as guardian of the inheritance of the younger line, showed herself faithful to the older tradition. She was extremely solicitous to maintain the independence of the duchies. In questions of national policies, moreover, she often held opinions of her own, and expressed them—particularly in the earlier years of the reign—with the greatest freedom. In this respect Duke Johan was usually more complaisant, partly as a result of his ambiguous position as half-brother to Sigismund of

Poland. Sigismund did not make this position any easier when he let it be understood that he considered that he had claims on Johan; and the duke seems more than once to have become the object of Gustav Adolf's suspicions. The secret agents of the arch-enemy did in fact display a disturbing preference for Johan's duchy. The Örebro Statute in 1617 was pointedly aimed at him, and it was in vain that he criticized it as too extreme in its consequences. It was forced through apparently against his will.

When the Riksdag Ordinance laid it down that even the hereditary princes should publicly justify their replies in the chamber—an absolute novelty very repugnant to Johan—it revealed the government's intention to facilitate the task of overcoming the duke's opposition. At least once during this Riksdag exchanges took place between the king and the duke in the presence of the assembled Estates. Johan did not cut a very dignified figure: "Duke Johan mumbled a few words which were inaudible at the back of the hall." It is at all events the fact that the Riksdag Ordinance deposed Johan from the place of honor on the king's right hand which he had formerly occupied, and transferred it for the future to Karl Filip. The older man was deeply angered at this "degradation"; but his protests went unheeded. Posterity has but a vague picture of Duke Johan of Östergötland. His real opinions never emerged. Luckily for Sweden he was a man of peace, though he could show valor in the field. Illness and an unhappy marriage cast a shadow upon his later life.

The leadership in the struggle of the hereditary princes against the monarchy fell as a rule upon the queen mother. In theory, as in practice, it was a struggle in which important issues were involved. The problem was to balance the interests of the central government against the rights of the two dukes as governors of their extensive domains—i.e. in the one case Södermanland, Närke, and Västmanland, and in the other, Östergötland with a considerable slice of Västergötland. The conflict reached its climax in 1617, and notably contributed to the tension which marked the Riksdag of that year. Special difficulties arose over the determination of what form the knight-service due from the nobles should take in the case of the duchies. The dissensions came to an open breach at the Riksdag of Örebro early in this year. Matters

went so far that the king caused the queen mother's most prominent adviser, Dr. Chesnecopherus, to be imprisoned, and extracted
from him a humiliating apology for the language he had employed. The unsolved problem came up again later in the year
at the coronation Riksdag, but once more without result. At last,
in accordance with a suggestion contained in Gustav Vasa's will
—which the Vasa dynasty revered as a law binding upon the
family—it was agreed to refer the question to a jury drawn from
the Estates.

The matter was thus submitted to arbitration. For one reason
or another, however, the arbitration never took place. As far as
Johan was concerned the question was settled by his death in
1618, for that event involved the lapse of his duchy to the Crown,
in the absence of heirs. Karl Filip survived him by less than three
years, and never entered upon the independent control of his
duchy. He was an impulsive and pugnacious young man, and
his somewhat unrestrained mode of life gave his mother some
anxiety. Gustav Adolf had more than one brush with his brother;
but as time went on their relations became more cordial, and the
funeral oration which the king pronounced over his brother's
grave is eloquent of a sincere and personal sorrow.

Thus by the middle of Gustav Adolf's reign the territorial
power of the princes had disappeared, never to return, to the
great benefit of the country. That Gustav Adolf entirely disapproved of it as an institution is abundantly clear. "In this matter
only was King Gustav at fault," he writes in his *History,* with
reference to his grandfather's will, "for agreement among brothers
is oft to seek, and it is rare to find power and unity together."
Many of his contemporaries, moreover, have assured us that after
the death of Johan and Karl Filip the king took a firm resolution not to endow his own sons, if any should be born to him,
with independent duchies. His daughter Kristina later adhered
to this rule when she succeeded in getting her cousin Karl Gustav
chosen as hereditary prince and heir presumptive. The resolution
of the Riksdag in 1650 laid it down that in future the kingdom
was never to be split up, but henceforth was to form a single
unit. Thereafter Sweden had only titular duchies.

[5]

"WE, THE undersigned, the Council and Estates of the Kingdom of Sweden": so ran the traditional preamble to resolutions of the Riksdag. It was a formula which long continued in use. It expressed the fact that the Råd was anciently the kernel of the Riksdag. The Råd itself was an element in the Estates. It formed a basic constituent in all recognized forms of the representative body. The meeting and its composition might vary; but the presence of the Råd was indispensable. Above all, the nobles saw in the Råd members their "foremen." Solidarity as between the Råd families and the rest of the privileged order was one of the most important securities for a stable society. It can hardly be denied that this way of looking at things involved a tendency towards the formation of an Upper House; but in Sweden it never became more than a tendency. The other Estates, too, felt themselves to be entirely dependent upon the Råd. The resolution of the Arboga Riksdag of 1597 had declared that for a decision upon matters of State to be considered complete, valid, and definitive, it was necessary for all the Estates to be present, and particularly the Råd.

Already before Gustav Adolf's time, however, this connection between the Råd and the representatives of the people had begun to grow looser, although the outward forms still persisted. In the main this was a consequence of the dual capacity of the Råd, as on the one hand an administrative council (though this aspect was still not fully realized), and on the other an integral part of the Estates. It could not be both to an equal extent; the more strongly it emerged in its former aspect, the weaker it became in the latter. To this must be added the fact that the bond between Råd and Estates had in the end been violently broken during the disturbed period which, at the end of the sixteenth century, had cleared the ground by revolutionary methods for a new order of things in the country. The Råd as revived in 1602 lacked the sense of authority inherent in its predecessors, and preferred to take shelter beneath the wing of the monarchy.

The events of 1611 might certainly have involved a return to conditions which would have permitted the Råd to force their will upon the king in questions of national policy. We are already familiar with the contents of the Charter as touching this question. We know, too, that development took place upon other lines. It became apparent that forms of government were sufficiently elastic to permit the preservation of the uncontested direction of affairs in the hands of the monarch. But this could only be by way of cooperation, and under the seal of mutual confidence. It very soon became clear that for this, too, the necessary conditions existed. The explanation is largely to be found in the fact that Axel Oxenstierna, apparently from the very beginning, became the leading spirit in Gustav Adolf's Råd. A new epoch had begun. It was only very gradually that the queen mother Kristina came to realize this fact. There is evidence from the early days of Gustav Adolf's reign that she sought—apparently without success—to awaken Gustav Adolf's suspicions against the Råd.

The connecting link between Råd and Estates is still plainly visible at the Nyköping Riksdag of 1611. When they presented their conditions to the king on that occasion, they appeared as parties in close collaboration; but thereafter their paths diverged. The Råd emerges in the sequel as a corporation quite distinct from the Estates. Its place is by the king's side. Råd and Nobility stand no longer in the same mutual relation as before. After this date it never happened that, at a Riksdag or assembly, the Råd joined the Nobility in an answer to the king's proposals, or returned one on its own account. We do not even know how far its members took part in the discussions and resolutions of their order in their private capacities as nobles, though it is quite probable that they did so. At all events, the "Ordinance for the House of Nobles" of 1626 decided that members of the Råd had no vote in the Estate of the Nobles. Their rôle was now that of negotiators between the king and his kingdom.

The outward forms of collaboration between king and Råd underwent an important alteration in Gustav Adolf's time. The first five years of the reign, as far as we know, produced no innovation. King and councillors met at the usual Råd meetings, of which a greater or lesser number might be held in the course of the year. Here the king put forward proposals which the Råd subsequently examined at its private sessions, finally drawing up

a so-called "opinion," which gave a written résumé of its views
on the question at issue. With 1617, when a short but continuous
period of peace began, came a new phase in Gustav Adolf's relations with his Råd. Cooperation, in fact, became more obviously
direct than before. The king now comes into closer and more
regular contact with the council chamber, often presides there,
and himself leads the discussion. We cannot fail to notice how
well this agrees with the aims which had guided the two men
responsible for the Riksdag Ordinance—i.e. the king and his
chancellor. Undoubtedly the two things are clearly connected:
Gustav Adolf desires to draw closer his relations both with the
Råd and with the Estates. In the Råd, as in the Riksdag, his
object is to determine which opinion has the "best foundation."
This is now done by means of systematic discussion intended to
throw light on the question from various points of view, positive
and negative. To that end set debates are arranged, and the minutes of the Råd are laid side by side with its "opinion." Thus a
logical treatment is secured, and an increased sense of responsibility for measures concerted and decisions taken. It can hardly
be doubted, moreover, that the presence of the king exercised a
good deal of influence in the same direction. Johan Skytte informs
us that the king frequently took up his pen to make notes of the
views expressed.

The Råd member usually belonged to the old aristocracy. For
the greater part of the year he lived in the provinces on his estates. When a meeting of the Råd was held, a writ was sent to
him in person; though often it was only possible to secure the
attendance of those who lived near the place of meeting. The Råd
had thus no fixed composition. But in this respect also a significant
alteration is to be noted, an alteration which may be said to have
led to a definitive transformation in the functions of the Råd. In
the spring of 1621 such of its members as lived in Stockholm
were commissioned to act as a regency during the king's absence
in the field. The commission was renewed seven times in all,
from 1625 onwards upon an extended basis inasmuch as all
members of the Råd who were not prevented by other duties
were henceforward to meet in the capital to transact current
business in the king's place. By virtue of the authority delegated

AXEL OXENSTIERNA
Oil Painting by D. Beck

by Gustav Adolf upon his departure to Germany in the spring of
1630, the Råd—or rather a section of it—carried on the internal
government for the rest of the king's life. These specially appointed regencies of Gustav Adolf's time are a sort of transition
stage leading up to the permanent Council Chamber which became the rule during Kristina's minority (1633-1644), and which
acquired the character of a regularly constituted Council of
Regency.

The most important feature of all, however, was the fact that
a growing number of Råd members was kept in the capital by
important official duties. Nothing did more to modify the inherited conception of the nature of the councillor's office than
the hitherto unprecedented demands which were made upon
officeholders by the central government. The pillars of the central
government were the five great officers of state: steward, marshal,
admiral, chancellor, and treasurer. The idea that the business of
government could be divided into five main branches answering
to the offices of the five (who were also members of the Råd) is
fully developed by the end of the reign of Karl IX, and became
the basis for the work of organization which took place under
Gustav Adolf. The results of this work take formal shape in
the Form of Government of 1634; but the main walls of the
edifice were built during the king's reign. The Supreme Court
for Svealand under the presidency of the steward was the first
to receive that collegial organization which provided the main
principle of the work of reform; next followed the Treasury and
then the Chancery—the *anima regni*. The reforming ideas of an
earlier age in this way came to realization, and in the course of
a few decades the whole character of the Swedish Råd was radi-
cally altered. Henceforward it became primarily an administrative body, concerned with the most important branches of the
State service. The members of the Råd ceased to live like independent sovereigns on their estates: they had become the cogs—
indeed the motive power—in the never-pausing machinery of
State.

At the time of Gustav Adolf's accession the Råd comprised some
twenty members. It is not very easy to be quite definite about
the identity of all of them. Apart from Axel Oxenstierna, who,

although one of the youngest members, always took the leading
part, this first list, which gradually thinned out as time went on,
contained men of only second- or third-rate ability. Even the
two members who were of higher rank than the others, Counts
Magnus and Abraham Brahe, were men of this type, though
Count Magnus held the high office of steward for the whole of
the reign. The generation of councillors of which these two
brothers may be considered fair representatives lacked neither
industry nor zeal; but with gifts of real statesmanship it was
less liberally endowed. In subsequent years an approximately
equal number of new members—twenty at least—was appointed
at various times. But among these, too, there was no one who
could rival the influence of the chancellor, whose unique capacity
for work, many-sided knowledge of State business, and adroit-
ness in the solution of difficulties gave him an unassailable position. Peder Galt, King Christian's agent in Sweden, remarked in
a report written in 1622 that Oxenstierna "reigned alone," and
was overwhelmed with the burden of his duties. In the view of
this observer there were some, and among them Magnus Brahe,
who viewed with disapproval the steady increase of his influence.

Several of the men who now entered the Råd were nevertheless of considerable eminence, and the new recruits were more
vigorous than the councillors who had surrounded Gustav Adolf
at the outset of his career. Among those who were called to the
Råd in the earlier half of the reign were Jakob de la Gardie,
Karl Karlsson Gyllenhielm—newly returned from his long captivity in Poland—Johan Skytte, and Gabriel Gustavsson Oxenstierna, the younger brother of the chancellor. Last but not least,
they included a generation of men whose acceptance of the title
of councillor may be said to have completed the reconciliation of
former enmities. In Gustav Adolf's Råd were to be found the
sons of the men who had fallen victims to his father's drastic
settlement with the aristocracy. No less than three of the sons of
that Gustav Banér who had been executed at Linköping—Svante,
Per, and Johan—took their seats in the Råd in the latter portion
of the reign. The king had intended to confer the same appointment upon their brother Axel, his declared favorite and especial
friend; but he never found an opportunity to nominate him be-

fore his death. Erik Sparre's son Johan, who had been brought up in exile, held first the important post of Speaker of the Estate of the Nobility (1627) and was subsequently appointed to the Råd. Young Per Brahe was also promoted in this way, which soon became the normal procedure.

The newly ennobled Johan Skytte, Gustav Adolf's former tutor, who was called to the Råd in 1617 at the Riksdag of Örebro, stood rather apart from the others. The high aristocracy always regarded him, despite his title of *friherre,* as a *novus homo.* The antagonism between him and the Oxenstiernas was at times very great, and towards the end of the king's reign, when Skytte was acting as governor general in Livland, it seems to have grown greater. In the Råd debates he was sometimes deputed to play the part of leader of the Opposition. This was the case in the autumn of 1629 during the discussions on the projected German war, against which he urged a variety of considerations. How far he was expressing, on this and other occasions, a seriously meant disapproval would seem to be extremely uncertain; for to Skytte, whose mind was of a rather donnish cast, academic disputation was a more natural form of procedure than it was to many of his colleagues. That his views diverged in more than one respect from those of the old aristocracy is, however, undoubted, particularly in view of his attitude during Kristina's minority which followed the king's death. It is difficult to decide in what degree the principles for which he may be supposed to have stood were supported by others within the Råd or by the ruling classes in general. In the confidential correspondence of the Oxenstierna brothers there are references to "Skytte and his gang." It is certain that after the king's death Karl Karlsson Gyllenhielm takes the same line as Skytte, and comes forward as the spokesman of those who distrust the tendency towards the growth of the power of the aristocracy. For him, as a scion of the house of Vasa, the tradition of Karl IX had naturally an especially sacred and binding force.

The fact that it is difficult to put one's finger on the real bones of contention between the members of Gustav Adolf's Råd does not therefore mean that such differences were non-existent. But in so far as they did exist, they had no prejudicial effect. Men were aware that the times demanded a united front. The imperious authority of the king, which grew steadily with the passing of the years, bound the Råd together as a united whole. There might, indeed, even in the Råd, be occasions when his projects were received with hesitation: there might be moments when the domestic sky grew dark with clouds. For instance, at the end of 1630, when Gustav Adolf's position in Germany still seemed anything but secure, his letters to the Råd became decidedly heated. He accused them of "unseasonable scruples, and perchance small care for the public weal—always the great failing of our nation." But this was exceptional. Viewed as a whole, the history of Gustav Adolf's collaboration with his Råd is remarkable for its extraordinary fruitfulness and solidarity.

[6]

GUSTAV ADOLF has often been credited with a marked tendency to favor the nobility. This view, accurate only within certain limits, has its roots in the seventeenth century. In the time of Karl XI's minority, in particular, when rival views of politics and society were coming into sharp conflict, belief in Gustav Adolf's boundless affection for the nobility was exalted in certain quarters into a dogma. Influential politicians in the House of Nobles dropped into the habit of appealing to the enlightened ideas and wise measures of the great king to buttress all sorts of claims on behalf of their own Estate. They liked to regard him as "the nobility's king" *par excellence,* as the all-wise champion of an ideal of society in which the center was a numerous and thriving aristocracy with ample privileges and incontestable precedence over other classes by simple right of birth. On the other hand there have been those who have held that such approval was rather to his discredit than otherwise, or have at any rate condemned as weakness what they considered to be his undue complaisance to aristocratic class interests. It is not difficult to read such views between the lines of Jonas Hallenberg's great work, which, although it was published so long ago as the last decade of the eighteenth century, and was unhappily never completed, is still a fundamental authority for the internal history of the reign.

Under the immediate impression of the king's work, the judgment had been rather different. Men such as Jakob de la Gardie and Per Brahe made no bones about their decided opinion that the "heroic king" had on occasion been rather high-handed, and had paid small attention to the privileges of the nobility. This view, which involves an important modification of that alluded to above, presents no difficulty if we try to survey what really happened under Gustav Adolf's rule in regard to the correlation of the privileges of the nobility with their duties towards the State.

It is undeniably true that, in the form in which they were put forward to the king in the Patent of Privileges, these noble rights were decidedly extensive. They were confirmed with some alterations on the occasion of the coronation in 1617; but it was some years before the amended Patent appeared. When at last it was promulgated, it became clear that the Swedish nobility had obtained a charter that for many years to come was to be the basis of those social privileges which were the concomitant of noble rank. This privilege legislation was intended to protect the judicial security of the nobles individually, and the exceptional position of the nobles as a class—both of which had been somewhat precarious under Karl IX—and also to extend by a number of new regulations the economic advantages which were reserved to them. From the point of view of the nobles, the new privileges signified a great, indeed a decisive, advance.

In the situation as it stood when Gustav Adolf came of age and took up the work of government it was scarcely open to the monarchy to reject the demands made by the Estate of the Nobility. There are, however, some indications that the king was not altogether satisfied with the scope of these privileges. A draft proclamation dating from the beginning of the reign, even if it does not actually curtail the rights of the nobility, does at least put a restrictive interpretation upon them; and we have some notes in the king's handwriting regarding certain points in the Patent of which he disapproved, which stand in close relation to the renewed discussions of 1617. The modifications which were then introduced dealt mainly with the judicial security of the individual noble: the regulations dealing with this matter were now applied in such a way as to provide better safeguards for the executive government—a change which was no doubt to be connected with the drastic Örebro Statute.

Gustav Adolf's Patents give significant confirmatory evidence of the reconciliation between the monarchy and the first Estate, a reconciliation which, after the crisis of Karl IX's reign, was certainly indispensable if the new order was to have solidity and stability. They put the nobility in the position of an official class upon whom the charge of public affairs was peculiarly laid: more than ever before, these public services appeared as the especial prerogative and possession of the aristocracy, and not simply as irksome duties. The goal to be aimed at was a fixed salary scale for government officials. All the more important offices were reserved to nobles; and it was laid down as a general principle that "no person of base birth is to be promoted over their head." Later on, this harsh provision became the object of increasing resentment from the unprivileged classes, and in the class struggles of the middle of the century the nobles themselves appeared anxious to modify its original sense.

The man really responsible for the Patents was Axel Oxenstierna. Yet he is also to be regarded as the foremost champion of the alliance between king and nobility which was so markedly a characteristic of the succeeding period. It was he, too, who in harmony with the king—and indeed at his request—gave to the Swedish nobility its political organization in a form which on the whole remained unaltered until the suppression of the Riksdag of four Estates in 1866.

Before this organization took place the Swedish nobility was hardly a definite or self-contained body. It was not without justice that Gustav Adolf remarked at the coronation Riksdag that no one really knew who was, and who was not a noble. There were still two conflicting theories as to the way in which noble status might be acquired: the old, indeed somewhat outmoded one, whereby nobility was conditioned by the performance of knight service to the Crown; and the growing opinion that possession of a coat-of-arms in itself gave a family a title to nobility. The future was to belong to the latter principle—the principle of birth. The compromise as a result of which the nobility was in-

duced in 1622 to give its consent to the "Little Toll" involved a
great victory for this principle, since on that one hand the conditions for nobility by birth were tightened up, and on the other
the obligation to perform knight service was made less burden-
some. The principle of nobility by birth definitively triumphed
in the *Riddarhusordning* (Ordinance for the House of Nobles).
After years of preparation, in which the chancellor had taken
an active part, this was at last drawn up in the summer of 1626.

The House of Nobles now became a society of noble families.
It also represented the totality of the Estate considered as a
branch of the national representation. Henceforward it was to
be the rule that every nobleman of legal age was bound to obey
the king's summons to the national assembly. It was a principle
difficult to carry out with any approximation to completeness,
and it was on other grounds little liked by the nobles, who on
several occasions, and most recently at the Nyköping Riksdag
of 1611, had attempted to emancipate themselves from this general obligation to attend. By the terms of the *Riddarhusordning*
only the noble who represented his family as the head of the house
was to have the right to a voice at the meetings of the Estate;
so that every family had one vote. To this division into families
there corresponded another based partly on a new order of precedence. The division of this first Riddarhus into three classes, each
with equal influence irrespective of the numbers of families contained in it, clearly mirrors the desire of its originator to establish an equilibrium within the order which should redound to
the advantage of that element in it which comprised the highest
ranks of society. How far the conscious imitation of Continental
models influenced this division is not easy to say: at all events
the segregation of the Counts and *Friherrar* and their families in
the first class, of the untitled Råd families in the second, and of
the other noble families in the third, persisted until the Age of
Freedom. There was certainly no lack of foreign precedents either
for the Riddarhus itself, or for the office of speaker (*lantmarskalk*)
which was instituted at the same time. In all other respects, the
Swedish Riddarhus, which was to be the stage for so many historic dramas, presents a distinctively national appearance.

It was only natural that the Swedish nobility should grow in numbers and power under Gustav Adolf. Elevation to the peerage and naturalization of foreign noblemen were both indispensable methods of bestowing an adequate reward upon merit. Neither was abused: the increase in numbers was indeed very notable in comparison with the preceding period; but it remained at a lower yearly average than that for the whole of the succeeding period up to and including the reign of Karl XIV Johan (1818-1844). At the death of Gustav Adolf the total number of patents of nobility conferred up to that time can be put in the neighborhood of 250, of which 68 date from his reign; whereas Kristina alone created 433 new nobles in less than ten years. Although the foreigners who were introduced into the Riddarhus under Gustav Adolf were not so numerous, their influx illustrated the rapid growth of the power of Sweden. The names of the newcomers are mainly German, though there are also British and Russian names among them. Patents of nobility were conferred upon native Swedes more generously than before, and the fact was not lost sight of that "ennoblement would be less of a burden to the Crown than grants of money or lands," as somebody once remarked during Kristina's minority. Meritorious military service was always the shortest road to a patent of nobility; but that distinction might fall also to the lot of men who had made a name for themselves in the civil service. A good example is the case of Johan Adler Salvius, one of the most capable men in the new Swedish diplomatic service which Gustav Adolf had created, and also one of the most distinguished writers of his time. Already a sprinkling of great merchants and manufacturers appears among the new creations, though representatives of the spiritual Estate, who before the end of the century were to take their places in the Riddarhus, were not as yet to be found there.

An office-holding nobility, in the exact sense of the term, was coming into being. As yet it was small in numbers: there was plenty of room for anyone who had a fancy for devoting himself to this or that branch of the public service. The Swedish government, confronted with greatly increased responsibilities of every kind, had such a wealth of employment to offer to men of solid ability that there was for the moment no fear of overcrowding. On the contrary, as the king remarked in 1620 in the course of a letter to the clergy about the need for educational reform, there was—and continued to be—good reason to complain that "the land has become unfruitful and barren of serviceable men." Even though the times were hard he continued to experience "a greater shortage of men than of money." From the fact that the nobles had first claim on the higher positions it followed that the new official class was in essence aristocratic, although it is true that the frontier between noble and non-noble was here indefinite and easy to cross. Above all, the reorganized military system naturally demanded the cooperation of the nobility, which had always been looked on as the military class. In the course of a speech delivered to the Riksdag in 1625 with the idea of demonstrating the advantages of a standing army, Gustav Adolf pointed out the attractive prospects offered by such an arrangement: "The nobility and gentry would benefit, not only because their relations and children could be exercised and trained here in this country in the military art and in the manly and knightly virtues, but also because there would be so many appointments, posts, and commissions, that probably more than 500 gentlemen could easily be employed, and thus recoup themselves richly for their trouble." It is a good picture of the military organization of seventeenth century Sweden, with its aristocratic corps of officers.

Nevertheless, the basis of the social position of the nobility remained the family lands, rounded off by gifts or enfeoffments from the Crown, as compensation for assistance rendered either in the way of military service or in other ways. There was in this respect a sharp distinction between the leading families comprised in the first and second classes of the Riddarhus, and the great mass of the lower nobility, who often struggled along in quite a modest style. Many of the petty nobles of Småland and Finland were scarcely distinguishable from the peasantry; and intermarriage with commoners had been relatively frequent down to the time when the caste system was definitely established. In general it is well to beware of applying to the Swedish nobility of Gustav Adolf's time the criteria which are valid only for those social developments which were themselves the consequences of the new order of things.

It is true that the mode of life of the magnate class underwent an important change as the result of that development of the central government which has been briefly outlined above; but this change was not so rapid that the spell of custom was wholly broken. Illuminating evidence of the attitude of contemporaries is afforded by Rudbeckius' funeral sermon upon Magnus Brahe in 1633. Although Magnus had been the greatest noble in the kingdom, his panegyrist found it quite natural to reckon it among his virtues that he took a more serious view of his responsibilities than those numerous landlords who "go home, look in on the women of their family, breed beagles or greyhounds, course hares, put down poison for foxes and traps and snares for wolves, and when the weather is bad stay at home and smoke tobacco." The type of Swedish gentry that the great bishop draws for us with such delicate irony was much the same in Gustav Adolf's time as in Gustav Vasa's—apart from the newfangled habit of smoking. When the Frenchman Ogier visited the marshal de la Gardie, at his country-seat a few years after Gustav Adolf's death, he found to his astonishment that it was as unpretentious as the summer residence of a Parisian merchant: whitewashed walls without hangings, hard wooden seats to sit on, no cloth on the table, no garden, no park. It was not until the 1640s and 1650s that any great alteration in living conditions first became general.

The *Riddarhusordning* of 1626 was in many respects a constitutional innovation in statutory form. Yet it regulated only the internal affairs of the Nobility, not their relations to the other Estates. In reality, the period that followed it was marked to an unprecedented degree by more rigorous demands on the part of the Crown upon those classes who were exempt from taxation. And it is by no means inconceivable that the king entertained the hope that the *Riddarhusordning* would facilitate the enforcement of precisely this kind of demand. With the Råd on his side the king might feel fairly confident, since the higher nobility, closely connected with the Råd as it was, had by this enactment obtained a preponderance in the counsels of their Estate.

Times had been changing of late. When the Älvsborg Ransom was granted by the nobles in 1613, the king at their request had promulgated in the form of a charter a solemn assurance to the effect that the consent of the Estate to this heavy imposition should be considered as exceptional, and that their privileges were not as a result of it to be called in question in the future. At the Riksdag which met early in 1627, when the procedure laid down in the *Riddarhusordning* was for the first time observed, the nobility and gentry requested a new assurance in approximately the same terms. The Estate wished it to be established that it had consented to waive its right out of particular devotion to king and country, and for no other reason. Such language was no longer to Gustav Adolf's taste. He refused to give any specific assurance, and bluntly told them that he saw no need for sentimental attitudes: "What you have done is a matter of duty and fidelity." The nobles were taken aback; but they contented themselves with this explanation, and with the insertion of a reservation in the Riksdag's resolution formally stating the exceptional nature of the levy—the heaviest that had ever been imposed upon the nobles, who now paid almost as much as the commons.

It soon appeared that what the nobles wished to consider as a purely occasional concession was to be demanded of them again. And the times were such that the privileged class found it increasingly difficult to resist the king's demands. The Nobility set the example for the other Estates. The Swedish aristocracy was therefore very sensibly affected by the burdens which were laid upon the country. Internal recruiting went on without respect for rank or person: for instance, laborers were taken for military service from the chancellor's estate at Tidö. Knight service, though less strictly enforced than of old, had still to be rendered. In 1631 the nobles complained that a great part of their farms lay "untilled and waste": five levies for the army had been held within four years; a sixth was granted by the Riksdag committee which assembled late in the autumn of 1632; and the nobles were unable to obtain any assurance that the unpopular demand would not be repeated. The regency government that followed Gustav Adolf's death found it advisable to lighten these burdens.

It is in the light of these facts that we must estimate Gustav Adolf's attitude to members of the privileged order of the Nobility. It is undeniably true that, as his reign proceeded, the great benefits which he conferred upon them were offset by steadily increasing obligations.

[7]

OF THE unprivileged Estates, the Clergy, by reason of their widespread influence, took first place. Indeed, so great was this influence that it seemed on occasion to balance that of the nobles. In matters concerning the welfare of the kingdom, as Jakob de la Gardie testified in 1635, it was usual to ask the advice of the Clergy immediately after the assent of the Råd had been obtained. Gustav Adolf is credited with a phrase—which subsequently became famous—describing the position of the pastors: "the tribunes of the people," he called them. It was the fact of their connection with the great tax-paying yeomanry that, more than anything else, gave weight to the opinions of the spirituality. In the eyes of contemporaries the pastor was the natural spokesman and protector of the peasant. He had "the hearts of his hearers in his hand." No other class stood, by blood and daily intercourse, in such intimate connection with the great mass of the people.

When the king made his speech of welcome to the Estates, it was the archbishop, according to the Riksdag Ordinance of 1617, who was to lay before the throne the good wishes of all three unprivileged Estates. This was a mere formality, but it was also an unmistakable indication of the social status which the clergy enjoyed, and the leading rôle which in consequence they assumed. The time had not yet come when the Burgesses could dispute with them the political primacy among the lower orders. In regard to the relations between Clergy and Peasantry there are, indeed, not a few evidences from Gustav Adolf's diets of how well each order appreciated the community of their interests. For instance, in 1612 they made a concerted demand for a drastic reduction in the extent of royal lands alienated to the nobility, hoping by such a measure to increase the resources of the Crown;

in this matter the Clergy took the lead, and pressed their demand
more vigorously than the Peasantry. During the heated discussions
in the Riksdag chamber in 1624, when the chancellor was ruth-
lessly urging his demands upon the deputies of the Peasantry,
there was a curious interlude. The archbishop stepped forward,
followed by the bishop of Skara, and drew Oxenstierna aside for
private conversation—though to judge from the Minutes it must
also have been audible to the whole assembly—and earnestly insisted that the government must show some consideration for the
difficulties of the commons. The Clergy displayed the same care
for the interests of the Peasantry at the meetings of the Riksdag Committee which were held during the king's absence in
Germany.

It was only natural that the men who were governing the country should try to get into closer touch with the church authorities
whenever any new political projects were in contemplation, or
new demands and impositions were preparing. Hence the bishops,
particularly those of the Mälar district, were summoned comparatively frequently in order that the government might take them
into its confidence, and receive the benefit of their opinion in
return. In relation to the rest of the clergy the bishops occupied
much the same position as that of the Råd in relation to the
nobility and gentry. Now and then they were explicitly commissioned to see to it that only "reasonable and understanding" priests
were chosen as deputies. There were, indeed, occasions when this
cooperation broke down; but normally it was extremely useful to
the government which as far as possible showed itself anxious
to give every consideration to the demands and viewpoints of
which the episcopate was the champion in the church's name.
This no doubt explains why Gustav Adolf's plans for a centralized
government for the Swedish church, upon which the laity should
have representation, were hastily interred, when in 1624 his
scheme for a General Consistory met with strong opposition from
the bishops and the general body of the clergy.

Furthermore, the Clergy insisted with particular emphasis on
the fact that they were a privileged Estate. They had been so, in
the words of a memorandum presented in 1627, "since the beginning of Christendom." It was now possible to regard Gustav

Adolf's Charter as the real legal basis for the position of the church within the State. Important provisions in that Charter were intended to make it impossible for the monarchy to interfere unduly in church affairs, and especially in ecclesiastical appointments—as Karl IX had done, in spite of frequent protests. But the church had no real legal organization, since the Church Ordinance of 1571 was too vague and defective to be adequate. A revision on the basis of existing conditions was recommended by the Clergy; but their scheme never obtained the king's approval. And the scheme for a General Consistory, for which the civil power thought the time was ripe, had to be deferred in consequence of the hostility of the spirituality to this new "caesaro-papism." It was brought forward again in Kristina's time, but with no better success.

The fact that the Swedish church of this period was a folk-church in the full sense of the term did not prevent it from having a strong hierarchical tinge, the most apparent feature of which was the dominant position of the episcopate. The official authority to which the bishops laid claim as the "leaders of God's people" was considerable, and it tended steadily to increase. In their sees they wielded almost absolute power. It was not merely the performance of priestly duties that fell under the judicial control of the bishop: in conjunction with his chapter he had jurisdiction also over the morals and family life of the layman, and could interfere in all sorts of ways in the everyday life of the people.

The fact that the long-sought uniformity in doctrine had at last been obtained did not prevent the widest divergences upon questions of custom and observance. The regulations which the bishops laid down within their sees were therefore anything but uniform. Different sees thus used different service-books, and had different regulations for schools. But this very lack of uniformity assisted in giving an impetus to the work of reorganization which certainly did take place. Each one of these episcopal pastors made it his object to convert a portion of the wilderness into the vineyard of the Lord. They held catechizations and visitations; they maintained decency and order. Their outlook might be limited; their strategy in the battle with evil might be simple and transparent; but they deserved very well of their country. They mitigated the boorishness of the rustic. They took, as a rule, a warm interest in education. And the fact that in many districts episcopal legislation linked up with the idea of local self-government was not devoid of importance for the future.

The generation of men that sat on the episcopal bench in Gustav Adolf's reign was a generation that stood firm in its faith. Its mind was at peace with itself. Discharging their functions with a vigor which at times bordered upon arbitrariness, but warmed by their zeal for the salvation of souls, these men, who had grown horny-handed in God's husbandry, represent—if one may judge from the great majority of them—much that is most fruitful in the cultural efforts of the age. Peter Kenicius, the archbishop of Uppsala for the whole of the reign, is perhaps a less clear-cut character than some of his colleagues. There can be no doubt, however, that his long tenure of office was an important factor in the almost uninterruptedly harmonious relations of the civil and ecclesiastical authorities. He emerges as a modest and peaceable prelate of the old school, who combined with moderation in action a strict adherence to principle. Among contemporaneous occupants of episcopal sees Laurentius Paulinus Gothus of Strängnäs, Johannes Rudbeckius of Västerås, and Isak Rothovius of Åbo—who all three continued to be active during the following period—may fairly take precedence in our remembrance. Rudbeckius, whose earlier work as court chaplain has been dealt with already, stands out in popular opinion as the typical spokesman of the church of the earlier seventeenth century. And rightly so. It was he, more than any other, who developed the idea of the church's independence. Axel Oxenstierna, the only man to whom he was prepared to give way, once Gustav Adolf was dead, said of him that he had inherited a goodly portion of the mantle of St. Peter.

The servants of the church lived simple lives. We are told that the only ornaments in the archbishop's house were the pewter plates hanging on the wall. The country parsons had always to be prepared to give hospitality to travellers, particularly if they were upon the king's business; but otherwise their mode of life differed little from that of the peasantry. It is true that already at the beginning of Gustav Adolf's reign the worthy pastors who came up to the Riksdag were complaining of the sartorial ex-

travagances indulged in by many of the servants of the Word—
"high courtiers' hats, scandalous great lace collars, and so on"—but
such splendors do not seem to have been very general. The clergy
were certainly not free from the sin of covetousness: on occasion
the most ingenious intrigues might be developed in an effort to
obtain vacant cures. Many ambitious young men in orders sought
for places as tutors or chaplains to noble families. Axel Oxenstierna
in time acquired a whole suite of protégés in this way; several
of them became bishops. The unstable element of the clergy comprised the great army of field-chaplains, and those who had been
unable to obtain a cure—a class of men frequently unruly and
only too often a cause of sleepless nights to their superiors.

The church had charge of the nation's schools. The whole educational system had long found in the bishops and the clergy its
best defenders and supporters. The bleak age of Karl IX had not
been propitious for such as tried to plead the cause of education
and learned studies; but the School Ordinance which the clergy
drew up in 1611 marked a step forward. By the side of the "provincial schools" cathedral schools were to be founded as centers
of higher education. Gustav Adolf's early awakened sense of the
value of education promised better times for the champions of
the schools, and their hopes were not disappointed. The king
became the driving force behind the movement; and from his
discussions with the clergy was born a program which was to be
fundamental to the organization of the Swedish *gymnasia* (1620).
These latter, as is well known, take their origin from his reign.
When his program was put in execution, there proved indeed
to be some alterations in the original design, and this is to be
considered as a reassertion by Paulinus and Rudbeckius, who took
the lead among the bishops in this matter, of the church's right
of control.

The purely ecclesiastical character which marked the Swedish
educational system did not commend itself to Gustav Adolf. "All
such as are employed either in schools or academies," runs a declaration in the king's name, "have either taken orders or directed
their *studia* to that end, so that the instruction in religion is relatively satisfactory; but since the teachers themselves neither know
nor care anything about matters pertaining to administration or

civil life, they are not competent to give any instruction in these matters." It was not for nothing that Gustav Adolf desired that students in the new *gymnasia* should read and expound the ancient Swedish laws. He shared with Oxenstierna, Skytte, and others of the Råd a warm desire to establish a nursery for national culture upon lines different from and broader than those pursued in an institution designed to train men for the priesthood—which is practically what the country's only university was. The views of the government, no less than those of the church, claimed consideration. This was probably the main motive which prompted the great reform in the University of Uppsala. Another reason, which must have had great weight, was anxiety about that aspect of national defense which depended upon spiritual weapons. Experience had unhappily proved that forbidden seats of learning abroad, and not least those of the Jesuits, were exercising a strong attraction through the advantages they could offer to the youth of the country, with its thirst for knowledge and its interest in novelty.

The vigorous expansion of Sweden's university, to which Gustav Adolf contributed with a truly royal bounty, was, therefore, at once an invitation to the profane Muses, and a tribute to the protective power of a unifying religion. One other motive was certainly present—the maintenance of the country's prestige abroad; an object which Gustav Adolf and his lieutenants had very much at heart.

With the reconstituted University of Uppsala as model, and under the supervision of Uppsala's first chancellor, Johan Skytte, the young University of Dorpat took shape towards the end of the reign, as a center of Protestant culture at the gates of the barbaric East.

[8]

"As FOR you of the bourgeoisie," said Gustav Adolf in his farewell speech of 1630, "I may wish that your little cottages may become great stone houses, your small boats great ships and merchantmen, and that your cruse of oil may never fail."

The Estate of Burghers not only stood a step lower down than that of the Clergy; its opinions counted for less than those of the

Peasantry, in spite of the fact that it took a greater part in politics. No Estate, moreover, had so often to swallow snubs and reprimands. The settled populations of the towns, the merchants and artisans, formed indeed to outward appearance a very compact body, but dissensions on all sorts of local issues crippled its action; and the almost universal weakness of the trade guilds was bound to react unfavorably on the authority of the Estate. The inhabitants of the towns, moreover, can hardly have comprised more than one twentieth of the total population of the country.

On the other hand the development of urban life lay particularly near to the heart of the government. By instructions and exhortations and intervention it attempted to remedy the irritating abuses which were brought to light every day. The towns in fact were at once the apple of the king's eye, and a thorn in the side of his ministers. They were the objects of an anxious solicitude which unfortunately bore but tardy fruit. They felt, too, that they were continually dependent on the government, whom they pestered unceasingly with all sorts of contradictory demands. Belief in the effect of benevolent legislation was mutual, although opinions often differed as to the method to be pursued. Hence it happened that the towns and their deputies, at meetings of the Riksdag or special assemblies of merchants, had more than once to endure sharp reproofs.

This relative solidity of the Burghers as a class was primarily the consequence of that line of demarcation between urban and rural industry of which it was almost heresy to doubt the necessity. In actual fact the distinction had been found very difficult to maintain; but nobody doubted that more effective regulations would ensure its proper observance. Again, the distinction between "staple" towns and "up-country" towns was far less clear in practice than the age's ideas of good order could approve. "Staple" towns, they held, should by definition be "based on sea-borne trade"; "up-country" towns, on the home market. Gustav Adolf's trade and navigation legislation was intended to clear the ground for a fixed, and if possible definitive, system on mercantilist principles. Its essential ideas involved no novelty. The intention, however, was to obtain a decisive settlement, once and for all. And the towns, "stagnant, decayed, crumbling" as they were, were by that means to be restored to prosperity.

The driving force behind the movement was apparently the chancellor. His hand is to be traced in a series of schemes which were submitted to interested parties, and which include provisions concerning the conditions upon which the government was prepared to grant the right to carry on navigation to foreign countries, and to receive foreign ships ("active" and "passive" navigation); the conditions for obtaining access to markets of various sorts; and in general the functions of the towns in respect of their own and foreign countries. At first the king regarded it as a matter for special legislation, in which only the government and the Burghers need be concerned. The procedure ran on these lines at the Riksdag of 1614, when a new Trade Ordinance was adopted and ordered to be put in force. When its application met with opposition from a variety of quarters—there were even complaints from foreign powers, and concessions had soon to be made in regard to certain details—it was found to be necessary to bring up the matter afresh. This was done at the Riksdag meetings of 1617, but on this occasion not only the Burghers but the Estates as a whole were permitted to express an opinion; for the king hoped with the help of the other Estates to break down the obstinacy of the towns. He succeeded—by rather high-handed methods—in carrying his point, after having himself addressed the Riksdag in confutation of the arguments or excuses of the Burghers. He rejected absolutely the view that the new statute increased the burdens of the people: if only the municipal authorities conducted their affairs with more zeal, there would certainly be no reason for anyone to complain.

The men who in the debates on this question—as upon other occasions—set the tone in the Estate and determined the line of action, were mainly representative of the recognized old "staple" towns, with Stockholm at their head. The capital, whose population was still under 15,000, generally took up a dominant position, not least in virtue of her traditional monopoly of the Bothnian trade. When the Estate of Burghers began about this time to have a sort of Speaker it was accordingly taken for granted that one of the burgomasters of Stockholm should assume the post of honor. The spokesmen of the interests of the "staple" towns, significantly enough, did not hesitate to brand as "illegal" the new Norrland towns of Hudiksvall and Härnosand, which had been founded at the end of the sixteenth century. The king took so little notice of this affection for the ancient and the customary that in the revised Trade Ordinance he even hinted at an intention to create in the immediate future new towns in the northern parts of the country, "since the land is so large that the peasantry cannot get to market with their produce without great loss and damage."

It is against this background that the majority of cities founded in Gustav Adolf's reign must be viewed. The object was to restrain by this means the endemic—and really ineradicable—"peddling," through restricting trade, which had hitherto had free access to the country districts, to the new commercial centers. In this way the existing industrial regulations would obtain the respect which was due to them. This motive—though it really was more of a pious hope—may certainly be considered as decisive with respect to the six coastal towns in Norrland, from Söderhamn in the south to Torneå in the north, which were granted privileges between 1620 and 1630. All these towns coincided with, or lay in the neighborhood of, old local trading centers. There can be no doubt, however, that this was not the only motive. It can hardly have been by accident, for instance, that the founding of new cities—most of them on a very modest scale—coincided in point of time with the period when the new military organization was being carried through.

Of all these new towns Göteborg, incomparably the most vigorous of Gustav Adolf's foundations and the particular object of his favor, occupies the first place. Old Göteborg, which Karl IX had founded on the island of Hisingen, and which from the beginning had been a thorn in Denmark's flesh, had been burnt to the ground in the course of the War of Kalmar. When Gustav Adolf, after the recovery of Älvsborg, founded a new Göteborg on a site to the south of the estuary and nearer to the sea, the town was really a completely new creation of his own. Its privileges, which were in some respects unique, were granted in the summer of 1621 after consultation with Dutch trading interests whose cooperation the king was anxious to secure; and from the beginning it was abundantly clear that he intended to take the new harbor on the Göta River under his powerful protection. The advancement of its development until it became a "well built, well ordered, populous, and properly constituted" town, was always a capital point in his program. And in fact it was not long before Göteborg took a leading place among the towns of the kingdom, whether new or old.

Apart from Göteborg, the immediate fruits of this comprehensive urban policy were comparatively insignificant. The sum total of the progress shown by the new Norrland towns could certainly not compare with the advance made by Norrköping alone, after Louis de Geer had established there the headquarters of his almost nation-wide undertakings towards the end of the 1620s; although before that time it had been quite insignificant. The majority of the older towns gave the impression of being little more than large villages. In spite of the importance which the trading class generally attached to the maintenance of the dividing line between town and country, there was little in their own way of living to distinguish it from "country life"; the care of vegetable gardens, meadow land, or fisheries occupied as a rule a prominent place in the representations which the town addressed to the government. Even in Stockholm goats were to be seen in 1616 grazing on the grass-grown roofs near the Saltsjö or the Mälar. Under Gustav Adolf the capital lost the character of a fortified town, which it had kept from the Middle Ages, since the unguarded walls were allowed to fall into ruin after the War of Kalmar. On the other hand, Stockholm, with its dockyards and its arsenals, was in this period rising to great importance as a naval station. Towards the end of Gustav Adolf's reign the nobles began to reside there in increasing numbers, and to embellish the town with their houses. The most notable merchants were usually Germans or Dutchmen. But Stockholm's great expansion, which was quickly to double its population and its area, occurred in the decades immediately after Gustav Adolf's death.

The greatest city in the Swedish dominions during the latter half of Gustav Adolf's reign was not Stockholm but Riga, which had been conquered in 1621. It is noteworthy that the king attempted to incorporate the burghers of the Livonian capital into the Swedish national representative assembly. A formal agreement on this point was concluded in connection with the surrender of the town, and to the Riksdag of 1622 it sent deputies who were ceremoniously welcomed and took their seats in the Estate of Burghers. This, however, was their last appearance. The fact that such an incorporation was never suggested in the case of Reval is sufficiently explained by the well known spirit of independence which animated its citizens. They insisted proudly upon the fact that they were a Baltic city, "saying that they would not be the bought slaves and offal-eaters of any Swedish or Finnish town," as a report dating from 1613 has it. We have already seen (*supra,* p. 102) how the king on one occasion succeeded in reducing the men of Reval to obedience.

The peculiar position of the towns in relation to the rest of the country had for years found eloquent expression in the fact that their inhabitants lived under their own law—the "Town Law"—which dated from about the same time (*c.* 1350) as the *Landslag,* and had by this time become obsolete in more than one respect. A new arrangement of municipal offices upon a unified and efficient system was one of the objects at which Gustav Adolf was aiming. In the efforts which were made in this direction we can see too the influence of the practical sense of Axel Oxenstierna. For instance, it was he who was really responsible for the great legislative project approved by the king in 1619, which was intended to modernize the internal organization of the Swedish municipal system on the basis of a reinforcement and expansion of the Town Law. This statute, which deals with "the administration and foundation of towns," was indeed never formally promulgated, but the government followed out the principles it laid down, and applied them in greater or lesser degree in the separate grants of privileges for old and new towns. Although the plan for national legislation on behalf of the towns remained a mere essay, the Statute of 1619 was to leave its mark on much of the development that followed. It corresponded to the forms that had been evolved for the government of Stockholm; though naturally these could not be applied with equal success to the small towns, which as a rule lacked the energy necessary to carry them out.

To remedy the weakness of the municipal administration, the central government resorted to the creation of posts for men of judicial and administrative capacity, who were to be associated with the leading magistrates in important cases. These "royal burgomasters," however, belong mainly to a later period, when they were to play an important part in politics, as well as in urban government. The bourgeois class still lacked men with the qualities of leadership. There is hardly a memorable name among them. As we have seen, the capital forged ahead only after Gustav Adolf's death. But a few decades brought great changes not only to Stockholm but to many of the smaller towns. By the middle of the century, many of the old-fashioned merchants were looking back with regret to the quiet times when—to cite a pamphlet of the period—burgomasters did not "speak French and Italian, and go about with a book beneath their arm."

[9]

THE Peasantry—the "humble subjects of the king," as they sometimes called themselves—differed essentially from the other Estates. The direct political influence they exerted was affected by their feeling that they lacked authority, and by their general disinclination to take the initiative in affairs of State. To receive rather than to offer advice was the basic rule of the fourth Estate, which was always keenly sensible of the fact that it depended in the first place upon the royal authority, and in the second on its colleagues of the other orders. On the other hand, the Peasantry was an element in society which had to be reckoned with, if only because of its control of taxation. In every enterprise which demanded supplies of men or money or both its views must carry weight.

The first Danish diplomat to be permanently accredited to Sweden, Peder Galt, has left us, in a report dating from 1624, a description of the position of the peasant classes in the country. Just as the present government, he says, was established with the help of the peasants, so it continues to be upheld by them. It is true that they often come forward with complaints, but they allow themselves to be talked over into remaining in a state of proper obedience. In essence, the judgment is a sound one. The revolutionary dynasty of Karl IX had from the beginning found its steadiest supporters in the lower classes. Gustav Adolf, too, was able to build upon the alliance which they had concluded with the monarchy. It was an old and ineradicable habit of the peasants to "go to court" with their troubles: in the presentation of grievances the Estate long saw its most important function at meetings of the Riksdag. Even in quiet times these complaints might be frequent and persistent. To see in them merely expressions of discontent would be a complete mistake: they were quite as much expressions of confidence and trust in the king as the "father of his country." And this was the true interpretation of the relations between all the Vasa kings and the Swedish peasantry. The reign of Gustav Adolf was no exception. Quite as much as his father, who is known to history as the king of the peasants, he made it his business to remedy grievances of the yeomen farmers, though, like Karl IX, he could be critical when criticism was needed. He felt himself to be in this as in other respects the guardian of that system of personal government into which he had been initiated from his earliest years.

The fact that the monarchy and the aristocracy had now reached a friendly settlement by no means implied that the former was prepared to sacrifice the rights and interests of the common people. On the contrary, it is rather characteristic of Gustav Adolf that he sought simultaneously to favor the noble and befriend the peasant. He saw no irreconcilable contradiction in this. He took great care that the legal position of the peasant population should suffer no deterioration through the ambition of the nobility; he hastened to espouse its cause whenever the occasion demanded, which was not seldom. A large number of ordinances and injunctions gives ample proof of his consistent attempt to punish abuses and keep an eye on the best interests of the commons. But on the other hand, when he considered that he had detected insubordination or sharp practice on the peasants' side, he was not disposed to overlook it.

None the less, symptoms were already apparent under Gustav Adolf of the economic and social transformation which was to lead to the great social crisis of seventeenth century Sweden. Thus, soon after 1620, there occurred the first sale to the nobility of the revenues which the Crown derived from tax-paying lands (*frälse-köp*). This policy, which was determined by financial considerations, was as yet carried out on quite a modest scale, but at the second Riksdag of 1627 it called forth from the Peasantry a reaction of alarm. The king on that occasion gave an express promise to take care of the inherited rights of the tax-paying peasants who were to be affected by such sales. From another point of view, the sale of revenues, which in the regency that followed was erected into a system—largely from necessity—certainly coincided with the tendency, common alike to Gustav Adolf and to Axel Oxenstierna, to base the fiscal system as far as possible upon payments in specie.

It is an incontestable fact that the Swedish peasantry had to bear an increasing burden during these years. The fiscal demands, which, as we have seen, had considerably increased, must, however, have been eased somewhat by the more equitable repartition which the government tried to enforce, and by the fact that on the whole more orderly methods of collection were introduced. There continued, indeed, to be complaints of abuses great and small, and in this connection the conduct of the tax-farmers of the Crown lands was a frequent object of attacks. Where extortion and irregularity could be established, the government did not fail to intervene, either directly or through its subordinate agents. The provincial government was remodelled and modernized with a thoroughness which made this one of the most important reforms of the reign. The offices of lord lieutenant or sheriff were reorganized on a more logical basis, and were entrusted with practically the same functions as they perform today. By these means the government was able to exercise a benevolent supervision. At the same time the peasantry received the right to collaborate in the levying of taxes through their own appointed agents, the parish clerks, who had the right to be present when the peasant paid his contribution to the king's bailiff. In spite of considerably higher taxation, there was a steady diminution in the amount of arrears. On the other hand there was a marked decrease in the tax yield, and deserted farms were numerous.

If the demands which Gustav Adolf made were great, he himself never attempted to pretend the contrary. He knew very well the thoughts of his peasantry, and he did try to take their sentiments into his calculations. One of the most important everyday tasks of the government was either by persuasion or some other means to "put the peasant in a good humor." As a rule they put up a stiff resistance before agreeing to concessions. But, even in times of great stringency, the voice of compassion was sometimes allowed to prevail. "The hand-mills may remain as they are," writes the king from his camp in Germany. "The aching arms of the grinders are mill-due enough."

In political outlook the peasantry was strongly conservative. It viewed with suspicion more than one useful scheme of reform proposed by the government—largely because it was always afraid of fresh taxation. It was for that reason, for instance, that the Estate of the Peasantry asked the government to drop a new Poor Law which was certainly benevolent in intention, and this in spite of the fact that the peasants themselves admitted that it was "well enough drawn." In order to do away with the ill-rewarded exertions which the so-called parochial collection imposed upon poor parish clerks the Estates in 1624 voted a new money tax to be paid according to a fixed scale by every resident in the district. The idea was that this "clerk-money" was to be divided up among the children of poor peasants studying in the nearest town-school. The tax, however, provoked opposition from the people, and the parochial collection remained in force until well on into the next century.

It is worth noting that the ability to read seems to have been quite widely disseminated in the country districts in Gustav Adolf's time. According to the account given by Anders Bure in his commentary annexed to the *Atlas* of 1626, most of the peasantry in Norrland could read printed books.

The social life of the Swedish peasant, as it is known to us from reliable sources, still followed ancient usage. The old Nordic names were still current both for men and women; the old customs, varying from district to district, were still faithfully observed; and the ties of blood were strong enough to preserve the old rules of family law in undiminished force in many parts of the country. The court registers of Småland and Västergötland in Gustav Adolf's time reveal folk customs so fiercely primitive that they are at times reminiscent of the Iceland of the Sagas. There was a notable assurance in the way in which the peasant was accustomed to approach his superiors, and the gulf between the peasant and the nobleman seemed less deep than it afterwards became. A description of a tour through Sweden in 1635 tells the story of a peasant deputy who had told Gustav Adolf to his face that "If my wife were as well dressed as yours, King Gustav, she would look just as lovely and attractive as the queen." We hasten to add that this peasant is alleged to have been a Dalesman.

The Dutchman Willem Usselinx, who founded the Swedish South Sea Company at Gustav Adolf's instigation, published in 1626 an account of the great undertakings which were in contemplation, and in this account gave also a description of the Swedish land and people. It must have been approved by the king, for in the same year it appeared in an official Swedish translation. Among the great advantages that Usselinx found in Sweden, as compared with other countries, he reckoned not the least to be the human material of which the population was composed. He was impressed by the ability of the Swedes to turn their hands to many things. "The inhabitants of this country," he says, "are a hardy folk, able to endure heat and cold; they are teachable, adaptable, bold sailors, as may be seen from the fact that they venture out in frail little craft not only among the skerries but into the open sea. With all this they are obedient to their rulers, and little disposed to mutiny and revolt, in which particular they excel many other peoples and nations. Nothing but practice is wanting to make them expert sailors, for they have no lack of intelligence, aptitude, or courage. . . . One perceives that the peasants follow all sorts of trades. They are carpenters, joiners, smiths, bakers, brewers, weavers, dyers; they can sew shoes and clothes, etc.; and in this they surpass all other European nations, for in other countries hardly anyone ventures to turn his hand to any trade to which he has not been apprenticed. Their wives and daughters make pretty things by weaving and sewing and by other pleasant arts, from which it will appear that they are sufficiently intelligent and ingenious."

"Some are of the opinion," adds our author somewhat critically, "that this nation is beyond measure addicted to eating and drinking and sloth, and that for this reason they do not take to any regular employment. How that may be I leave to each one to judge for himself. But if it were so, I would still give the palm in these respects to the English, who are particularly prone to such vices."

The picture of the living conditions of the people which is presented in the innumerable schedules of grievances dating from this period gives on the whole an impression of poverty and harshness. It need hardly be pointed out that these sources are distinctly one-sided. Men readily resorted to sweeping statements when they brought their complaints and requests to the government, even though their addresses were couched in the most deferential terms. This was especially the case with the peasantry, but the burghers were very nearly as bad. More than once the complainants were convicted of exaggeration, and indeed of unsubstantiated allegations. It was the regular thing in these cases to paint the situation a little blacker than it really was, and many were unable to resist the temptation to make it very much blacker—indeed quite desperate. This need not rule out the existence of genuine abuses which gave just cause for protest. Many official documents speak of them in terms which are not to be mistaken. The king at various times frankly admitted that the fortitude of the people was being severely tested. He made it his principle, while not losing sight of his ultimate goal, to see things as they really were, and not through rose-colored glasses.

The position at the time of Sweden's entry into the German war was described in gloomy terms. "The land is so exhausted," writes Gabriel Gustavsson Oxenstierna in 1630 to his absent brother the chancellor, "that it seems on the verge of collapse, and if this goes on for a couple of years longer, we shall be able to say that we have won the lands of others at the cost of ruining our own." The war budget of this year absorbed nearly three-quarters of all the State's expenditure. Afterwards, however, the situation rapidly improved; the corresponding figures for 1631 were five-eights, and for 1632 one-third. The clergy admitted with gratitude in this latter year that no "extraordinary" war taxes had been demanded from the people since the king's departure. The function of the home country was now mainly to equip, feed, and transport the troops which were sent over to Germany to make good the losses of the armies. The heaviest burden in these years was the drain of men. Failure of crops, which was repeated in several of the following years, increased the distress. Previously the country had had a series of good harvests, which had kept up the spirits of the farmers.

To the foreign traveller who had opportunities for comparison, the rural population of Sweden did not, however, give an impression of poverty and destitution. Charles Ogier, the French secretary of legation, notes in 1634-1635: "I do not remember in the whole of Sweden to have seen a naked or ragged person. Just as the rich here have no superfluity of this world's goods, so the poor do not perish in misery. Even the poorest peasants are not clad in hemp and linen, as they usually are with us, but in clothes of black wool, for that is the color of the Swedish sheep. On their feet they have leather boots instead of wooden shoes, on their heads nightcaps, and on their hands woollen gloves; and thus they are well prepared to brave the bitter cold which ravages this country."

[10]

TOWARDS the end of his career, Gustav Adolf in a burst of confidence attempted to sum up for Oxenstierna's benefit the tale of his joys and his sorrows. As the chancellor, quoting from memory, told the Råd in 1641, he first mentioned the fact that "he could look back on five hundred years of Swedish history, and not find a king who had not had to meet revolts of his subjects, either at the beginning of his reign, or in some part of it, or at the end of it; while His late Majesty had not had a single one, although he had extracted more from his subjects than any king before him. This he took God to witness he had done not for pleasure, but for the advantage and security of the realm."

The tradition of the latter part of the seventeenth century, which loved to dwell on Gustav Adolf's memory, cherished especially the irrefutable proof of his confidence in every one of his subjects. As Per Brahe reminded them in 1668, he could sleep in any man's bosom. It was a phrase attributed to the king himself. In 1682 it was reported that the great king Gustav Adolf had said that "he was so supremely confident of the love and fidelity of his people, that he could safely lay down his head and let it rest upon the knee of any one of his subjects if need be, which no other potentate could readily make bold to do." Happier relations between king and people could scarcely be conceived.

We recall Peder Galt's half-grudging admission that the staunchly royalist temper of the Swedish peasant, no matter how great his exasperation, emerged triumphant in the end. Usselinx testified even more unreservedly to the same effect, when he accounted Sweden fortunate in that she had a population less prone to violent courses than that of most other countries. Yet Gustav Adolf's internal government does not appear in its true light if it is conceived as presenting a picture of perfect acquiescence and unruffled calm. Deep in the heart of that strenuous and troubled age was a feeling of tension; and it would be a mistake to suppose that the harmony was more perfect, the good-will more continuous in its spontaneity, than such a condition normally admits. Certainly detached observers more than once asked themselves uneasily how it would end. And contemporary reports from other sources show that though such ideas were oftenest met with in the camp of the enemy, they were not unknown elsewhere.

At no time during the reign was there any agitation on a universal scale. On the other hand there were local centers of disturbance of which the activity or inactivity provided as it were a barometer indicative of the state of public opinion. As under Gustav Vasa, Dalarna and Småland were the focal points of popular discontent. Apart from the difference in the seriousness of the movements, there was this further distinction that discontent was not now directed, as in Gustav Vasa's time, against the government itself, or against the king personally.

With the Dalecarlians Gustav Adolf had several sharp conflicts. They had felt themselves to be particularly closely associated with his father during the years of crisis after 1590, and could always count on his favor. The change of rulers gradually brought a revulsion of opinion within the province. It was not long before the Dalesmen, who in the ordinary course of events were not much affected by the claims and privileges of the nobility, began to realize that the wind had changed. They grew apprehensive of reprisals for the acts of violence which they had allowed themselves to commit at the time of Sigismund's last expedition to Sweden. As fate would have it, Johan Skytte, who was always anxious to be accounted a friend of the people, became the object of their suspicions; for his father-in-law, Jakob Näf, had been murdered by them in the course of a rising in 1598. During 1613 and 1614 feeling was running high in Dalarna. Soldiers raised in that district deserted in droves from the army in Finland, and when the government took steps to punish these derelictions of duty there were violent upheavals at a number of places in lower Dalarna. At the same time the parishes around Lake Siljan were seething with excitement. The word went round the countryside that they were to rise in a body and "slay all the nobles," upon whom they laid the blame for everything that was amiss.

The threat of trouble from Dalarna had at the time of the first Riksdag at Örebro reached an alarming height. At first the young king seems to have resolved to make an example by drastic severity; but he revoked his intention, or was forced to abandon it, so that the punishment actually meted out seems to have been lenient enough. The Dalesman Dean Terserus—the influential and respected "Master Elof of Leksand"—faithful to the traditional duty of his order to "preach men's follies out of them," was tireless in his efforts for peace, and powerfully assisted in calming the agitation. Gustav Adolf himself went up to Dalarna more than once in an attempt to bring the common people to a better frame of mind. We find him there, for instance, in March and November 1613, in February 1614, and again in March 1615. It is a great pity that his speeches to the people on these visits have not been preserved. Incidentally, he paid his first visit to Dalarna as early as the summer of 1605.

The situation in Småland after the devastations of the War of Kalmar was extremely critical. A vivid picture of the position is given in the letters sent by the then vicar of Angelstad, Jonas Rothovius, to the chancellor, with whom he had been on intimate terms since the days when they had studied together in Germany. Here if anywhere we may see the Swedish priest of the seventeenth century in his rôle of spokesman of the people. Rothovius was never tired of bringing forward their manifold grievances, and demanding that something should be done to meet them. In his complaints he spares neither recruiting officers nor royal bailiffs; indeed, he accuses the latter on one occasion of allowing themselves to be bribed with "silver tankards and oxen." He keeps a sharp eye on "some of the newly created nobility, not to mention the old established aristocracy"; and on the whole this son of the people, who before his early death had risen to be bishop of Kalmar, seems to have considered himself as good as most of the provincial nobility. He speaks on behalf of the whole of his district. "If the peasant in his great misery does not now ask and obtain help," he protests in the autumn of 1613, "then no other possibility remains but that this country shall become a desert."

Rothovius's account of the strained relations between the Småland peasantry and the bailiffs can be substantiated over and over again. But there is no parallel to what happened in the spring of 1616 at the Västbo county court. A band of infuriated peasants massacred the accounting clerk of the detested bailiff in the presence of the sheriff, and in spite of all his efforts to save him. "We have nothing to lose," shouted the furious mob, "for they have taken away everything we possess." Gustav Adolf considered the occasion demanded his personal appearance to judge the guilty parties on the spot. In a case of this sort he felt himself bound to prefer rigor to clemency. It is said that he declared that he would not place his crown on his head—we remember that the coronation had not yet taken place—until the culprits had been suitably punished. The leaders in the affair were sentenced to be broken on the wheel, and every male person in the whole district between the ages of fifteen and sixty had to pay a special fine. But the bailiff, too, was condemned to death, having been found guilty of such grave derelictions of duty that no other penalty was considered adequate. Several of those implicated had fled abroad; these were now "outlawed over the whole kingdom of Sweden." Of those who had been imprisoned some were set free, as being less guilty than the others, "since it is only with reluctance and from absolute necessity that we take the life of any one of our subjects."

The introduction of the "Little Toll" in 1623 provoked grave disturbances in the capital itself and in its environs. Before their instigator, a simple tradesman, could be brought to justice he had died of the plague, which this year raged in Stockholm with great violence, and obliged the king to reside for some months in the interior of the country. Much more serious, however— at all events in its opening stages—was the revolt which broke out in the following year in Möre. It seems in great measure to have been directed against the foreign officers in the Swedish service, who did not understand how to handle the peasant soldiers. The disturbances began as a military mutiny, but spread to the peasants of the neighborhood. They found a leader in a certain Jon Stind, who is alleged on reliable authority to have been a member of the same family as the celebrated Nils Dacke, who eighty years earlier had raised the whole province of Småland against Gustav Vasa, and had even entered into negotiations with foreign princes. The king later spoke of it as an attempt at a new "Dacke war." The rising was nipped in the bud. Stind, called in derision the "king of Småland," was brought in irons to Stockholm to be executed; a band of vagabonds from the woods who had hastened to join him received short shrift; and some peasants who had taken a more conspicuous part in the conspiracy were transported with their wives and families to Ingria.

With that, the king ordered all examination and investigation to stop. He was in fact extremely anxious to induce the other peasants of the district to believe that he had complete confidence in their innocence. "In the last few years," he wrote to the assessors of the county court, "you have exerted yourselves in our defense and in that of our country more zealously than the rest of our subjects, so that we have cause to commend the men of Möre for their good-will. Let it now appear, faithful subjects, that you are still of the same mind." The king's action upon this occasion is a good example of his method of dealing with the peasants when they began to grow restive. He was, moreover, inclined to suspect that Sigismund's agents had fomented the troubles at Möre; for simultaneously with the outbreak "odious speeches and rumors" were being disseminated in Småland concerning the speedy return of the king of Poland to his ancient heritage.

The attitude of the Dalecarlians continued to be a cause of anxiety to the government. The Danish agent in Stockholm even expressed the opinion that if they had succeeded in finding a leader in 1623 they would have "led the government a rare dance." The method upon which the government relied for subduing the obstinate province was, as after the troubles at Möre, to deport those guilty of more serious insubordination to the colonized areas of Ingria. Another method, which was less harsh and more effective, was personal persuasion on the spot by the king. It was partly with this object, partly to follow the development of the Kopparberg mines, that he made a number of trips to Dalarna between 1620 and 1630, in the course of which he talked to the stubborn peasantry much as his grandfather had done. Nevertheless, from time to time there was trouble. Thus at the beginning of 1627 a German adventurer, a tailor by the name of Mattias Pfennig, succeeded in calling to arms the whole parish of Orsa. This popular movement was, however, an isolated outbreak in which the discontent prevailing in the forest regions found a vent. The rebels began to march; but they permitted themselves a halt on the road, whereupon the provincial governor, summoned by courier, rushed up his troops and surrounded the entire party.

The king, however, considered the episode to be of so serious a character that in March he went up himself to the Kopparberg accompanied by the queen, and remained in the district for some weeks. Bishop Rudbeckius was summoned from Västerås to assist in the investigation. Five or six of the Dalesmen who had been particularly prominent in the movement were condemned to death; but in the case of four of them the king was later graciously pleased to commute the sentence to transportation to Ingria. Those who had been held as security for the recapture of the fugitives were to receive the same punishment, if these latter did not surrender themselves for trial. A royal letter of protection was dispatched to the rest of the province, prohibiting anyone from reproaching the faithful subjects of the Crown with the gross misdeeds of the guilty parties.

The motive behind the movement seems to have been a desire
to free the district from the burden of taxation; but an element
of religious enthusiasm was also present. In previous years
Mattias Pfennig had in fact assumed the rôle of a popular
"prophet," claiming to be "King of the Jews and Swedes." He
was executed in Stockholm that spring, after the king had returned from his enforced sojourn in the Dales. Gustav Adolf now
considered that the province—the cradle of the dynasty—was at
last definitively reduced to order. "You are like the Dalecarlians,"
he was heard to say to the gentlemen of Estonia in 1629; "they,
like you, prided themselves on their liberties, and would submit
to no restraint; but I have brought them so low that I can twist
them round my little finger. I shall have to do the same with
you, if I am to get any further!"

The peasants of Finland were more quiet. Yet there were complaints in plenty; though to be sure they date mainly from the
earlier years of the reign. The most usual grievance is the out-
rageous behavior of the soldiery, and this in spite of the fact that
the authorities did their best to check this abuse—well knowing
that it was a matter on which the king held strong opinions. A
detachment of troops left to itself in a remote district almost felt
itself to be in enemy country. A company of local Finnish soldiers sent out to recover deserting recruits had distinguished
itself in 1620 by its appalling proceedings in the interior of the
country. When the peasant deputies from the north of Tavastland complained of this lawlessness to Karl Eriksson Oxenstierna, the lord lieutenant, they threw out menacing allusions
to the possibility of another "Club War" like that of 1596-1597,
when the peasants of north Finland had carried out a regular
campaign against the government. "They told me to my face,"
he wrote in his report to the chancellor, "that there had been
risings in the country for less cause, and said that if there was no
alteration there would be risings again."

However, it is certainly quite unjust when certain Finnish historians moved by excessive national feeling, attempt to exhibit
Finland in Gustav Adolf's time as a province particularly mal-
treated and harassed. Compared with the majority of Swedish

provinces, Finland might on the contrary consider herself to be in the main secure, well cared for, and even favored.

A new and foreign element was introduced into the population by the coming of the Walloons, whom the nascent industrial development of the country attracted to Sweden in considerable numbers. They remained, naturally enough, strangers to the customs and outlook of their new home. In general, moreover, they do not seem to have shared the feelings of the Swedish nation at the news of Gustav Adolf's death. The fact that he had seriously impaired the military prestige of their countryman Tilly stuck in their throats. While the church bells were tolling for the king, the Walloon charcoal-burners at the Österby ironworks could be heard winding their horns and firing their muskets in their forest encampments. At the forging mill a characteristic argument arose, which was afterwards noted down in the minutes of the parish meeting. The miller, who was "French," had permitted himself a number of remarks of the most provocative description. Among them the following: "Your king would have done better to stay at home in his own country, and not go off to our country killing folk." But the same report also contains the exclamation of a Swedish peasant woman who was visiting the mill when the news arrived: "God help us poor folk now that we have lost our good king." It was a cry from the heart of the plain people.

Gustav Adolf, who on his own confession drove his subjects harder than any king before him, left a memory revered by the Swedish peasant. At the diet of 1633, the spokesman of the Estate of Peasants thus expressed himself: "We have lost our father and our country's father, beneath whose gracious, pious, and Christian rule (under God) we lived and dwelt within our borders in peace and security, and went about our business, sowing and reaping, harvesting and gathering into barns, with a quiet mind."

THE PROBLEM OF THE BALTIC

THE PROBLEM OF THE BALTIC

[1]

AT THE beginning of the seventeenth century, the leading power in the Baltic was undoubtedly the kingdom of Denmark-Norway. Even if we leave out of consideration its distant appendages—Greenland and Iceland—its extent was very considerable. Gotland and Ösel were Danish possessions, giving support to Danish interests and pretensions far up into the Baltic, and the entrance to that sea was wholly in Danish hands. To the north, this great stretch of territory reached to the extremity of the continent of Europe. Its immense coastline, in which Bohuslän, Halland, and part of Skåne were included, gave easy access to the west. To southward, the duchies of the Jutland peninsula included a considerable German-speaking area, while many of the secularized bishoprics of North Germany presented tempting and by no means unattainable objects for the dynastic ambitions of the Oldenburg house. Apart from such new acquisitions, Denmark had already a vital connection with the Continent, whose main currents of thought and politics lost little of their strength before sweeping the Danish shores. Similarly, Denmark's control of the Sound brought her into intimate relations with the seafaring nations and their vigorous cultures.

Norway's chief assets were a genius for seamanship and a lucrative deep-sea fishery, the products of which enjoyed an extensive market. There was, in addition, a not inconsiderable export of timber. Denmark, the dominant partner, was moreover a rich country according to the standards of that age—richer than she was to be in later years. Rising grain prices in conjunction with an increasing demand from overseas had given the noble landowning class great capital resources, and stimulated it to a spirit of enterprise beneficial to native agriculture, though not, perhaps, to the peasant who labored on the land. Splendid country seats dating from the last decades of the sixteenth century bore witness to the prosperity and good taste of the aristocracy, whereas in Sweden there was no similar outburst of building activity among the nobility until the full noonday of the Age of Greatness.

Among the Danish nobles who did homage to Christian IV upon his attaining his majority were many distinguished for their all-round abilities, active interest in culture, and lively patriotic feeling. All the signs seemed to point to a powerful future for Denmark. On her borders there was but one rival with whom she needed to reckon: Sweden—a Sweden which still included Finland.

In any comparison between the two states, Sweden, in the opinion of most observers, was distinctly at a disadvantage. The mining industry, though it had been for centuries one of the country's most important resources, had not yet entered upon its boom period. The exploitation of the forests provided mainly for domestic needs, and left little over for export. Its shipping could not be compared with that of Denmark-Norway. Agriculture showed a deficiency as often as it showed a surplus. As to the fruits of intellect and culture—which were garnered only by the select few—it was plain that here above all Sweden was in a backward state: she could boast of no Arild Huitfeldt or Tyge Brahe. In literary culture, in the world of books, Sweden's part was as yet but a meagre one. Social development in Sweden had for long been hampered by political interruptions and internal discord, and this had resulted in conditions far less settled than prevailed in Denmark. Even that national valor once so dreaded by her neighbors had (or so the Danes considered) been broken by the Seven Years' War of the North (1563-1571). On top of that came the War of Kalmar, the significance of which for Gustav Adolf's development we have already noticed. No doubt the war had not fulfilled the most audacious expectations of Denmark; but still less had it decided in Sweden's favor the burning question of the military potentialities of the two nations when locked in single combat.

The rivalry between Sweden and Denmark is a leading motive in the history of the period. It was not altogether inexplicable. There was an accumulation of rancor on both sides, not least in the hearts of the masses; for the masses, though they knew all about the blessings of peace, could easily be stirred by national animosities and caught by political catch-phrases. The Älvsborg Ransom left bitter memories with the Swedish people, and there is evidence of their survival into much more recent times. Denmark's statesmen, though they had begun to question the value of a policy which aimed at the restoration of the supremacy of the Danish monarchy in the North, had no doubts in their minds when it was a question of keeping Sweden in a position of inferiority; for although Sweden never recognized what was not, perhaps, a very conspicuous fact, it remained true that her inferiority was practically uncontestable. Swedish statesmen, on their side, could not fail to realize that in the long run they would have to solve the problem of freeing the country from the danger of encirclement by her neighbor. The doctrine of natural frontiers is a good deal older than the French Revolution.

Karl IX seems to have attempted to inaugurate some such solution in his Arctic policy. The project was bold enough: the Swedish-Finnish realm was to be rounded off to the north and east so as to reach to seas which, if cold, were at least open. It was a great conception, the conception of a statesman perhaps, but it was foolish in so far as its author dreamed of carrying it out without infringing Danish-Norwegian rights already buttressed by treaties; and at the peace of Knäred in 1613 it was shattered for ever. Gustav Adolf's foreign policy lacked this northern aspect. Even Jämtland and Härjedalen, which the Swedes had overrun in the course of the struggle, were retroceded at the conclusion of peace. A broad tract of Norwegian territory still drove a wedge east of the watershed towards the Baltic coast, threatening some day to isolate Swedish Norrland. After Knäred, however, there was hardly attention to spare for matters of this sort; for some years all other considerations had to give way to the redemption of the lands about the mouth of the Göta River—Sweden's single narrow window to the west. There on the west coast every foot of land was precious. Gustav Adolf called Älvsborg the "apple of his eye." After repeated attempts he did succeed, by strenuous efforts, in saving it for Sweden; but the success of these efforts would have been more than doubtful if he had not found in Holland the support he needed for his financial operations. One favorable effect of the Treaty of Knäred was the alliance which that power concluded with Sweden in 1614, with the obvious intention of preserving the balance of power in the North.

The relations between Christian IV and Gustav Adolf form a richly eventful chapter of history. As a rule, they were determined by their common wish to hold one another at a distance; but within these limits they gave scope for *rapprochement* and *detente* in irregular alternation. This mutual mistrust did not prevent the two kings from seeing that cooperation might be of advantage to both countries. On occasion, moreover, their belief in the common interests of Protestantism could kindle into flame. But the most disturbing feature of the situation was that Swedes and Danes found it more difficult than most other peoples to sink their differences and present a united front. They still felt that there were old scores yet to be paid off between them. Gustav Adolf in 1617 spoke openly to the Estates of "our old enemy the Jute."

Sweden's political problems, and her attitude towards them, differed fundamentally from Denmark's; for, quite apart from conflicting interests in the North, they demanded a solution which would clearly be prejudicial to Danish interests. Danish statesmanship could work under far less disturbed conditions. In Denmark there was no parallel to the deep-rooted bitterness with which the dynastic conflict within the house of Vasa had complicated Sweden's foreign relations. As far as the people of Sweden were concerned that quarrel was now over; but outside the country it still remained undecided. It hung like a dead weight on Sweden's policy; but on the other hand it compelled her to resolute action. The Oldenburgs had more elbow-room and freer hands. Christian's dealings with the outer world did not have to be limited by other considerations than such as wisdom might suggest or conscience dictate. The power he represented was from the beginning regarded by Europe at large in a very different light from Sweden. Into his relations with Poland and Spain he could infuse such measure of confidence or distrust as might seem good to a Protestant sovereign at liberty to choose his policy. Apart from religious considerations, and the friendships and enmities they brought in their train, Christian held a neutral position. Gustav Adolf could never do that. Their relations had begun with a desperate grapple; subsequently they were frequently of no very friendly kind; and not the least factor making for irritation was this difference in their political outlooks.

This basic situation explains, on the other hand, why, of the two, it was Gustav Adolf who generally sought to draw the other over to his side. There was never any possibility of Denmark's being induced to take sides with Sweden against Sigismund; but a strict neutrality was not irreconcilable with a more or less benevolent attitude. When, early in his reign, Gustav Adolf suggested that they should act together with other powers to keep an eye on Protestant interests, he was actuated by the subsidiary consideration that Christian would thereby be prevented from pursuing a policy injurious to Swedish interests. When in 1619 Gustav Adolf put forward the view that the two Northern monarchies were the main props of the evangelical cause, the general state of Europe, and particularly the obvious feebleness of English policy, gave his contention a good deal of justification. It would be unjust to deny to King Christian and his advisers a lively Protestant consciousness; but for them the question appeared in a rather different light from that in which it presented itself to the Swedes. The Danes stood in close proximity to the events on the Continent; but on the other hand they had none of that sense of occupying the post of danger which was increasingly present to their neighbors to the north. This latter aspect of Swedish policy, its origin in the circumstances of the time, and the historical significance of its effects, will be dealt with in more detail in another connection.

Christian IV was sixteen years older than Gustav Adolf, and survived him for fifteen. It was his tragic fate to see the balance of power in the Scandinavian North tip decisively against the dual monarchy over which, for more than half a century, he bore rule. The change came in the reign of Gustav Adolf, and he was indeed its main agent, for it is undeniable that the alteration was a consequence of his intervention in world affairs, although no doubt the fatal consequences for Denmark only became apparent later. The turning point was Sweden's participation in the Thirty Years' War; but some years before that event—indeed, even before the disastrous Danish intervention in Germany—those who could read the signs of the times detected a significant shifting of the balance.

As long as the Älvsborg Ransom was not completely paid off Denmark felt herself to have the upper hand. There were times when it appeared probable that the Swedish people and its government would be baffled by their onerous task. At certain moments, indeed, peace hung in the balance; at the end of 1617 Gustav Adolf was almost convinced that an appeal to arms could not be avoided. King Christian took a menacing tone in his letters, and refused to budge a hair's breadth from the rights secured to him by the peace treaty. However, the danger passed away. At the beginning of 1619 the two kings met at Halmstad to negotiate for a lasting friendship between their countries. They were seen to embrace "frequently." But the sky soon became overcast again. Complaints from both sides, arising mainly out of obscure customs disputes and conflicting mercantile interests, reached an alarming pitch, and meetings and negotiations seemed of no avail in the search for a settlement. At last matters boiled up to a serious crisis. By this time (1623) Gustav Adolf had determined upon the arbitrament of war if he could not obtain a hearing for Swedish claims by any other means. A breach was avoided by the virtually complete surrender of Denmark in the summer of 1624. No factor had more powerfully contributed to this result than the knowledge of the well-drilled army—completely reorganized in the years immediately preceding—which Sweden now had at her disposal. Denmark abandoned her attitude. The defeat of her policy made it clear that the position in the North had undergone a radical alteration since the War of Kalmar. Hardly twelve years earlier King Christian and his fleet had sailed up to Vaxholm, at the very gates of the Swedish capital—the concluding episode, this, in a fierce saga which seems almost to take us back to the age of the rimed chronicles.

Simultaneously with these complications—which, as we have seen, were settled to Sweden's advantage and almost at her dictation—the ambitions of the two monarchies had clashed in a field which Danish statesmanship had long regarded as its particular preserve, and which the Oldenburgs tended to view as their legitimate sphere of dynastic influence—North Germany. Gustav

Adolf had many connections with this district through ties of blood: the prince bishop of Bremen was his uncle; his near relatives governed Holstein; the dukes of Mecklenburg were his relations by marriage. The Hansa towns, with Lübeck as their traditional leader, might be counted among his other friends from sympathy and commercial interests. The aim of Gustav Adolf's policy was the formation of a group of powers with Swedish support and in the last resort under Swedish leadership. He envisaged a North German alliance, which was to form a barrier against the threat of Catholic expansion, but which was also to serve the purpose of keeping Denmark in check. In the years round about 1620 several negotiations richer in ideas than in results were set on foot for such a union of the princes and towns on the coasts of the North Sea and the Baltic. They might perhaps have produced more effect if the war with Poland had not intervened and thereby chilled the courage of the contracting parties still further. The project may be considered the forerunner, on a more modest scale, of the great evangelical league whose formation was to be the last, the unfinished, work of Gustav Adolf's statesmanship in Germany.

The most natural sphere of Swedish-Danish rivalry was of course the Baltic. Large portions of this sea had for years been considered by the Danes as their territorial waters. They had never really been able to reconcile themselves to the fact that the collapse of the Military Orders in Livland, about the middle of the preceding century, had given Sweden an opportunity to gain a firm footing on the Gulf of Finland. And now they had to stand by and see these Swedish positions beyond the sea steadily extended southwards. "God forbid that such a thing should happen," exclaimed King Christian at the news of the attack on Riga in 1621. Riga fell. Christian's feelings may well be imagined. He continued, indeed, to claim supremacy over the Baltic (*dominium maris Baltici*) within extremely extended limits. By a declaration promulgated by the Danish Rigsraad[1] on his instructions, Danish waters were defined so as to include the seas between Bornholm and Gotland on the one hand, and Sweden on the other, and to

[1] Council of the Realm.

stretch thence across to Ösel and Kurland, together with the seas
off Prussia, Pomerania, and Mecklenburg. It was plain, however,
that Sweden did not recognize these pretensions. Gustav Adolf's
naval demonstration against Danzig in 1623 caused great uneasiness in Copenhagen, particularly as it was suspected that
the enterprise would be repeated. The Danish ambassador to
Stockholm, Peder Galt, reported that Gustav Adolf had allowed
it to be known that he considered himself to be "a sovereign of
the Baltic." These differences with Denmark did not, indeed, lead
to open disputes; but they contributed very greatly to produc-
ing the severe crisis which was eventually settled in 1624. King
Christian was now of opinion that the limits of concession had
been reached. "I will not allow him," he said, referring to Gustav
Adolf, "to become more powerful in the Baltic than he is at
present."

The interest in the Baltic common to the two Northern powers
was not, however, only a source of dissensions; some years later
it became plain that it could also constitute a bond between them.
Christian IV's armed intervention in the weary struggle in Germany had, as we know, ended in bitter disappointment. In the
end he was driven to take refuge in the islands; all Jutland fell
to the enemy; and the whole of North Germany was left to its
fate. Old plans for an Imperial navy in the Baltic and North
Seas now quickly began to revive. In this critical situation Sweden
and Denmark at last composed their quarrels. Early in 1628 they
concluded an alliance. Together they lent assistance to Stralsund,
now hemmed in by Wallenstein, and the only town on the south
coast of the Baltic to keep alive the spirit of resistance. Their
collaboration, however, did not extend very far, nor did it prove
to be very durable. It was not Gustav Adolf's fault that this proved
to be the case. For his own part he was fully determined on a
resolute resistance. He urgently exhorted his neighbor of Denmark to stand by him, and not to withdraw from a struggle which
had hardly begun. At their interview at Ulvsbäck in February
1629, when he met Christian for the second and last time, he
brought all the ardor of his eloquence to bear. He might have
spared his breath; Christian was disheartened, and his country
was exhausted; all he desired now was peace. And peace he

succeeded in obtaining—on relatively favorable terms—by turning to his advantage the alteration in the temper of his victorious adversaries, who, now that Denmark was out of the game, were preparing for a stroke at Sweden. Gustav Adolf considered that Christian's conduct fell little short of treachery: when the Råd was debating the possibility of intervention in Germany, in the autumn of 1629, he remarked of Christian that "he pulled his own foot out of the fire, and stuck mine in it."

At this time, and in the months that followed, Christian IV conceived it to be the capital object of Danish foreign policy to avert Swedish intervention in Germany. Without delay he set on foot efforts to bring about a settlement by peaceful means. But in these efforts he overlooked (or tried to ignore) the profound seriousness which underlay Gustav Adolf's view of the great European crisis. Gustav Adolf's way now lay clear before him. Nevertheless, he would have welcomed an opportunity to state the Swedish conditions for such a settlement, and it was scarcely Gustav Adolf's fault that the attempt to open negotiations with the emperor failed. Sweden's terms were such that the chance of a bloodless settlement must appear infinitesimal, for Gustav Adolf demanded that Protestant North Germany be restored to its pre-war position. The negotiations, which it had been agreed should take place under Danish mediation, broke down in the summer of 1630 before the envoys of the parties could even arrange a meeting. By that time a Swedish army under the king's command stood on Pomeranian soil.

How deep the mutual distrust of the two kings had once again become may be seen not least from the fact that before the German campaign Gustav Adolf was toying with the idea of a preventive war against Denmark. The events which followed Gustav Adolf's landing in Germany thrust Christian more and more into the background. The Lower Saxon Circle, however, in whose deliberations Christian was always anxious to have a say, gave the Swedes some trouble; and in other quarters too Swedish statesmen met with opposition which they did not hesitate to attribute to Danish machinations, or, in the last resort, to King Christian's personal jealousy of his more fortunate neighbor. The Råd in Stockholm assured the king (February 1631) that in the event of war the Estates would "come about the Jutes like bees, being that they are much embittered and desirous thereto." In the spring of 1632 the tension was so acute that the outbreak of war could be expected almost at any moment. Matters were smoothed out diplomatically, however, and on the whole this front remained quiet until Gustav Adolf's death; but the state of feeling on either side boded no good for the future. The Swedes felt that they now had the means at their command to break the spirit of their enemy, if it should come to a rupture. They could take Denmark in the rear from Germany. It was by that road that Torstensson was to travel in 1643.

[2]

WHEN in the summer of 1613 the young Duke Karl Filip arrived at Viborg, accompanied by the delegates who were to negotiate with the Russians on Sweden's behalf concerning his election as Tsar, the popular ferment within the Muscovite dominions was already coming to a head. It was soon to be plain that the national movement for unity, which had had its origin in the Volga provinces, and was supported by the Cossack party and by the nobility (though until recently they had been enemies) would sweep away any support for a foreign candidature. Michael Romanov had been crowned in Moscow before the Swedish prince reached the frontier. The opportunity had been lost for good, though this was not generally realized at first.

To Swedish statesmen the prospect of an imperial crown for Karl Filip had naturally never been a matter of very vital concern. Their advances to "that barbarous and unruly nation" had, all along, been designed principally to forward the territorial and mercantile interests of their own country. It was no part of their plan to smooth the way for a Russian dynasty of Vasas by compromises or concessions. Moreover, Gustav Adolf had informed de la Gardie that it was his duty to "keep a tight hand on the reins" and hold Novgorod "within proper bounds." He had not an atom of confidence in the Russians. He considered that he had a very good notion of their national character, and believed that when dealing with them, even under conditions of peace and

STOCKHOLM CASTLE IN THE MIDDLE OF THE SEVENTEENTH CENTURY

friendship, it was essential always "to keep in view the possibility of having to fight." His policy was innocent of illusions.

The fact that Novgorod, with its Swedish garrison, clung obstinately to Karl Filip's candidature, and hailed him as a new Rjurjik, could be dismissed as of no significance, since it was clear to everyone that there was no longer any prospect of a unanimous election in his favor. At the beginning of 1614, when it was futile to wait any longer, Karl Filip went home. The attempt, by way of compensation, to induce the authorities in Novgorod to unite their future destiny with Sweden's met with resolute opposition; while the newly founded national Tsardom in Moscow was simultaneously recruiting armed adherents in alarming numbers within the area under Swedish protection. Everything pointed to a united effort to settle the question, and it was scarcely to be expected that it could come about by purely peaceful means. When Gustav Adolf later in the year carried out his purpose of invasion, his intention was to "offer the Muscovite peace in one hand and a sword in the other." The object of his later Russian policy, in short, was to secure for Sweden pledges which could be used to extract the most favorable possible peace terms. To that extent the way out of these tedious complications was now clear.

The king, however, encountered obstacles which delayed a settlement, and which resulted largely from what he called the "shameless behavior and gross insolence of the Russians." The Russians seemed to be well aware that the weight of numbers was on their side, no matter how poor their military efficiency if it came to a pitched battle against the invaders. On the other hand, the consciousness of the vastness of Russia's internal resources encouraged Gustav Adolf and his advisers to persist in view of the fact that those resources were for the moment crippled. They knew that the war was unpopular with the other powers; they knew, too, that feeling at home in Sweden was in favor of an early peace. Yet they had no intention of allowing this opportunity to slip through their fingers: they were resolved to strike while the iron was hot. The Muscovite must not be allowed to escape until "his wings are clipped, and things have been made a bit more difficult for him," as Axel Oxenstierna emphasized. (This was in the autumn of 1615, shortly after negotiations for peace had been initiated under the mediation of England and, for a time, Holland.) If he were let off now, when he was beaten to his knees, he might in the future develop a power dangerous to Sweden and other neighboring States, so that "in the end, when it is too late, we shall bitterly repent it." It was this policy, therefore, which was less concerned with the present than with the future, that was pressed forward relentlessly to its conclusion.

The events of the war may here be passed over. The siege of Pskov—which coincided with the episode of Margareta Slots —was the last military enterprise undertaken by the Swedish forces. Even this had to be abandoned in the end, though Gustav Adolf was able at a pinch to cloak the failure under a reference to the fact that the mediating powers were already at work. Interest now centered on the bargainings of the negotiators, which proved a lengthy and stubbornly contested affair. Sweden started from a position which was upon the whole very favorable, since, besides Novgorod, she held a number of other important key points in western Russia. The danger that the Russians and Poles might effect a reconciliation and together turn against their common enemy could not, however, be ignored, and this fact helped to moderate the claims which were advanced from the Swedish side. In the last resort, the essential point was the demand for protection for the country's eastern frontier, so that (in the words of the Råd) the enemy should be "utterly cut off from the sea." The question of compensation for the help which Karl IX had previously given Vasilij Sujskij had therefore eventually to give way to these considerations of future advantage. At last, at the end of February 1617, the treaty of peace was signed at the little village of Stolbova.

The Treaty of Stolbova was undoubtedly one of the most important ever to be concluded by Sweden. It endorsed the abandonment of Karl IX's Arctic policy already implicit in the Treaty of Knäred, and it gave Sweden instead an unbroken coastline round the whole of the Gulf of Finland. Not only did this form a valuable strategical land-bridge, particularly now that it was secured by the possession of the whole of Ingria, but it signified also, while it lasted, a settlement of the problem of controlling the most important trade routes to Russia—a settlement wholly in Sweden's favor. At the same time, the incorporation of the fief of Kexholm pushed forward the eastern frontier of the Swedish-Finnish state to the shores of Lake Ladoga. The Treaty of Stolbova is the basis upon which the modern limits of Finland are determined, the basis of claims which were to be asserted after years of mutilation, when the link with Sweden had been broken for ever.

Of the value of this peace, which thus rounded off in a natural manner the eastern frontiers of the kingdom, no one had a livelier or stronger appreciation than Gustav Adolf himself. "Why should we Swedes be so foolish," he said, "as to permit the Russian to sit as it were on our front doorstep in Livland and Finland, when we can put Lake Ladoga, a thirty-mile belt of marsh, and the swiftly flowing Neva, between us?" When he put his question to the Estates at the Riksdag of Örebro in 1617 peace had not yet been concluded, though it was already in sight. In August, he met them again, when they assembled to celebrate his coronation. At the previous meeting he had been concerned to defend his policy; at this he presented an account of its fruits.

The peace, he said, was honorable. It was more than that: it was a providence of God. "For what could be more honorable than to have repulsed our mighty neighbor, with whom for centuries, and, so to say, from time immemorial, our relations have been dangerous and uncertain, and to have brought him so low that he has been forced to abandon for ever that nest of banditry whence he was wont to inflict such injury upon us?" He told them of Russia's power, of the vastness of her territories, and pointed out that the Tsar was "the reigning Lord of a great part of Europe and Asia, which are the earth's chief continents." Until this day, the overweening enemy would never have believed that "the valor of Sweden, the manly character of her subjects, could (under God) have so far compelled them that they must conclude with us such a peace as this is. . . . Finland is now divided from Russia by the great Lake of Ladoga, as broad in its extent as the Åland Sea, or the Baltic between Estland and Nyland—and no Poles have ever succeeded in crossing these.

Therefore do I trust with God's help, that in future it may be a hard matter for the Russians to overleap this brook; but should they (which God forbid) succeed in crossing it, then Kexholm and Nöteborg, both fortresses well defended by nature and by art, will (after God) give them pause for an hour or two, and bar their passage into Finland." With similar clarity he emphasized the additional advantages of the new frontiers: "And so it would appear as though God Himself through Nature had in this victory designed to free us from our false foe the Russian."

Not the least encouraging prospect for the future in the king's eyes was the exclusion of his formidable neighbor from the sea. Hitherto it had been possible for the Muscovite to attack Finland by sea with his "innumerable sloops and shallops." "But from this by God's grace is he now inhibited, for he cannot put a single boat upon the Baltic without our consenting thereto." We remember that it was upon territory acquired by Sweden by the Treaty of Stolbova and still legally in Swedish possession that Petersburg was later to arise.

When Gustav Adolf said that the frontier so favorable to Sweden had been established "forever" the phrase had, in this context, a significance mainly terminological, and was conformable to the diplomatic language usual in eastern Europe, and to the unlimited validity which the contracting parties had accorded to the treaty. But everything indicates that he was firmly convinced that the settlement was to be final and permanent. He based this opinion upon a cautious estimate of the superiority which he considered Sweden to have gained by the peace, and he refused to believe that this advantage could not be pressed again, if necessity arose. Certainly he believed, too, that the Muscovite power, weakened by such a severe and protracted crisis, must now devote itself to the management of its neglected internal affairs, and, for as far ahead as anyone could foresee, would be compelled to adopt an attitude of reserve in its relations with other countries. In spite of their "shallops" the Russians had hardly shown much inclination to take to the sea. Even boyars in positions of responsibility, men who had represented the Tsar at the peace conference, confessed that they had never seen a warship. Gustav Adolf held that Russia by her very nature was a land power with her back turned upon the Baltic.

He did not, indeed, cease to reckon with Russia as a political factor of some weight. More than once during the following years he sought to induce the ruler in the Kremlin to make common cause with him against Sigismund. These schemes, however, took a relatively subordinate place in his active and enterprising statesmanship: they remind us of his tentative attempts at collaboration with the Turks and Tartars, with which, indeed, they were often connected. But Gustav Adolf was always anxious to be on good terms with the Tsar, once the definitive settlement had been reached. His Russian policy after Stolbova conscientiously sought to preserve neighborly harmony. The delimitation of the frontier was not completed until 1621, and was not settled without occasional attempts at sharp practice on the Russian side. Thereafter, however, the relations between the two countries grew steadily more friendly, and towards the end of the reign were even cordial; a contributory cause being that Russian policy was moving towards a breach with Poland. In 1631 Gustav Adolf appointed a permanent agent in Moscow; this was the first diplomatic representative to be accredited to Russia. The victory of Breitenfeld was celebrated by the Tsar with Thanksgivings in the churches of the capital, pealing of bells, and an imposing review of troops.

In 1622-1623 there had been talk of a close family alliance between Gustav Adolf and Michael Romanov. The Grand Duke—as he was still called in Sweden—wished to take as his wife Katharina of Brandenburg, the younger sister of Maria Eleonora, and accordingly asked for the good offices of Sweden. In Stockholm, where the gross manners of the Russian embassy were a matter of common talk, it was felt that there were more ways than one of viewing the question, though outwardly the government was benevolent. The contemplated family alliance, however, never took place: there were religious difficulties, for one thing. Katharina was shortly afterwards married off to Bethlen Gabor, the Protestant prince of Transylvania. Bethlen Gabor was an old adversary of the house of Habsburg, and almost a stock figure in the busy political intrigues of the time.

Yet deep in the hearts of Swedish statesmen remained a suspicion of their eastern neighbor. Jakob de la Gardie, who considered he knew the Russian intimately, later formulated the results of his experience in the following words: "Trust the Muscovite not at all when he speaks you fair, and but a little when he shouts and swears at you."

[3]

GUSTAV ADOLF's arch-enemy was his cousin Sigismund of Poland. The struggle between them, which was never really to be decided in their lifetime, was at once a family quarrel, a conflict of two States, and a clash between two ideologies.

Men said of Sigismund in his youth that it was his nature to resist stubbornly, but to give way in the end. In his relations with Gustav Adolf he had ample opportunity to show his talent for constancy; and never for one moment did he abandon the doctrine of his inalienable right to the throne of Sweden. At long last, indeed, he was driven to strike a bargain with reality, and admit that it was now no longer possible for him to upset the new order in Sweden; but he never consented to parley on the question of principle. From beginning to end he felt that it was he who had every right on his side. The wordly resources which he could command, as king of the "aristocratic republic" of Poland, were so entirely indeterminate, and so much at the mercy of circumstance, that he must have found his best resource in his own inner convictions. It is, moreover, fairly clear that for a considerable portion of Gustav Adolf's reign he believed that events might turn in his favor, and that Sweden might, by some happy chance, accept a return to the old order. When this hope later proved to have been illusory, when the usurper, against all expectation, sat ever more firmly in the saddle, he found compensation in the fact that he could reckon among his allies contemporary movements which were marching inexorably onward. And in the meanwhile he was himself by no means inactive. His propaganda seized every opportunity; his diplomacy spread its net for the destruction of his adversary; and though he turned his gaze primarily to Vienna, Madrid, and Brussels, he was too sagacious a politician to neglect to preserve a connection with

Copenhagen, and even with The Hague. At Berlin, moreover, in virtue of his feudal suzerainty over the duchy of Prussia, he could indicate his wishes in the most unvarnished language.

The first few years were a period of unbroken truce. Both Sweden and Poland had their hands full in Russia, where they pursued aims so divergent that it is remarkable that they never turned their arms against each other. During the whole of this period Sigismund was in reality the aggressor, in spite of the fact that there were no hostilities. His offensive was, indeed, mainly confined to the smuggling of proclamations and messages across the frontier at regular intervals. He did not hesitate to make an early attempt on Jakob de la Gardie, the Swedish commander in Russia, whom he endeavored to entice into his service—"trying to sound him out," as Gustav Adolf remarked. Apparently Sigismund counted on the good will of considerable sections of Swedish society, particularly among those noble families whom Karl IX had used so severely. Around him he had gathered a large circle of exiles, who supplied him, through devious channels, with more or less reliable information about the state of popular opinion at home.

This propaganda service continued for years, although it was rigorously punished by the Swedish government whenever traces of it could be detected. The campaign was cleverly managed from Sigismund's side. His long *Answer* to the Swedish act of deposition, for instance, which was published in 1617, shows great talent. It is now excessively rare; clearly all copies that could be secured were burnt. We may surmise that the seed did not always fall on stony ground. Subterranean agitation certainly went on here and there within the country. Finland and Östergötland seem to have been the areas of which Sigismund entertained the best expectation. The Danish agent, Peder Galt, who was no doubt inclined to take as gloomy a view as possible of Sweden's internal condition, could still, in 1624, feel justified in reporting that the country contained many who were at heart "Polish."

Sigismund made no secret in his propaganda of his intention to return at some future time to reclaim his inheritance, reward the faithful, and punish the deserters. There were moments when there was talk of an imminent Polish invasion, to be directed in the first instance against Kalmar. It is clear that Gustav Adolf himself reckoned with this danger; his parting speech to Queen Kristina and Duke Johan when he left for Russia in 1615 has a reference to it. During his long absence in the East, the rumors of an impending attack grew louder, and at last reached an intolerable pitch. It was whispered among the people that the king was kept in ignorance of what was preparing; no one (so the story ran) dared tell him, though everyone knew of it. Simultaneously the agitation, mainly directed from Danzig, reached its culminating point. At last the home government really took alarm. They earnestly implored Gustav Adolf to return home, since in the spring of 1616 he was still lingering on the Russian border. They laid special emphasis on "the dangerous rumor of the king of Poland's arrival in Sweden, which became current in the country last year, and is still general, and repeated every day."

Now Sigismund's chances of inducing the Polish Diet to fit out an expedition against Sweden were scarcely very bright, as long as Gustav Adolf did not meet with any major disaster; but it seems that Sigismund was counting on precisely such a contingency; and he was, moreover, keeping other means open which would make him independent of the support of the Polish magnates. There was for instance his plan—by no means a new one— of creating a fleet with Spanish help, to be stationed in the North Sea at Dunkirk, for the purpose of harrying the Swedish coasts. A more fantastic project was suggested to him by an Austrian adventurer, Count Althann, who offered to raise 14,000 men at his own expense for service against Sweden; compensation to be by drafts on Swedish resources, payable after the reconquest of the country. Althann, who had gone over from Protestantism to Catholicism, dreamed of a "Christian Military Order" the object of which would be the conquest, first of Sweden, and afterwards of the Turks. It is characteristic of Sigismund that he should have fallen in with this project, and at the beginning of 1617 a contract was drawn up in Warsaw between the king and this distinguished convert. For some time afterwards there was much talk of Count Althann and his order, which now had Poland's support, and the Swedish agents kept a close watch upon its activities; but, as the rebellion in Bohemia provided a new sphere of action for the pious zeal of these new crusaders, it gradually disappeared from view.

For Gustav Adolf, the question of how to deal with Sigismund's emigré protégés was as much a matter of domestic as of foreign policy. The sentence on Messenius, shortly after the king's return in 1616, and more particularly the Örebro Statute of the following year, were intended to make it clear to all that there were limits which could not safely be passed. The Statute was a measure the very existence of which was a fiery warning to all turbulent spirits. And immediately afterwards Gustav Adolf, being now secure on the Muscovite front, dealt his first blow against the possessions of the Crown of Poland. To some extent this attack could be considered as a reply to the progress which Poland and the Catholic Church had been making in Kurland, where the quarrel between Sigismund's vassals, the dukes, and the native nobility had recently precipitated Polish intervention, with consequences which might be dangerous to the balance of power in the Baltic. The results of the Swedish campaign of 1617 were not, however, of any great importance; for the Poles recaptured Dünamunde, and in consequence the plan to put pressure on Riga from that position came to nothing. The whole affair was an isolated episode, and was followed by a renewed cessation of hostilities.

The policy of continued truces was purely a matter of necessity. It left the situation unchanged. Sigismund's standpoint remained what it had always been. The increasing strength of the Catholic party in Europe more than compensated for the fact that with the passing of the years the ranks of the Swedish exiles gradually thinned, as more and more of them, particularly those of the younger generation, reconciled themselves with the Vasa who reigned in Sweden, and returned to their native country. A faithful nucleus remained, under the leadership of one of Axel Oxenstierna's cousins, the impetuous Gabriel Posse. To secure a peace on the terms that Sigismund required, Gustav Adolf would have had to sacrifice his crown. It was not until Swedish arms had intervened with pitilessly increasing pressure that Sigismund reconciled himself to further concessions.

It was with the feeling that the situation must sooner or later become impossible that Gustav Adolf assumed the tactical offensive. In doing so, he was not oblivious of the fact that he was engaging Poland's forces, and thereby preventing them from assisting the Catholic reaction which was mounting ever higher in Central Europe. He soon found, however, that the reopening of the war with Poland was considered by the rest of Europe as a deplorable and useless complication of the situation. He did not on that account swerve from his purpose. The fact that he took advantage of the difficulties in which Poland was involved by her war with the Turks—the common enemies of Christendom—provoked criticism which in many quarters was very audibly expressed. It was prophesied that Gustav Adolf would share the fate of Francis I at Pavia. Sigismund himself appears to have thought that the patience of the Swedish people would soon be exhausted, and that a general rising must be the result. Moreover, a certain revival of Polish machinations became apparent, partly occasioned, no doubt—as we saw in an earlier chapter—by the great uncertainty as to the succession in Sweden at precisely this moment.

By attacking in Polish Livland, Gustav Adolf intended to secure territorial pledges for a definitive peace, and thus settle the dynastic question once for all. The longer this question remained open, and the longer his adversary could draw encouragement from the favorable trend of European affairs, the more dubious would be the prospects of obtaining a solution satisfactory to himself and to Sweden. The question of the mere title was not the stone that upset the applecart; Gustav Adolf was prepared to concede that to his cousin as a kind of souvenir of the past. The acquisitions in Livland, steadily extended as the result of a series of successful campaigns, he was prepared to renounce provided that in return he could secure a peace, and not merely a renewal of the truce. It should, however, be added that he linked this offer with a demand for compensation for the heavy expenditure in which Sweden had been involved by the war, and that this demand, which naturally grew larger as the struggle continued, was finally put forward as an alternative to the formal transference of Livland to the Swedish Crown. The province had only recently become Polish territory; its population was Protestant; its culture predominantly German. It is a natural assumption that the idea of incorporating Livland permanently into the overseas dominions of the Crown early took shape in the minds of Swedish statesmen, and was grasped without difficulty by the Swedish Estates. Livland and Estland formed a historic unity. Its acquisition would give the earlier Swedish acquisitions in the Baltic a more natural frontier, would assist trade and communications, relieve the State's finances, and consolidate Sweden's political position in the Baltic.

The pressure which the Swedes exercised on the Lithuanian half of the Polish republic through these Livonian campaigns proved to be insufficient. In the negotiations which alternated with the military operations, and which resulted in several long truces, the Poles found ample scope for their genius for wasting time with formalities. "If it is a question of bandying words," wrote Gustav Adolf to the marshal of the realm, "then they have better writers than we have, and more skill in protracting business." If he was to effect his object of forcing a peace, the enemy must be struck in a more vulnerable spot. In the summer of 1626, therefore, he transferred his field army to Prussia, and in a rapid and decisive campaign occupied the country round the mouth of the Vistula.

The attack on Polish Prussia gave Gustav Adolf much to do, apart from the military operations, which in the following years were mainly confined to the coastal districts, where the two armies engaged in a war of positions over a more or less constant area. The king's task was to defend and round off the occupied districts in order to convince the Poles that he had a real grip on the vital artery of the country, and was no longer to be put off by pretexts. This object he realized, though not so definitively as he had hoped, for it still proved impossible to obtain a conclusive peace. He had not failed to consider the possibility of penetrating more deeply into the interior of Poland; but he abandoned this idea because the conditions upon which he was prepared to entertain it—support from the anti-Habsburg powers for an offensive movement against the hereditary dominions of the emperor—could not be realized, and because in any case the German war took a turn which destroyed the whole basis upon which the scheme had been founded.

The hostilities in Prussia were even more liable to injure important interests than the campaign in Livonia. England and Holland saw their lucrative trade with Poland in danger of diminution, and grew increasingly anxious to ease the tension—particularly since they wished to induce the king of Sweden to turn his arms directly against the victorious Catholics in Germany. Worst of all was the fate of Brandenburg, which now had to stand by and see the elector's own brother-in-law constructing strongholds—as a measure of precaution—within the limits of the duchy, while at the same time Poland enforced her irritating feudal claims, and demanded that Brandenburg contribute a corps to the Polish army. Gustav Adolf, however, succeeded in imposing his will upon Georg Wilhelm and his harassed subjects, laying down his conditions with that blend of friendly irony and reckless vigor which usually distinguished his proceedings in such cases. As a result, the feudal services of the Hohenzollern were of no great use to Sigismund. When in 1627 a Brandenburg-Prussian auxiliary force set off for the Polish headquarters it was plain that its morale was undermined, for on the march the troops all deserted to the side of Gustav Adolf—whom, in Lutheran East Prussia, they were forbidden to term king of Sweden!

The most serious disappointment and the most serious reverse that Gustav Adolf encountered in the course of the Prussian campaigns, was the refusal of the town of Danzig to come to terms with him upon his demand that they should observe "a safe and honorable neutrality." Danzig had been, and continued to be, the favorite resort for the intriguing Swedish exiles. It was the base of operations for all Sigismund's contemplated attacks on Sweden; it gave harborage within its walls to his preparations, which were now increasingly concentrated on maritime ends. Danzig was incomparably the greatest and richest city in the Baltic. In comparison Lübeck seemed merely to be preserving the vanished pomps of yesterday. The old Hanseatic League, to which Gustav Adolf, perhaps, attached undue importance, still attempted to hold together, but as a political force it had now but a shadowy existence. Danzig, on the other hand, was able to follow an independent policy on her own account. As a rule her watchword was caution, but on occasion she could act with decision. The settled objects of her policy were, on the one hand, to maintain and even to extend the city's franchises in relation to the crown of Poland; and on the other, to preserve the link between them. For most of Greater Poland's trade passed through Danzig's harbor. Gustav Adolf, who had an old score to settle with the city, soon found himself in open enmity to it, since the leading burghers rejected his suggestion that they should give a declaration of neutrality similar to that which Königsberg, the capital of the duchy, had given already. The pressure of a blockade failed to produce the desired effect. "I have taken the water from them," exclaimed the king, "I would I could take the air also!" The burghers, driven more and more to take the part of Poland, strengthened their defenses, and at last met the Swedes openly in the field and on the high seas.

Axel Oxenstierna, who in 1626 was appointed to the important post of governor-general of the area of Swedish occupation, testified on a later occasion that the king "had more respect for Danzig than for the Polish army." The strongly fortified town weathered storms like a rock: Karl X Gustav and Karl XII, like Gustav Adolf, could make no impression upon it. And in 1647 Oxenstierna, recalling the vain attempts to beat down its resistance, remarked that "the king of Poland has Danzig to thank for the fact that he still sits upon his throne." If the Swedes proved unable to utilize fully their strong position in the Vistula delta, that fact is to be attributed primarily to Danzig, although the cautious and calculating strategy of Koniecpolski was also a contributing cause.

The open breach between Sweden and the great mercantile city gave Sigismund a most welcome opportunity to use its harbor to fit out privateers, which harried Swedish shipping after the Swedish fleet had gone home in the autumn. Under the unwearied care of Gabriel Posse, a royal Polish navy had begun to take shape at Danzig—not altogether to the gratification of the burghers, who were always very sensitive on the subject of their privileges and independent status. Sigismund had embarked

upon this program of naval construction in reliance upon Spanish
subsidies, but these were slow to arrive. At last he decided, with
a view to more effective action, to unite his squadron with the
Imperial armament which was being organized at Wismar. To
Wismar therefore the Polish ships sailed, early in 1629; while
simultaneously Posse went overland to Wallenstein, who had
recently been created duke of Mecklenburg and been given the
ominous title of "General of the Baltic and Oceanic Sea."

The handing over of these ships, which had been eagerly
urged by the Spaniards and Imperialists, was a sign of the increasingly close cooperation between the Polish government and
the victorious Habsburg powers. In 1627 a small Imperialist
auxiliary force had marched off to the Swedo-Polish theater of
war; in 1628 a new detachment was put in readiness to assist
Sigismund, though it was not able to get away; and in the summer of 1629 Hans Georg von Arnim, Wallenstein's most distinguished lieutenant, arrived in Prussia with a considerable army.
Although the attack on the Vistula delta had awakened the Polish
nobility to a full realization of their danger, and led them to hasten
to the assistance of the king with liberal subsidies, the Imperialists
had no faith in their willingness or ability to hold out, and prevent the Swedes from invading German territory. And their
apprehensions were not groundless. One of the decisive reasons
for the fact that a peaceful settlement with Poland was soon
to be possible was that the Polish nobles, having at last convinced
themselves that the enemy had no intention of loosening his grip,
were anxious to put an end to a state of affairs that threatened
to cripple the lucrative grain trade down the Vistula.

The solution reached in the treaty concluded at Altmark in the
autumn of 1629 was a truce for six years. Swedish statesmen had
never made the retention of the Prussian conquests a condition
of peace; indeed, their chief concern was that the peace should be
definitive; but in the situation as it stood they must be less than
ever indifferent to the palpably great advantages which would
be offered by even a provisional and temporary occupation of
the Prussian harbors. The rich revenues from tolls—a source of
future discord with the maritime powers—would sensibly lighten
the burden of the German war, which had already been deter-

mined on by the Estates. It was, indeed, with a view to ensuring
an early outbreak of hostilities in Germany that Cardinal Richelieu had smoothed the way to a reconciliation between Sweden
and Poland through the intervention of French diplomacy. To
obtain such a relatively lengthy truce without being compelled
to abandon the rich stream of revenue was in itself an important
success; and it seemed, too, to provide sound security for the
acquisition of Livland when at some future date a formal peace
should be concluded.

King Sigismund on his side was not in the least disposed to
purchase peace at the price which Gustav Adolf steadily demanded: the abandonment of the claims of the Polish Vasa to
the Swedish throne. Why should he make such a sacrifice now,
when the Catholic reaction, intoxicated with success, was preparing to refashion Central Europe after its fancy? In the negotiations for peace into which upon former occasions he had been
compelled to enter, he had so far yielded as to agree to accord the
crown to his more fortunate cousin for his life-time, but his
consciousness of the uncertainty of the Swedish succession made
him less than ever inclined to deprive his own dynasty, with its
reassuringly plentiful supply of male heirs, of its legitimate right
to his own hereditary kingdom. The Treaty of Altmark consequently left the thorny dynastic problem in principle unsolved.

Sigismund had other anxieties than his loss of the Swedish
crown. He had his Polish crown to consider. Poland was in spirit
and in fact an electoral kingdom, and in the last resort there was
nothing to prevent the magnates from allowing their choice to
fall on a foreigner. With this danger before his eyes Sigismund
took measures to secure in good time the election of his eldest
son Wladislaw—that same Wladislaw who had once been offered
the crown of Sweden on terms unacceptable to his father, and
had later during the troublous times been hailed as Tsar of
Russia—an empty title, as events turned out. Sigismund wished
to see Wladislaw recognized as his successor before he died. According to contemporary accounts, Wladislaw was a very different
man from his father—less limited in outlook, and less bigoted in
religion; there was even talk of his secret leanings towards the
Protestant faith. It is at all events certain that the Evangelical

Dissidents in Poland, who had found times hard under Sigismund (though they had many men of importance in their ranks, including Prince Radziwill) viewed Wladislaw's candidature with approval. The strict Catholic party, on the other hand, were less enthusiastic.

Gustav Adolf surprised Europe by coming forward as Wladislaw's rival for the throne of Poland. This apparently extraordinary step is explicable only upon one supposition: that he wished to wrest a dangerous weapon out of the hands of his enemies. If Johan III's descendants could be excluded from the Polish throne by peaceful means, they would no longer be a menace to Sweden. It became therefore a prime object of his policy to prevent Sigismund's son from obtaining the crown. If his own candidature had this effect, he would be satisfied. The game could be considered won if the line of Sigismund were compelled to renounce all claims on Sweden under pressure of the divisions within Poland which Gustav Adolf undoubtedly intended to foster. And perhaps in the last resort his candidature was not quite without prospects of success. His attractive personality, the ever-lengthening list of his victories, must have appealed to the Polish weakness for the brilliant and the heroic; and there was, besides, discontent in many quarters with Sigismund and his government. Under certain circumstances, the name of Gustav Adolf might offer Radziwill's party a better rallying point than that of Wladislaw.

None the less, the plan failed in every particular. An unfortunate choice of the agents upon whom the king relied to influence public opinion, and the fact that he gave them too free rein, combined to do his reputation in Poland serious injury. After that, there was not much more to be done than to attempt to give the Poles a rather more favorable impression of the usual methods of Swedish diplomacy. After an interregnum of six months— Sigismund had died in the spring of 1632—Wladislaw was chosen king, three days before the battle of Lützen. The election was unanimous—an unparalleled occurrence in Polish history. Dissidents and Catholics voted together for Wladislaw, though the latter did so much against their will. It was a victory for toleration, and in reality it was wrung from them by their respect for

Gustav Adolf, though that particular result had been no part of his intention. The ardent Catholics would have preferred one of the younger princes, who were thought to be more orthodox. And Wladislaw ascended his throne without being forced to renounce the inherited claim of his family upon the throne of Sweden. A decision had been taken which was to be fateful for both countries.

The sequel falls outside our subject. In the next year, the word went round the peasantry in Småland that Sigismund's "Lutheran son" would suit Sweden very well. It was asserted that Gustav Adolf himself had had his eye upon him. How far this was a spontaneous popular feeling, or a last survival of the old emigré propaganda, it is impossible to say. Practically all the exiles had now returned to Sweden. Only Gabriel Posse and one or two more still held out to the bitter end. Even at the time of the Peace of Oliva (1660) there was still living in Poland a handful of Swedes who had left Sweden at the beginning of the century.

Wladislaw was chivalrous enough to admire Gustav Adolf. After his death, he did homage to him as "his near relation, and a man of the most transcendent abilities." After the Treaty of Stuhmsdorf in 1635 he begged of Maria Eleonora that he might be given, as a most precious gift, the sword of the fallen hero, "so that every day he might draw it forth from its sheath."

[4]

FROM the preceding sketch of Sweden's relations with Denmark, Russia, and Poland, it will have become clear that certain principles of Baltic policy played their part in every case, although they operated with varying force, and although the extent to which they were consciously pursued differed in different instances. In regard to Russia a full settlement had been reached when that gigantic land-power had, by the Treaty of Stolbova, been excluded from the innermost recesses of the Gulf of Finland; though it was still a question whether the settlement would stand the test of time. With respect to Poland, the transference of Livland into Swedish hands, though not as yet definitive, was in itself a very palpable advantage, particularly as it was accompanied by the temporary occupation of those Prussian harbors which furnished the Republic with her direct contacts with the sea. But Poland was no more a sea-power than Russia. Her overseas relations were in the hands mainly of foreigners or vassals, and among the latter was a town of the unfettered status and haughty independence of Danzig. Despite excellent intentions and numerous attempts, Poland's maritime aspirations had hitherto enjoyed scant success.

Sweden and Denmark, on the other hand, were vigorous Baltic powers. Each recognized the other's right to maintain a fleet in that sea; each denied that right to any other Baltic State. They divided between them—though in no very brotherly spirit—the dominion over its territorial waters. It has already been pointed out that Denmark from time immemorial had claimed the lion's share in this dominion. Christian IV, in fact, considered himself as the real suzerain of the Baltic. He put in a solemn protest, when in 1612 the Emperor Matthias declared that the Baltic belonged to the Holy Roman Empire: "His forefathers had possessed, and he himself still maintained, the fullest sovereignty over the aforesaid sea." Denmark was prepared to permit Sweden, with her extensive coast-line, to make herself *de facto* mistress within certain limits; for Sweden was the second "Baltic monarchy." The claims of the other powers were out of the question. And the special consideration to which Sweden was entitled found expression in the Treaty of Knäred (1613) when she was expressly guaranteed permanent freedom from the Sound-Dues levied by the Danes. When Gustav Adolf at the beginning of his reign—as in the treaty concluded with the States-General in 1614—reserved to himself and his country in general terms a *dominium maris Baltici* and the rights pertaining thereto, his claim no doubt foreshadowed a livelier interest in these questions on the part of Sweden; but it did not of itself imply any encroachment upon the traditional sphere of influence of his neighbor. It was only with the extension of the Swedish hold on the other side of the Baltic— the result of the dynastic settlement with Poland—that the situation underwent a change. There can be no doubt that Gustav Adolf hastened to use the opportunity, and viewed with satisfaction the consequent improvement in the naval balance of power. Char-

acteristic of this was his order to Oxenstierna, when in 1620 the
chancellor was to fetch the new queen and her mother from
Germany, to the effect that upon meeting with a Danish warship
he was to strike his topsail, if forced to do so, "for the sake of the
women," but only under protest. It is clear that the king was irked
by that precedence upon the high seas to which his neighbor laid
claim, and which in reality concealed a claim to the primacy of
the North. His naval demonstration in the summer of 1623, which
has been mentioned above, when as grand admiral he personally
assumed the command for the duration of a cruise which covered
the whole of the Baltic, was no doubt designed primarily as a
warning to Poland; but it took the form of a review of a "royal
armada" which was not prepared to give way, within the Baltic, to
any other power.

The foreign flags which appeared most frequently in the Baltic
were those of England and, above all, Holland. The English
found, particularly in Poland, a profitable market for their manu-
factures. To the Dutch, who stood out as the greatest maritime
people of the age, the Baltic trade had a significance which became
proverbial.

> *Whoso shuts the Sound to Ships*
> *Also shuts the Dutchman's lips.*

The Baltic region gave an inexhaustible supply of ship's timber
and all sorts of other commodities of which the free Netherlands
stood in need for their carrying trade, their commerce, and their
naval establishments. They found it a powerful source of strength
in their struggle against Spain. Almost as old as that struggle
was their anxiety lest their enemy should secure a foothold in
northern waters by the acquisition of bases upon their shores. Not
unnaturally Spanish policy did in fact seek to attain this object;
from time to time various projects with this end in view saw the
light, and during the period of reaction in the time of Johan III
Sweden herself was cast to play a part in them. Now and then
the meshes of this net of intrigue would become visible. After the
breach with Sigismund, the Swedes felt that they too were threatened. Karl IX, from his broad Protestant standpoint, did not
neglect to turn a beam of publicity upon these moves—he even

caused pamphlets to be written on the subject—and after him
Gustav Adolf felt himself called upon to utter a warning against
this "capital object of the King of Spain"—the establishment of
a navy in northern waters in cooperation with the Habsburgs and
Poland. It was a grateful subject for the propagandist, and it did
not lack a basis in reality, as we shall see.

Some few words may perhaps be added here concerning Sweden's relations with that Protestant power for whom the question
of the Baltic had most significance. From the time of the War
of Kalmar dates a visible revolution in the Northern policy of
the States-General. From Denmark they turn now to Sweden.
A number of things contributed to this result; among them, mistrust of Christian IV's ability to resist the enticements of Spain,
and the fact that the Dutch early came to count on the young king
of Sweden as a future buttress of the Protestant cause. This
actively pro-Swedish policy, which found expression in the treaty
of 1614, was not destined to continue to the end of Gustav
Adolf's reign. With the fall and execution of Oldenbarneveldt
(1619) the policy of close friendship with Sweden lost its strongest supporter. Maurice of Orange, though he avoided an open
breach with Sweden, adopted a more reserved attitude, and Dutch
statesmanship sought once more to draw near to Denmark. Swedish expansion round the Baltic, and the Prussian tolls in particular, aroused growing discontent in the Netherlands. At the time
of Gustav Adolf's landing in Germany a violent campaign was
being waged against him in Amsterdam, apparently with the connivance of the Danish government, and Sweden was being accused
of aiming at "absolute sovereignty in the North." However, Gustav Adolf's victories in Germany produced a notable revulsion
of opinion.

To return to the course of events in the Baltic. In Denmark, as
in Sweden, it was feared that as soon as the Catholic offensive
should reach the coast, the political character of the Baltic would
be jeopardized: it might no longer be possible, as it usually had
been hitherto, to consider it merely as a Northern inland sea.
This impression was a just one. The Northern powers were to
witness the military policy of the Habsburgs taking immediate

steps to carry out those maritime schemes which had so long been feared, and so earnestly prepared. From the autumn of 1627 Wallenstein deployed a ceaseless activity to this end; while the Spaniards broadcast promises and placed their expert knowledge at his disposal. Lübeck and the other coastal towns were subjected to strong pressure to induce them to assist the great enterprise. Wallenstein's plans were of the most grandiose kind: for instance, he conceived the idea of a canal between the North Sea and the Baltic. His policy at this time gives the appearance of being tinged with improvisation, an improvisation so limitless in its audacity that it might almost seem that his efforts were doomed in advance to failure. To contemporaries, however, the situation must have borne a very different aspect, in view of the startling transformations of the last few years. And in fact there can be no shadow of doubt that it was Gustav Adolf's action which alone destroyed the emperor's attempt to obtain a foothold on the Baltic. Even in the face of all his difficulties Wallenstein was able, with Spanish and Polish assistance, to turn the port of Wismar into an Imperial naval base. It was not until 1632 that the warships lying in that port fell into the hands of Sweden.

It was no part of Gustav Adolf's intention to use the desperate necessities of Denmark for the advantage of Sweden. Wallenstein dropped hints and made offers in plenty; but Gustav Adolf took no notice of them. The rivalries of the Northern nations took second place to the danger which was threatening the balance of power in the Baltic. Denmark now appeared, in Oxenstierna's phrase, as "a bastion to the Swedish realm." A brief reference has been made already to the collaboration between the two sovereigns brought about at this time. It proved less durable than Gustav Adolf had hoped, for Christian IV was weary of war, and had lost confidence in his own powers.

It was clear, however, from the beginning, that the maintenance of the security of the Baltic would come to depend mainly upon Sweden. It was certainly no accident that precisely at this juncture the claim to a Swedish dominion in that sea should have been formulated more clearly and more consciously than ever before. Thus, in its report of January 1628, the Secret Committee observed—and we should remember that the report was written by the king himself—that the emperor must be prevented from obtaining a grip on the Baltic, for the lordship of that sea, from pagan times downwards, had been in the hands or under the control of the crown of Sweden. The pretensions of Sweden had thus taken on a sonority and amplitude scarcely inferior to those of Denmark. From other sources it is plain that this claim must not be interpreted as a demand for a Baltic absolutism. Gustav Adolf's intention, when in 1628 he put a Swedish garrison in Stralsund, was described by him to Christian IV as "the preservation of the Baltic in its usual condition." A proposition to the Estates in 1629 gives a reasonably clear idea of the king's program, when it emphasizes the importance of ensuring that "The Baltic may be protected against hostile fleets, and especially that it may remain under His Majesty's control, so that no fleet other than His Majesty's and Denmark's may appear in it." Note the recognition of the traditional rights of Denmark; but note also that word "especially." It was the moment when Denmark was concluding a separate peace with the emperor. The fact that at such a time the king of Sweden asserted against all and sundry a right to be considered as the preeminent guardian of the Baltic needs no other explanation than the situation created by the Treaty of Lübeck. In the manifesto in which Gustav Adolf in 1630 explained to the world the reasons which had induced him to interfere in the hostilities in Germany, he proclaimed also the fact that from times beyond the memory of man Swedish kings had enjoyed a protectorate over the Baltic. Such a declaration did not fail to evoke sullen disapproval and open contradiction from Denmark.

The protectorate of the Baltic to which he had thus laid claim gave him, as a matter of international law, good grounds to demand the withdrawal of all Imperial naval armaments from the German coast. It was a demand which took a prominent place in his peace proposals of 1629-1630. The fundamental aim of this program was simply the pacification of North Germany and its restoration to its former political and religious position. This had for some years been a leading motive in Gustav Adolf's German policy. But he was bound to ask himself what security he could obtain meanwhile for eventual compliance with this demand, since it represented a maturely considered program from which he would not swerve except under compulsion. The idea easily presented itself of retaining Stralsund for Sweden, as a guarantee or even as compensation, perhaps for a considerable time, perhaps for ever. It is plain that from an early stage the king had also had an eye on Wismar; but the idea of handing over the duchy of Pomerania to Sweden did not develop until somewhat later. From the beginning of the campaign, however, it appeared to him only natural that the petty German states of the seaboard—Pomerania and Mecklenburg—should be compelled to submit themselves entirely to the exigencies of Swedish statesmanship, and to assume more extensive obligations than the States of the interior. Only so could a basis be laid for Swedish enterprises, a barrier be erected strong enough to withstand the tempest, a wall of defense for the Baltic be built up. It was a conception, as we remember, traceable to an earlier phase of Gustav Adolf's policy. The projected blockade of the northwest German coast, for instance, which dates from about 1620, is undoubtedly a link in the chain of ideas. And the king's attempt to draw closer the ties with Brandenburg through his marriage was clearly only one element in his plan to find a safe anchorage for Swedish interests on North German soil.

This is no place to discuss the various questions—some of them of the most complex kind—which present themselves in this connection. The acquisition of Pomerania—compared by Axel Oxenstierna to a "girdle round the Baltic"—was of essential importance in Gustav Adolf's plan for a final settlement. As ruler of these territories, Sweden would have a seat and a voice in the German Diet, and she would thus, as an Imperial "Estate," be able to participate directly in German affairs, to keep a watchful eye on her own political interests, and to make a stand for the cause of the Protestant world in general.

There is a quotation from Axel Oxenstierna which turns up now and again to the effect that the king fixed his ambition upon the creation of an "Empire of Scandinavia," which was to include Norway, Denmark up to the Great Belt, and the coastal lands of the Baltic. The quotation is not authentic. Yet it is true that the chancellor at first shrank from the immense commitments involved by intervention in Germany, and would have preferred to wage a purely defensive war with the Empire. His own words, moreover, show him to have been of opinion that there were tasks of sufficiently great importance awaiting the king's attention in the North. In 1636 he told the Råd: "I definitely advised the king not to venture with an army upon German soil. Had His Majesty taken my advice, he would have been *arbiter totius septentrionis* today." None the less, Oxenstierna was ready in 1636 to admit the king's superior foresight. "It is now certain," he continued, "that had His late Majesty not betaken himself to Germany with his army, the emperor would today have a fleet on the seas—for he had fourteen ships even then [in 1630]—and it would have been in his power, with no more than 2,000 soldiers, to take Copenhagen, and capture the king of Denmark himself. And if the emperor had once got hold of Stralsund the whole coast would have fallen to him, and here in Sweden we should never have enjoyed a moment's security." In such words—spoken soon after his return to Sweden—the great Swedish statesman strikingly summed up the political motives for Gustav Adolf's action in Germany. It remains to consider the question, which we have hitherto postponed, of those religious motives which also played their part in that great decision.

THE PROTESTANT CAUSE

THE PROTESTANT CAUSE

[1]

FROM the civil disturbances at the turn of the century emerged a Swedish kingdom which had attained religious unity in no ordinary degree. The strait doctrines of Lutheranism laid down in the resolution of the Assembly at Uppsala in 1593 soon effected a complete conquest of the country. It is a notable and apparently paradoxical circumstance that the final and decisive triumph coincided in time with a dynastic revolution, for submission to the princes of this world was a principle deeply rooted in the historic spirit of Lutheran theology. It was scarcely an accident that several of the leading Swedish churchmen of this period should have recoiled or hesitated at the prospect of a breach with an anointed and hereditary sovereign. Nor should we lose sight of the fact that Karl of Södermanland, who carried through the revolution, held theological opinions which were at least tinged with Calvinism, even if they were partially offset by the legitimist convictions to which we have already alluded. In a political point of view Calvinism was more liberal than Lutheranism, since it recognized the right of the subject in case of necessity to appeal to arms against a ruler who neglected his duty towards the church of Christ.

The pressure of events following logically upon one another had the effect of leaving contemporaries little time to ponder such theoretical differences. Sigismund was expelled from his kingdom. The decision implied a common responsibility for action taken. To ensure the survival of the work the nation must needs remain indissolubly united in common acceptance of what had happened. And so it was that Lutheran Sweden found herself committed to a point of view which, though it was not in any true sense Lutheran, tallied satisfactorily with her own vital interests. Upon questions of doctrine and ceremonial it had no influence whatever; but it gave a principle and a rule of action for Sweden's attitude to Europe and for her relations with foreign powers. The recognition of the right of resistance to a sovereign who failed in his duty was a condition of the existence of the new régime.

That régime offered no appearance of solidity so long as its adversaries refused it legal recognition. This was not a question merely of Sigismund's attitude. Behind Sigismund could be discerned a group of powers—the kernel of European Catholicism—who might only too probably be suspected of a design to make Sigismund's cause their own when opportunity should offer. The outcome of the struggle—half open, half secret—between the forces of Protestantism and those of the Counter-Reformation was bound to involve the fate of Sweden. No matter how often or how vigorously Sigismund might declare his resolve never to impugn the heretical creed of his hereditary dominions, the Swedes felt themselves to be in no position to take his word for it. For such a thing to be possible there must first be a stable equipoise between the two great religious parties, and that was discernible as yet only in the very distant future.

For long periods at a time King Karl was at odds with his clergy. The affair of Micronius, which has already been mentioned, was only one episode among many arising from this disagreeable tension. There was a sharp line of cleavage within the Protestant camp, and Karl was generally considered to stand on the wrong side of it. The Reformed Confession was by the contemporary Swedish church deemed a grievous heresy, if not an abomination. The young Oxenstiernas, who in the years about 1600 were studying at orthodox Lutheran universities in Germany, were there taught that Zwingli was an enthusiast whose violent death formed a fitting conclusion to a turbulent career. Superintendent Jonas Rothovius, the chancellor's tutor during boyhood, writes to him in 1620 in loud lamentation at the proceedings of the Calvinists in Bohemia, where, as he hears, they have done the Lutheran Church more harm in six months (i.e. during the brief reign of the Winter King) than the Catholics in half a century. Such was the strength, on occasion, of the feelings of hostility between the two Protestant confessions. As far as Sweden was concerned, however, the opposition between them was relegated to the background whenever it was really a question of shaping policy in accordance with the logic of a situation which grew ever tenser and more menacing as Protestantism girded up its loins for the battle with Rome.

As a layman theologizing from the throne, Karl IX was the cause of much heart-searching to his subjects; as spokesman of a policy clearly conceived in the broad interests of Protestantism, he met with no opposition. Nevertheless the paths he followed to this end led him mainly to the headquarters of Calvinism. Family connections, as we have seen, drew him in the same direction, and so did his sympathies and interests. The common foe of all Protestants was the house of Habsburg; and these West German States, with the Palatinate and Hesse at their head, felt keenly the pressure from Spain, whose possessions in the Netherlands and in Burgundy shut in this part of Germany on two sides. These States were the typical representatives of radical Protestantism and the party of action; that Protestantism whose fighting organization was created in 1608 by the founding of the Evangelical Union—a step to which the Catholics replied in the following year by the creation of the Catholic League. The Lutheran princes, in the main, stood outside the Union. The elector of Saxony, whose attitude may be considered typical of this Lutheran group, clung to a conservative idealization of the Empire, and took a certain pleasure in following in the wake of Imperial policy. Besides, in eastern Germany the lurking danger from the Turks meant more than in the west, where it had lost its hold on men's imaginations. Brandenburg, on the other hand, adhered in the fulness of time to the Union, and Johann Sigismund later went over to the Reformed faith (1613), though the political character of the electorate as we have traced it in connection with Gustav Adolf's marriage was little altered by the change. In this connection it will be remembered that the Hohenzollerns' dynastic interests in Prussia imported an additional complication into their relations with Sweden.

Karl IX's statesmanship shows one fundamental point of agreement with Gustav Adolf's: its vigilant anti-Catholic, or more accurately anti-Habsburg, tendency. It was Karl's deliberate endeavor to put his own dispute with Sigismund into its general European context. We know already that his trustiest political friends were mostly too distant to give him anything but moral support. With this end in view, he tried to draw closer to England and to the free Netherlands, from whom he hoped to obtain direct assistance. He cultivated relations too with the France of Henri IV; but here again they were hardly of an intimate nature. It was typical of Karl that he eagerly seized upon every symptom that seemed to point to a union of the Evangelical princes, and that his diplomacy was sometimes based upon assumptions in this regard which had no foundation in fact. A common front against the champions of the Papacy stood for him as the goal to be aimed at. He saw in such a policy the most practicable method of breaking down Sweden's isolation, and of eradicating the current notion that the Swedo-Polish struggle, so vast in its significance, was merely a local affair, devoid of relevance to the great Central European crisis which was so visibly coming to a head. He desired to identify Swedish policy with Protestant policy, as far as that was possible, and to that end he seemed to be willing to precipitate the course of events.

The results of his efforts were meagre. Yet the pulse of the age beats in his policy none the less, and the consciousness of acting in self-defense gave it a high degree of intensity. Lutheran Sweden found herself now in the forefront of the Protestant party of action—not by reason of her strength or reputation, but through her own inner tension, or as it were of her own momentum. Her enemies came gradually to learn the true spiritual affinities of this distant land on the fringes of Europe. Early in the 1620s a German Catholic pamphleteer was writing, "Sweden is dominated by the spirit of Calvin."

Among his own people Karl worked incessantly to inculcate a firm grasp of the necessity of erecting a barrier against the Papacy which its agents should find it impossible to surmount. His gift for propaganda found excellent scope in painting the proselytizing activities of the Catholics in the most lurid colors. Of the Inquisition he wrote on one occasion: "Man and woman, old and young, must dance towards the stake and the scaffold." And the war with Poland, though it found little favor with the common people, was in the king's eyes a war for the cause of true religion. The fact of its intimate connection with the central problem of the age thrust itself forcibly upon his attention, and more than once he lamented that even the clergy seemed incapable of appreciating this. Whether he was wholly convinced

GUSTAV ADOLF
Oil Painting by an Unknown Dutch Artist, about 1626

by his own arguments is perhaps an open question. But at least there can be no doubt that he felt that the ground would crumble beneath his feet, if Protestantism went down to disaster. Its cause was his cause. And his cause had become his country's.

[2]

To UNDERSTAND Gustav Adolf in his rôle of Protestant champion, we must have some knowledge of the standpoint from which he started out, and of the assumptions with which he identified himself from the beginning. The nature of his religious convictions has been discussed already; but before proceeding further we must say a word or two as to his views on ecclesiastical policy.

Gustav Adolf was always anxious to appear as a good son of the evangelical Lutheran Church. With his accession there was an end to all controversies over the articles of faith or the form of church service. In the matter of church government, too, he sought to avoid dissensions; thus he laid aside his plan for a general consistory when the clergy, led by the bishops, opposed it. His attitude to purely ecclesiastical questions may consequently seem somewhat lacking in subtlety, and over-submissive to authority; but in reality it displayed personal nuances of no small interest. These concerned, in the main, his relations with the other Protestant confession. Although, in contrast with Karl IX, he was plainly Lutheran in his basic convictions, he found room for points of view which were undoubtedly echoes of his father's theories. Thus we can discern an undefined leaning towards a conception of religious liberty which forbade him to apply restrictive regulations as stringently in the case of Calvinists as in the case of Catholics.

Abroad, there long remained a general disposition to attribute to Gustav Adolf semi-Calvinistic opinions after the pattern of Karl IX. One of the reasons for Johann Sigismund's liking for his future son-in-law was that he supposed him to be in this respect the true son of his father. The elector's own words put the matter beyond a doubt. Even as late as the German campaigns, the king's proceedings were closely scrutinized with a view to discovering his real opinions. When, after his arrival at Frankfurt, he caused a famous Lutheran divine to preach before him, and afterwards presented him with a gold chain, the fact was quickly noised abroad. "I write of this event," runs a description of the episode, "because hitherto there have been doubts whether he is a Calvinist or a Lutheran; but His Majesty is as good and pure an evangelical as any Christian who cleaves to the Augsburg Confession." The king's German court preacher, Johann Fabricius, found it necessary after his death to compose and print a "complete refutation" of the allegations of his leanings to Calvinism. The misconception had its real explanation in the fact that Gustav Adolf had taught men to see in him the spokesman of a broad Protestant policy of a sort that had hitherto found its advocates mainly in the Calvinist camp. And we may certainly add the fact, that all his proceedings were remarkably free from the narrow sectarianism which usually distinguished the lay representatives of contemporary Lutheranism.

During the negotiations about the Charter of 1611 the Råd and Estates had demanded the adoption of the Book of Concord[1] as a part of the body of recognized Lutheran doctrine. The Crown refused to assent to this request, which at bottom emanated from the clergy. And that was not all. The program of the Estates had likewise included the claim that, in general, adherents of other faiths should not be tolerated in Sweden. The Charter, in its final shape, considerably modified this rigidly exclusive application of the theory of a National Church, for it permitted private persons of other religions to carry on their lawful business in the country; "for no sovereign has power to direct or coerce a man's conscience." Even though the formulation of this principle was dictated by considerations of national advantage, it is none the less true that its frank polemic against the demands of the Estates must undoubtedly be taken as a defense of the personal standpoint of the young king. Nor should we forget that Johan Skytte stood at his side during the negotiations. A somewhat similar situation arose in 1617 when the Riksdag was discussing the Örebro Statute. Members of the Estates put forward the demand that not only Swedish papists, but all others who had allowed themselves to be perverted by heretical teaching

---

[1] The Lutheran Confession, published in Dresden, 1580.

should be considered as "severed members of the body politic," and that among those who were to fall under the penal provisions of the Statute the Calvinists should be included. Gustav Adolf took his stand on the Charter, and held himself at liberty to refuse the request of the Estates in this particular. It is therefore sufficiently clear that on occasion he was anxious to protect the adherents of the Reformed faith.

A remarkable and apparently reliable piece of information is to be found in the funeral sermon on the king preached by Johannes Botvidi. According to this account, Gustav Adolf had asked him "whether several religions could not be tolerated in the kingdom." He thereupon earnestly warned the king against any step of this nature, and enjoined him to beware "lest he kindle such disunion, strife, and enmity as might in time ruin and destroy both his country and the congregation of God." Before these arguments the king gave way, assuring him that "it shall never be so in my time." The preacher was concerned to point out the piety of the answer; posterity fastens rather on the searching question that had preceded it. It looks as if Gustav Adolf were taking soundings among the clergy, and abandoned the attempt in the face of such strong opposition.

Such incidents as the above are illustrative of one facet of Gustav Adolf's mind, but they have no other significance. Under his rule Sweden remained a State more unified in religion than before, if that were possible. His Charter had a definitive character in this respect, since it established without limitation or circumlocution the Augsburg Confession as the fundamental law of the State religion. Karl IX at his coronation had managed to avoid such an explicit avowal. When we remember that Sigismund was Catholic, Johan III catholicizing, and that under the first two Vasa kings the Lutheran idea had not yet struck root in Sweden as it was later to do—neither Gustav Vasa nor Erik XIV had pledged themselves, nor needed to pledge themselves, to any definite creed—then it may be said with some justice that Gustav Adolf was the first Lutheran king of Sweden. An inner unity which should be complete and full was now within reach. But that unity could not be considered secure, unless alien doctrines were excluded. Any alleviations of the law that Gustav

Adolf effected in this respect were therefore of very limited scope. Public worship for Calvinists he never permitted in Sweden, though undoubtedly his plans, as we have seen above, tended in that direction. In this matter he made no exception even for his own brother-in-law Johann Kasimir, or for Louis de Geer after he had settled in Sweden. And the ecclesiastical policy which Gustav Adolf at the close of his career attempted to carry out in the German lands he had conquered gave so decided a precedence to Lutheran interests, that on more than one occasion it was really directed against the Calvinists—or at least it was considered by them, with some justification, to have had that object.

Gustav Adolf's view of Catholicism was subject to some variation. In his last years it underwent a change in the direction of toleration in practice—a policy which had hitherto been quite alien to his attitude to the Roman Church. We shall recur to this question presently. Previously he had seen in Catholicism simply the mortal foe. The Rome of the Counter-Reformation comprised for him every conceivable abomination. Some sentences from his great speech to the Örebro Riksdag of 1617 may serve as witness. The speech is a violently phrased indictment and a resounding testimony to the irreconcilable bitterness of contemporary controversies. "This religion, if I may call it so, is not only in itself idolatry, the invention and fancy of men—clean contrary to the word of God in the Holy Scriptures wherein standeth written our way to salvation, but it embraces one principle which is especially damning: *haereticis non est servanda fides*—with heretics, as they call us, shall no man keep faith. And King Sigismund has made it clear enough in all his actions that he has well learnt to apply this popish maxim, as well against us as against others. . . . What can we expect of King Sigismund, who is not only wicked himself, but allows himself to be ruled by those Devil's minions, the Jesuits, who have been the instigators of the fearful tyrannies practised in Spain, France, and elsewhere? These Jesuits and their Inquisition have spared neither high nor low, man nor woman. In Spain, their burnings have been abominable. In the same country their assassins have not spared King Philip II's own son, Duke Carlos, for him they took off only because they suspected he was one with us in faith.[2] . . . The Holy Murder, as the papists call it, which by these same advisers of the king of Poland was planned at Paris in France,[3] and thereafter spread over most of that kingdom, teaches us what means of oppression these Jesuits and the kings who obey them employ against our religion."

His burning words strike us like some fiery blast from the furnace of the religious wars. And a little later in his speech Gustav Adolf recalled with indignation the great Armada's attack on England in 1588. But it was not only to the past that he turned his gaze. In this same speech he pointed out the dangers hourly threatening the Protestants of Poland, still at that date a numerous community. "In that country church after church is burnt down; the Protestants can assemble to hear a sermon only with the greatest danger, although by the law and custom of the land, and by the king's own promise, freedom of religion is recognized and permitted." As yet there is no word of the danger to Germany. It is the general, manifest danger of papal aggression that he is proclaiming. "Their confederation, which they call the Holy League, is in fact directed to this end, that through violent and treacherous means of every kind they may busy themselves to compel all those in whom the black darkness of popery has been dispersed, to turn again to the yoke and thraldom of Rome."

When the young king of Sweden spoke these words to his assembled Estates the outbreak of the Thirty Years' War lay barely a year ahead. Their strong polemical tinge can hardly escape observation; but it is a fair question whether they were not justified by events. A decade later, and the Catholic reaction had advanced to an undreamt-of strength in the very heart of Europe.

Similar utterances of Gustav Adolf on the subject af Catholicism occur with some frequency. In his unfinished *History*, for instance, he does not shrink from calling the pope the son of the Devil, and his legate Malaspina—well known for his part in events at the time of Sigismund's visit to Sweden in 1594—"Satan's

---

[2] Gustav Adolf thus shared the long-held, but quite inaccurate, belief that Don Carlos (d. 1568) harbored Protestant sympathies, and was murdered on that account.

[3] The Massacre of St. Bartholomew, 1572.

bellows." The first time Gustav Adolf saw the Catholic religion at close quarters was upon his journey to Germany in 1620, when for a ducat he bought the permission of a Dominican monk to witness mass in secret in the abbey church. Both Hand and Rusdorf mention this episode; the latter found the king stirred to the depths by the impiety and corrupt morals of the officiating priests. After the taking of Riga in the following year Gustav Adolf caused the members of the Jesuit College located there to be called before him. Among them he encountered the Norwegian Laurentius Nicolai—the famous "Kloster-Lasse"—who in King Johan's time had labored in Sweden in the Catholic cause.[4] The king is said to have burst into violent abuse—"You old limb of Satan!"—and to have asked him if he did not know that they who follow false doctrines in this life must expect punishment in the next; to which the aged monk replied with dignity that it was not his fellow Catholics but the Lutherans who must be prepared to render their account and receive their condemnation. Father Laurentius and his brethren were, however, allowed to leave the town under Swedish escort. The anecdote comes from Jesuit sources, but it bears the stamp of truth. On the other hand there is every reason to dismiss as malicious and fictitious a story whereby the king is supposed during his victorious Prussian campaign of 1626 to have laughingly contemplated his soldiers desecrating the Host in Frauenburg cathedral. The story stands alone and is in plain conflict with reliable first-hand sources.

That the battle with Rome and all she implied should have led to a sort of spiritual blockade was inevitable in the nature of events. The Örebro Statute of 1617, to which reference has been made more than once already, went very far in this direction. The product of a period to which King Sigismund's attempt to win adherents within Sweden gave a strong flavor of apprehension, this piece of legislation assumed an almost Draconian severity. It has been justly remarked that it was "Sweden's reply to the Counter-Reformation's forcible attempts at expansion." All

---

[4] As preacher in the old Franciscan monastery in Stockholm (now the Riddarholm Church), 1578-1580.

relations with Sigismund and the Swedish exiles were to be punished with death and confiscation of goods, if the accused were shown to have conspired against king and country, and otherwise with perpetual exile. Study at Catholic universities was forbidden on pain of banishment and confiscation, and connivance or other assistance by parents and guardians was to be put on the same footing as actual commission of the offense. To lapse into Roman Catholicism was to be likewise punishable by exile; all papists were enjoined on penalty of death to leave the country within three months. Those who persisted in remaining must be prepared upon discovery to answer a charge of high treason. This was *ad hoc* legislation, unmistakably designed to act preventively by terror and the threat of punishment. The limits of national policy and national religion were to be made to coincide. And the Örebro Statute was no provisional statute. On Axel Oxenstierna's suggestion, it was reenacted after Gustav Adolf's death.

The motives behind the Örebro Statute were mainly political. The celebrated religious trials which took place in Stockholm in 1624 are better called State Trials. The king and the chancellor personally took a part in the hearings, for the government at first scented a comprehensive conspiracy against the safety of the State. That the judicial proceedings had less of a religious than of a political character is sufficient explanation of the fact that the German Jesuit Heinrich Schacht, although proved to have attempted to spread Catholic propaganda in Sweden, escaped with deportation, as being a foreign subject. The sentence imposed singled out three victims, of whom two—Zacharias Anthelius, the burgomaster of Södertälje, and Göran Bähr, a chancery official—were crypto-Catholics. The case against them, apart from their apostasy, was that they had smuggled the Jesuit into the country in disguise; and the fact that the latter had already successfully scraped through his cross-examination did not improve their chances. In addition, Bähr was convicted of offenses against public morality. The third victim, Nicholas Campanius, rector of the college at Enköping, although he had been sincerely reconverted to Protestantism, was gravely compromised by his admission that during his long residence in Poland he had accepted help from King Sigismund. This unfortunate found not a few to intercede for him; but Gustav Adolf was adamant, and refused pardon.

It is indeed incontestable that punishment was meted out with the utmost rigor of the law. It is vain to attempt to whitewash the business to satisfy the susceptibilities of a later age. Gustav Adolf appears unashamedly as the merciless and implacable upholder of the doctrine of "State necessity" as he understood it—and his interpretation coincided pretty accurately with national feeling; but on the other hand the Catholic Church can certainly count nobler martyrs than the two pitiable creatures who, after long and successful dissimulation, fell victims at last to the false position in which they had placed themselves. A few others of those implicated, among them young Arnold Johan Messenius, son of the prisoner of Kajaneborg, received lighter sentences. It is perhaps worth noting that in the same year Catholic priests and members of Catholic religious orders were forbidden upon pain of death to remain in Denmark.

The Treaty of Stolbova in 1617, which gave Sweden the county of Kexholm and the district of Ingria, involved the incorporation of a considerable Finnish-speaking population of Greek Orthodox faith. The fusion of these districts with the rest of the kingdom in religious matters was the more urgent because in this instance the difference in faith went deeper than other divisions, and cut across racial and linguistic affinities. Measures were indeed taken to extend the frontiers of Lutheranism in these parts; but under Gustav Adolf they were always marked by obvious circumspection. The king was anxious for peace and concord with the Greek Church. He endeavored therefore to combat the opinion—deeply ingrained in the Swedish people—that the Russians should not be accounted Christians at all, and a disputation upon this theme was held in Uppsala University in 1620. In dealing with the Greek Catholics he was at pains to insist less upon points of difference than upon elements which in spite of schism were common to both. He was anxious to make good his contention that Protestants and Orthodox had, up to a point, common interests in face of the danger from Rome. Karl IX had been no stranger to such ideas; but in Gustav Adolf they took shape as a definite program. Tendencies such as these, though they are set against an obvious background of political interests, must nevertheless be recognized as having a distinctly ecumenical implication. A certain interplay of religious forces was already apparent. Within the old Christendom of the East forces were stirring which just at this time were aiming consciously at a reformation. One of the most decided partisans of this new outlook was Cyril Lukaris, patriarch of Constantinople from 1620, who was well versed in Baltic politics, and who became in course of time a warm supporter of the increasingly vigorous Protestant policy of Gustav Adolf.

[3]

How far Gustav Adolf is to be considered a "champion of the faith," and how far a "politician," is a question which in a strictly historical aspect misses the point. It was only natural that the safety and advantage of his country should shape his decision upon all occasions where it was a question of employing national means. Yet there was a firm inner core of religious motive within this demand for security. Like his father, but with more conscious purpose, Gustav Adolf strove to bring the interests of Sweden into harmony with the general interests of Protestantism. In one sense his policy was a policy of national interest, but at bottom it implied the consistent application of a philosophy of life to the problems of statesmanship. If this philosophy did not perhaps invariably act directly upon his policy, there was, nevertheless, always an indissoluble connection between the welfare of Sweden under the new dynasty, on the one hand, and the success or failure of the attempts to safeguard the Reformation throughout the world, on the other. As a modern Catholic historian testifies: "For Gustav Adolf there was an almost complete coincidence between his own interests and those of Protestantism." Such was his fundamental position; and naturally, with his ardent and sanguine temperament, he felt that his policy was Protestant through and through.

The king's effort to attain perfect unity between the objects of his own ambition and the doctrines of the Protestant Church was often hampered by a certain reluctance in his co-religionists to approve his ideas. While Gustav Adolf contended with the

greatest pertinacity that his attempt to reach a settlement with
Poland was a blow in the interests of the Protestant cause, since
it engaged one wing of the enemy, this way of looking at it was
generally thought to be of dubious validity. The Protestant powers
would have preferred Sweden to disentangle herself as soon as
possible from these eastern complications and put her forces at
their immediate disposal to whatever extent might be necessary.
Moreover, they could not forget that Sweden was hostile not only
to Catholic Poland, but also, as a rule, to Protestant Denmark.
However deeply rooted in the consciousness of the Scandinavian
peoples the historic antagonism between them, it was felt to be
unnatural and deplorable in view of the common faith which
linked them together. The position was admitted to be a paradoxical one. In a proclamation to the Norwegians during the
War of Kalmar, Gustav Adolf deeply lamented that he was forced
against his will to turn his arms "not against any idolatrous,
heathen, or barbarian king or country, nor even against the pope
of Rome and his supporters, but against a land and people that
are at one with us in Christian faith and doctrine; and thus to
give our detractors, and the enemies of our faith, cause to rejoice
at our civil strife."

Abroad, through his diplomacy, and at home, through his active
propaganda, Gustav Adolf preached incessantly the gospel of
Protestant unity; and in both respects there were times when his
preaching took on a note of urgency. He felt he was doing his
full share in the business of standing sentinel against the Catholics. Johan Skytte, who was sent out in 1617 to work for a "general
league against the hosts of popery," told the English ministers
that the king of Sweden, as practically the only defender of the
evangelical cause in North Europe, was forced to shoulder unreasonable burdens. We are already acquainted with the great
indictment of Jesuit-ridden Catholicism which he presented to
the Estates in the course of this same year. Other examples could
easily be given. It is not possible, nor is it necessary, to introduce
here even a brief account of Gustav Adolf's struggles during the
following years to bring the evangelical powers round to his view.
We have proof enough that he did not confine his efforts to other
countries. Only some almost inexplicable misconception could

have led Droysen, whose outlook was purely German, and was
quite uninfluenced by Rome, to state in all seriousness that not
until 1629 did Gustav Adolf "for the first time" explain to his
people the religious side of the great struggle, and the danger to
the Protestant faith which it involved. As far as the king's utterances are concerned, there are innumerable evidences to the contrary. Gustav Adolf was not guilty of the smallest neglect in this
matter. This extraordinary distortion of the facts—which still
appears occasionally even today—is refuted a hundredfold by his
own words. It is sufficient to look for proofs where they may be
had for the taking—i.e. in his numerous messages and speeches
to the Swedish Estates.

The orders convoking the Riksdag are in themselves a rich
source of material for this purpose; and an even richer are the
royal proclamations at the Riksdag meetings. But the best indication of the state of popular opinion which the Crown sought to
cultivate is to be found in the edicts appointing Days of Prayer
to be observed by the nation. These edicts were proclamations,
reaching everybody's ears. They gave currency to the views which
the government desired to foster in the minds of each one of its
subjects. It is assuredly no matter for surprise that they speak
in plain unvarnished language of the dangers which were clouding the religious horizon of the age. Thus in 1615 the nation is
warned in stirring tones of the intention of the Papacy and its
creatures to use every means to root out the true worship and
quench the light of the Gospel, "even though for the compassing
of that end they overthrow governments and destroy kingdoms."
It was no mere rhetorical flourish, when in the spring of 1623
a proclamation asserted that "a general persecution and an open
war of religion" had broken out in some countries—"particularly
in Germany, whereby whole principalities and lordships, which
in former time cast off the yoke of Babylon, are now once again
come under it." This was at the conclusion of the first act of the
Thirty Years' War, the main result of which had been to deliver
over Bohemia and the Palatinate to the Catholic reaction. The
proclamation, in moving words, reminded the nation of these
facts. "We learn also of places where the holy word of God has
now for many years been preached in purity, plainness, and

honesty, that popish idolatry is brought in there again, and the abomination of desolation set up in God's Temple, to the accompaniment of fearful harryings and destruction; whereby many cities are laid waste, many noble houses and families cut off, and the blood of the innocent and harmless poured out beyond description. . . . This persecution draws nearer and nearer to our neighbors, so that a more grievous affliction may lie before us, and many may suffer it who least think to do so, ourselves included, if God in His mercy do not protect us." The evidence seems to indicate that this passage was written by the king himself.

In the following year, 1624, the situation is depicted in equally gloomy colors. "Where but now the light of God's word was freely preached, are abominations and image-worship. Where once man was free to serve the Lord and keep His ceremonies, there is now persecution, oppression, and slavery. And, to be short with you, the papists are now so high in courage and in the hope of subverting all who truly call upon the name of God, that in their hearts they hold us and others of our faith to be already as it were swallowed up and consumed away." In this increasingly perilous situation the Swedish people had thus double reason to seek the compassion of the Most High, who, in the words of the writer, "may be as a wall of fire around us, and bring to naught the counsels of our enemies and them that hate us."

With lamentations and accusations of the ordinary sort these proclamations have little in common. They fulfil a definite purpose; they form an element in a deliberate policy based on unswerving fidelity to the faith.

It was in 1623 that Gustav Adolf put into shape his great plan for common action by all the enemies of the house of Habsburg, with his own campaigns against Sigismund as a principal element. A Swedish advance through Poland to the Silesian frontier was to put new heart into the oppressed Protestants of the hereditary dominions, force the emperor to withdraw his army from Germany, and ease the pressure on the evangelical party in the Empire. For this plan, the ultimate object of which was the restoration of that equilibrium between Catholics and Protestants which had existed before the war began, it was Gustav Adolf's hope to enlist in the first place the support of Holland. The "diversion" via Poland occupied a conspicuous place in the negotiations of the next few years, but it never became anything more than a mere suggestion by Sweden. Yet on the whole the idea offered extensive prospects; if it had been realized, it is possible that the Protestantism of the Imperial hereditary dominions, formerly so vigorous, but now doomed to perish, might after all have been saved. There could, however, be no question of Gustav Adolf's engaging Sweden's armies unsupported in so vast an enterprise.

His offer in 1624 to intervene directly in Germany through a landing on German soil had no better success in obtaining acceptance, for it soon appeared that his demands upon the support of the western powers exceeded what they were prepared to give, and in addition his insistence upon the supreme command for himself was not acceptable in all quarters. Christian IV of Denmark, less clear-sighted and less exacting, took his place in the battle, upon such terms as could be agreed on without much delay. Gustav Adolf now turned his attention to the acquisition of the Prussian coastline, and in the summer campaign of 1626 this object was achieved. He continued to cling to his diversion plan, but he was not able to break down the opposition to it. And the posture of affairs in Germany soon altered so rapidly that every attempt to remove the seat of hostilities to another theater of war and another "front" became obviously pointless.

It is abundantly clear that Gustav Adolf had no faith in a favorable outcome of the war, thus reopened by Christian's intervention, and now definitely centered in North Germany. A plain expression of his views about it is to be found in the Proclamation of a Day of Prayer promulgated in May 1626—a document which bears the unmistakable hallmark of the king's religious policy. Persecutions against the people of God are now raging all over the world. Humanly speaking there is little hope of the "resurrection" of the oppressed. The papists might indeed seem to have reason enough for mutual distrust, but as against the Protestants they are kept together by one common purpose. "Thus their power is in itself great, but it waxes and increases the more by the ruin of our friends. On the other hand, if we consider ourselves, and those who are at one with us in religion, or for other

reasons hold the pope in abhorrence, we discern neither earnest-
ness, zeal, nor patience to fight in our defense, still less that unity
and concord in resistance which our foes display in attack, apart
too from all the other burdens and troubles with which God at
this time has seen fit to afflict his congregation." He speaks here
in the name of the Protestant world; and in a Proclamation for
a Day of National Intercession, dating from the following year,
the passage is repeated unchanged. It provides an authoritative
summary of the king's view of the condition of Europe, and
shows it to have been a view colored by disillusionment and deep
disquietude for the future of the "evangelical cause."

"The evangelical cause" is a concept which appears again and
again in the political negotiation of the time. It implies, without
more precise definition, the obvious measure of common interest
and common need as between Protestant states when face to face
with the other great religious faction. "The common cause"
(*causa communis*) is another name for the same idea. Gustav
Adolf employed these and similar expressions more often than
most of his contemporaries. He applied them in all good faith
to his own aspirations and his own aims. This came the more
easily to him because of his uncompromising enmity to Rome
and his consequent need to find a practical link between Swedish
policy and the general interests of Protestantism. If the Protestant
cause, as the years went by, came ever more frequently to be
termed "the cause of the oppressed and needy," Gustav Adolf, as
we have seen, was well aware of the reasons that had produced
this unhappy alteration. He was anxious, too, that the Lutheran
people of Sweden should not for one moment be lulled into a
false sense of security. At Christmas 1625 an order went forth
that on all Sundays and festivals a special form of Intercession
for all sufferers for the faith throughout the world was to be used
in all Swedish churches. This service was also introduced into
the army prayer books. "Look graciously, O Heavenly Father," it
ran, "upon those of our religion who are sore beset by papists, and
persecuted by them in life or safety. Grant them Thy fatherly
help, that they may be delivered from such affliction." Two years
afterwards, that is, towards the end of 1627, when all northern
Europe resounded with the triumph of the Imperialists, he pub-

lished a royal patent inviting the oppressed of all countries to seek in Sweden a harbor of refuge from the storm.

As events followed hard on one another, they gave irrefutable confirmation to the king's idea of the dangerous situation of evangelical Christendom. The prescience of his judgment seemed borne out by the logic of the situation, as it gradually revealed itself. That danger was approaching, that it was close at hand— that was precisely what he had always told them. And it drew nearer and nearer, sweeping new regions into its scope, closer and ever closer to the frontiers of the country. "I today, thou tomorrow," as Gustav Adolf with an undertone of deep serious- ness remarked in a letter of 1621 to Duke Adolf Friedrich of Mecklenburg. The allusion was to Friedrich of the Palatinate, whose unhappy fate many of the German Lutherans viewed with some indifference. In due time the duke of Mecklenburg shared his fate and his exile. At last the triumph of the emperor assumed the form of a real revolution. All Germany to the shores of the North Sea and the Baltic seemed delivered into his hand. "As one wave follows another, so the Catholic League batters at our gates."

It is unnecessary to recapitulate the well known events that marked Sweden's gradual intervention in the war. That fear of the growth of Imperial power in the Baltic played an enormous part in the decision is as undeniable as anything can well be; but that there was consequently implied any weakening or abandon- ment of the religious struggle as a motive for action, and as a real- ity of politics, can only be contended by those who are the victims of preconceived ideas. It was no accident that Gustav Adolf in a proposition to the Estates in 1627 should have spoken of "the Christian Church in the Baltic," or that he should have loved to speak of "the papists" in this connection. To contend that the well attested feeling which drove the nation into permanent hos- tility to the Roman Church was now subordinated to a purely secondary factor in a situation which the lessening of the distance between the two sides had suddenly exacerbated is to put a wholly false interpretation upon the history of the preceding decade. The critical observer will not fail to note, that before Gustav Adolf took the step which plunged him into the German war—and it was the greatest and most hazardous step he ever took—he was able to reckon, as he had not usually been able to do in previous years, upon an acquiescence by the Estates in the validity of the principle at stake.

In 1637, in the course of a debate in the Råd, we find Axel Oxenstierna declaring that the defense of religion was not the primary reason for the king's intervention in Germany. It is important to notice how the chancellor himself develops this remark in the sequel. The main reason, he says, was in fact that Sweden and her Protestant friends might rest secure and undisturbed in politics and church; it was a question not so much of religion as of *status publicus*, in which religion was itself included. Oxenstierna's contention is thus not that political reasons were predominant, independently of religious motives, but that the latter were bound up in the former, in other words that both motives operated in inextricable combination. Such a line of thought was entirely natural in that age. What the chancellor was concerned to deny was the idea that religion was fought for as an end in itself, divorced from the welfare of the State and the interests of the country. The battle for the faith is indeed fought out with the weapons of the spirit, but the State is none the less bound to safeguard religion and protect it against threats and violence from within and without.

Gustav Adolf was a statesman of this way of thinking. To expect anything else of him would be to apply utopian standards to his work as the champion of Protestantism. With all his hardy enterprise he was still obliged to keep his aspirations within the limits of the attainable. His responsibilities to his country compelled him to it, however much his love of action and his imagination might drive him to extract the utmost from his opportunities. The program for a settlement with the emperor, which was kept ready from the autumn of 1626 onwards, might seem bold enough in view of the actual posture of affairs, but it was at least untainted by visionary extravagances. Gustav Adolf fixed his attention in the first place upon the restoration of the *status quo* in those parts of North Germany where it had been so violently disturbed —Upper and Lower Saxony—and in particular in the Baltic coastal region. When it was a question of Sweden's immediate objective, the problem of the Palatinate had to take second place.

It was taken up only in connection with more extensive, but less definite, combinations, in which England's attitude always played an important part. To that extent, therefore, the issue was decided by purely Swedish interests.

And yet the Gustav Adolf who went over to Germany in 1630 will always seem more than a mere politician weighing risks before undertaking a gamble, and calculating chances in the moment of crisis. Axel Oxenstierna perceived the deeper, more inaccessible complexities of his character, when in a famous passage he spoke of the *impetus ingenii* which drove the king to action, and of the *dispositio divina* which he obeyed on such occasions. Gustav Adolf and his chancellor had at first had differences as to the wisest procedure to be adopted against the emperor, for Oxenstierna would rather have seen a defensive war in Germany based on Stralsund, which in 1628, under circumstances which have become historic, had concluded an alliance with Sweden. Gustav Adolf, however, went on his way, unfettered by doubts or difficulties, as though discerning from afar the course he was to follow. His parting words to the Estates recall a scene without parallel in Swedish history. In the memorial sermon on the king which he preached in Åbo cathedral, Bishop Isaac Rothovius tells of the profound impression which his "pathetic oration and moving speech" made upon those who heard it. "There was not one that could refrain from tears. He spake also of all that has come to pass since that day, as with the lips of a prophet. Who shall not weep upon these things?"

[4]

AT THE moment when Gustav Adolf, with his people behind him, decided upon the invasion of Germany, Protestantism was threatened in the land of Martin Luther by dangers the magnitude of which it is not easy to grasp. Politically it was crippled, morally it was to a large extent broken. Its ability and its will to resist seemed alike extinguished for ever.

The solution upon which all who counted for anything on the Protestant side were now tacitly agreed, was to avoid making bad worse by giving cause for fresh disorders, and to save what could still be saved. "Necessity knows no law." It was possible that in the long run something might be achieved by adaptation to changed conditions, no matter how onerous those conditions might be. After the peace with Denmark in the spring of 1629, the problem of securing tranquillity for the German States seemed to turn on whether it was possible to put a stop to the abuses and extortions of the soldiery, which continued even though the tumult of war had now died away. The prospects of a solution to that problem appeared to be reasonably bright. The party of the victors showed signs of cracking. The arrogant tyranny of Wallenstein's Imperial soldiery had made it ill-liked by Maximilian of Bavaria and the other Catholic princes of the League. The cry for peace was a strong cry—a cry that bound old antagonists together.

Yet everyone knew the price at which such internal peace must be bought. The Imperial Edict of Restitution of March 1629 had made that clear. The effect at which the Edict aimed has been compared by a trustworthy Catholic historian to an earthquake shaking all Germany. Its application would have involved a reversal of the entire course of development in favor of Protestantism which had taken place during the last seventy-five years, based as it had been on the great religious peace of 1555; though admittedly that peace had from the moment of its conclusion proved an ambiguous arrangement, and had been constantly disputed.

Great territories in different parts of the Empire, which since that date had fallen piece by piece under the sway of the Reformation, were by the Edict of Restitution to have been brought back to Catholic control and the Roman faith by a mass execution: two great archbishoprics (Magdeburg and Bremen), twelve bishoprics, more than five hundred abbacies, monasteries, and churches. The dynastic power of the Imperial house, cloaked under the authority of titular bishops, would have been planted firmly in the furthest north of Germany. The Calvinists would, once and for all, have been put outside the scope of the religious peace, and left as "schismatics" to protect themselves as best they might. The adherents of the Augsburg Confession were indeed to be treated as contracting parties; but they were made to feel also that their whole position in the Empire was endangered. Even the elector of Saxony, that loyal trimmer, who had hitherto kept himself well on the lee side of the emperor, and had salvaged some planks for his own vessel from the Bohemian shipwreck, was at last beginning to harbor doubts. Almost every princely house, and virtually every town on the Protestant side was sensibly affected by this revolutionary ordinance. It had, indeed, been promulgated without the direct cooperation of the Papacy—a fact which did not fail to produce friction between the Rome of Urban VIII and the Vienna of Ferdinand II; but since it was laid down in the Edict that possession of one of the reclaimed territories involved the right to determine the religion which was to prevail in it, the shifting of the balance of power became from a religious point of view a question of life and death for a large section of the German Protestant community.

It was not long before the execution of the Edict was set in motion. An army of soldiers and priests stood ready to make it a reality. And on the Protestant side, at first, the bonds of union snapped asunder. Each one sought to protect himself and to avoid the hardest knocks.

"In Germany the whole country is oppressed and enslaved." The words come from the king's proposition communicated to the Swedish Estates in the summer of 1629, and in the circumstances they can hardly be said to be an exaggeration. "Our ill-wishers and enemies, lay and spiritual, flourish; while our friends, and all who are escaped from the Romish bondage, are fallen into peril and misery. . . . Whoso has a heart honest in devotion to God, religion, and liberty, his eyes must weep, his heart bleed, to hear of such sorrow and misery among his friends and those of his faith; and he must be forced to consider and conclude what fate awaits him in such a case. There is now no kingdom in Europe more free than is the land of Sweden. But now disaster draws nearer and nearer to us, and day by day the evil increases."

Gustav Adolf's plan to make his appearance on German soil this year could not be carried out. Wallenstein, resolved at any price to prevent his dreaded interference, threw a whole army corps against him in Prussia in order to immobilize him there. The effect of this was partly to postpone the expedition to the following year, partly to embitter the struggle, and so provide the king with fresh arguments for intervention. Yet even when he crossed to Pomerania in June 1630 he had not quite abandoned the hope of a peaceful solution. He was, however, resolved not to deviate from his program in order to obtain such a settlement. He would carry on negotiations sword in hand. This peace program, settled in its main outlines some years before, always included the demand for a "restoration" of conditions in North Germany to the position before the last great upheavals. During the discussions in the Råd which preceded the king's departure from his country, the question was raised as to whether the peace program ought not to be extended also to cover upper Germany. Gustav Adolf, however, allowed the matter to drop, with the explanation that what was now impossible might become possible at a later date. "We must help those who are still capable of help."

He landed with his army on the soil of Germany without having the support of a single ally; indeed, he was received with obvious chagrin by the disheartened spokesmen of the German Protestant party. Engrossed in their efforts to restore the *Reichsfriede* through collaboration with the Catholic Estates, and to ease their burdens through obtaining Wallenstein's dismissal from the supreme command—in which they were surprisingly successful, despite the Swedish attack—the majority received Gustav Adolf at first as an unwelcome guest, from whose visit only new misfortunes were to be expected. Many of them imagined that the meddling Swedes could be headed off, if an emergency settlement could be reached upon the controversy which had arisen as the result of the Swedish alliance with Stralsund. Gustav Adolf had his own methods of dispelling misapprehensions and hesitations of this sort. "Neutrality!—what sort of talk is that? For or against—there is no middle term!"

From out the heart of the Protestant masses a welcome of another sort rose to greet him. All the discontented in the Empire, wrote Wallenstein significantly in the summer of 1629, waited for the king of Sweden as the Jews awaited their Messiah. Several years before his armed intervention Gustav Adolf's name had been upon the lips of many, as a promise of hope in the evil day. Dark prophecies in the Scriptures seemed to grow luminous when applied to him as the new, the last, the ultimately victorious defender of the true faith. Was it not written that a saviour should arise in the North, a conquering warrior who should break the powers of darkness? Mystical ideas of this sort about Gustav Adolf early gained a footing here and there in Germany. They are to be discerned already at the time of the unrest of 1627; and the relief of Stralsund, whose fight against palpable odds appeared to the average Protestant as a fight for the Light, gave them a rapidly increasing currency. The Swedish king, therefore, with his well known genius for success, became for ever-widening circles the man of destiny, the chosen hero, the "Lion of the North." Broadsheets spread the belief far and wide. Men waited for the coming of the great ruler of the peoples. Portents in the heavens seemed to indicate his speedy advent. In the hour of his victory this sentiment irradiated him like a great aureole, enhancing the splendor of his personality. What posterity, rightly or wrongly, has called "the Gustav Adolf legend" here takes its origin. It traces its source to his contemporaries themselves; it is no mere distortion of later historians.

Whatever judgment may be passed on Gustav Adolf's motives in intervening in the Thirty Years' War, it may at least be considered established that he counted in all sincerity on being able to work for the good of Protestantism. The larger the scope of such work, the better. Thrown back upon his own resources, and consequently compelled to devote attention in the first place to what appeared to be Swedish interests, he dealt in his first peace program only with North Germany. It is easy to perceive that such a limitation, dictated by practical considerations, must to a certain extent suppress the religious aspect of the struggle. It was a difficult matter to emphasize that aspect as strongly as might have been wished, when simultaneously Protestants in other parts of the Empire seemed to be left in the lurch. The king, however, as we have seen, had from the beginning kept in view an extension of his aims, if his campaign should be successful and his diplomacy could assume wider scope; projects at present out of the question might become realities in time. And in the fulness of time that was precisely what happened.

For months before the great turning-point in the war, he had had his eye on the goal. "A great door is opening before us," he wrote in January 1631 to the Count Palatine Johann Kasimir, "so that we may go forward in our Christian plans and raise up many of those Protestants who are now in bondage." He was thinking here of Magdeburg, the proudest bulwark of Lutheranism, the beleaguered mistress of the Elbe. We know the sequel—a tragedy upon an appalling scale. Magdeburg crashed into smoking ruins before the allied Swedish army succeeded in forcing the obstacles and coming to its relief; and the grand plan, hitherto a "fundamental" for Gustav Adolf's strategy, fell with it to the ground. But the victory of Breitenfeld in September 1631 was, all the more clearly for what had gone before, a turning-point. Contemporary Europe was not again to see so decisive a day.

The vanquished general of the League, hitherto considered invincible, had stood out above all others as the executor of the Edict of Restitution. So complete was his defeat, that it set a barrier against re-catholicization which held firm forever afterwards. "In a single battle the situation was reversed," admits the latest and most authoritative historian of the Papacy. "The Catholic restoration, which had girded itself to the task of a comprehensive recovery of northern, central, and southern Germany, saw itself once and for all stopped in its course, and stricken with a mortal wound." This is no more than the sober truth.

It is only natural that Rome has never been able to forgive Gustav Adolf for it. Hence her polemics against him, hence her desire to attack openly, or under various disguises, his actions and his motives. But, whether it is deplored as a crowning disaster or hailed as a crowning mercy, his work lives by its results. In spite of all subsequent changes, it proved impossible to put the clock back. The last chance for that had gone by.

In the autumn of 1631, as he was marching triumphantly south from Breitenfeld, Gustav Adolf came for the second time to Erfurt, where once eleven years before he had observed Catholicism at close quarters as he toured Germany in search of a bride. The town was, as it is today, predominantly Lutheran. Here he addressed the town council and representatives of the burghers, together with his assembled staff, upon the demands which the evangelical community was making upon all of them, and particularly upon himself. He took the well-worn but always apt image of a ship's crew striving manfully in tempestuous seas.

"Not otherwise should we," he continued, "one and all gladly throw ourselves into the task, that the ship of religion and freedom, hard driven though she be, may be delivered and brought in safety to the haven of her desire. But the call of Heaven bids me save not only myself but my kindred by blood and faith in the common cause, and commands me, rather than abandon them, to set all things temporal at hazard, even to my body and my life." This was carefully calculated propaganda. But it was no ordinary propaganda. It made its great popular appeal because it struck the note of personal sacrifice.

[5]

WAS it for freedom of conscience that Gustav Adolf was fighting?

It is a question which has been answered negatively or with hesitation, even by those who in other respects give him a high place in history. The true answer seems to be that in the course of his struggle he attained at last a standpoint which may be said without misinterpretation to have been that of freedom of conscience.

When with the assent of his people he took up arms in an effort to stem the tide of events—for that was his real aim— he knew himself to be acting in his own defense. Purely political arguments contributed much to that decision; yet the protection of the evangelical faith was an integral part of his conception. Tolerance for such as differed from him—at any rate as far as Roman Catholicism was concerned—had never been part of his policy. By inheritance and from his own experience he felt himself to be its avowed foe and chief antagonist. Yet at the climax of his career his behavior presents a very different aspect.

The fact that he had now a Catholic power as his ally, in the shape of Richelieu's France, helped to cause this change. By the Treaty of Bärwalde he had engaged himself not to molest German Catholics in the exercise of their faith. The question seemed hardly at that time (January 1631) of burning importance. Nevertheless it is clear from the fact that Gustav Adolf had already decided to stand as a candidate for the electoral crown of Poland after the death of Sigismund (which it was expected could not be long delayed) that he had already made his choice and resolved on his attitude, irrespective of the doubtful chances of the German war. It was natural, no doubt, that he should look for support first to the relatively numerous Polish Dissidents; but the whole idea of his candidature, whether really seriously intended or no, must be taken as a recognition of the fact that he saw no reason why Protestants should not live peaceably side by side with the Catholics who formed the great majority of the inhabitants of Poland. To destroy Catholicism root and branch was in itself a scheme too foolhardy to win acceptance from such a political realist. From this point of view, therefore, he could with a clear conscience declare, to those Catholic powers who were enemies of the Habsburgs, that he was not waging a religious war. To charge him with self-contradiction in this matter is to betray an imperfect understanding of his true purpose.

The nearer Gustav Adolf drew to Catholic Germany in its own home, the more bound he was to accept consequences which were logically inevitable. In Würzburg and Mainz the standards of the Örebro Statute were scarcely applicable. Was then the recognition of the principle of toleration, to which he so often committed himself towards the close of his life, forced upon him by circumstances? If by "forced" we mean that he felt it to be cramping or hindering him, then the answer is No. Everything tends to show that it represented his sincere conviction, that it was part of a conscious philosophy. He felt convinced that it was the only policy for a statesman who aimed not only at destructive but at constructive action. For all his violent opposition to Rome in his earlier years, he had never been a religious fanatic. His moderate attitude towards Calvinism, and his view of the Greek Church, had already placed him among those who were able to rise above the narrow spirit of their age. And apart from all religious sympathies and antipathies, there was a dynamic element fundamental to his character which drove him in the same direction. When he considered that he had staked his honor he was not the man to be content with half-measures. The discipline he demanded from his soldiers, for instance, did not lose its validity because the people it protected were not in the habit of alluding to the pope as Antichrist. And finally—how was he to accomplish his work, the scope of which had so suddenly expanded, if he did not concern himself to establish a lasting peace between the religions of the Holy Roman Empire?

Thus in the end he threw away all reservations even in regard to Catholicism, and in language and action took a humane tolerance for his watchword. He did so the more openly in proportion as he felt himself increasingly independent of Richelieu. To the uses and customs of pious Catholics he extended secure protection as long as military necessities permitted. He gave shelter to priests and monks. The pastors and servants of Catholic communities were allowed to retain their offices, though occasionally limits were set to their freedom of action. In view of the experiences of the preceding years of warfare such treatment was unexpected. "We have suffered no interference in the exercise of our religion," avowed the Jesuits of Mainz in a later petition to the chancellor. In Munich the king was even to be seen in conversation with fathers of Loyola's Order. His behavior made a strong impression, for he had been preceded by rumors of his design to exterminate the faithful by fire and sword. The Capuchins, in particular, seem to have preserved a kindly remembrance of the heretical conqueror. A Bavarian monk on one occasion frankly exhorted him to turn Catholic, and according to the monastic annals he did not seem to take it amiss. What a contrast to the scene in Riga, eleven years before!

Henceforward he gave forcible and outspoken utterance to the basic principle of toleration: to do no wrong and inflict no persecution on any man for the sake of his creed. Thus after his entry into Augsburg he personally assured the Catholic members of the town council of his protection, "since *dominium conscientiarum* belongs to God alone, and each man must answer to Him for his faith." And in Augsburg his court preacher Fabricius, in words strongly reminiscent of the king's, proclaimed the value of religious freedom, and its necessity in a large community. "It is not reasonable nor Christian," he said in his sermon on April 14, 1632, "to massacre, kill, or exterminate false believers only for the sake of their false faith and doctrine, as the murderous Jesuit bloodsuckers contend. For such as will not freely turn to the true faith may be left in peace, and should not by force be compelled thereto, since God demands willing worship, and since every man must render account to the Lord for the manner and substance of his belief." This was in fact a declaration of policy on the king's behalf. Indeed, Gustav Adolf's words, and they were widely reported, breathed a spirit of tolerance from which every sting of controversy had been removed. He refused to hate those pious souls "who sought to serve the Lord according to their understanding and after the fashion of their fathers."

Even the zealots in his own camp learned to know in him the guardian of religious liberty, and—not less—the champion of the rights of the State. When he was earnestly entreated to introduce the Book of Concord into the see of Magdeburg as a pattern for priests to emulate, he declined, explaining that he was not minded to take his examples from the papists, who forced men to their religion. "Consciences would only be oppressed thereby." In many parts of the Protestant world the Swedish victories had produced a violent movement of hostility to Rome, which was reflected in a shoal of pamphlets. It was now or never, they urged; this soul-destroying popery must be beaten to its knees, and the Holy Roman Empire delivered from its yoke. It is apparent from this contemporary literature that the demand for general liberty of religion already counted a growing number of adherents, to the alarm and indignation of a hot-headed and vocal section of extremists within the Lutheran Church. Representatives of this section made no secret of their opinion that both Catholics and Calvinists must be bound "on pain of fine or banishment" to attend services in the true faith. Such demands stood, of course, in irreconcilable antagonism to the whole trend of Gustav Adolf's policy as it appears from his words and actions at this time.

On the other hand it is by no means impossible that he was prepared to encourage a dissolution of the bonds that bound the German Catholics to the Holy See. This idea appears *inter alia* in a pamphlet published before his death, with the object of crystallizing the demands of the Protestant nobility of the Empire. Its author was Filip Reinhard von Solms—a man who certainly stood high in the king's confidence. For Solms, the goal to be aimed at was the realization of a religious peace between

the Protestant and Catholic States of the Empire based on complete mutual toleration, but also upon the condition (certainly a
very radical one) that German Catholicism should organize
itself as a national church independent of Rome, while retaining
its doctrines in other respects, and also its forms of service. It is
worthy of note that in Gustav Adolf's plans for the reorganization
of southwestern Germany to bring it into closer connection with
Sweden, a leading position was reserved for Solms.

In contrast to many of his contemporaries, the king saw in an
arrangement which permitted adherents of the various confessions to live in peace with one another a really practical solution of
Germany's religious problem. He rejected the sovereign's right
to determine the beliefs of his subjects, but at the same time he
recognized—in the main, at all events—the existing frontiers between the two confessions. He was not prepared to give Catholicism another opportunity in regions where it had already relaxed
its grip. In so far as he could weaken its external power through
alienating the ecclesiastical lands, which he held by right of conquest, to secular lords and corporations, he availed himself of
the opportunity; in particular he sought to win over the cities to
his cause by means of such gifts. To the Lutheran faith, on the
other hand, he did give preference in so far as he strove to endow
it with fresh vitality in regions where it seemed to be declining,
and in general to secure the most favorable conditions for its
development.

Most significant in this respect was the constructive work which
was carried out under Swedish guidance in the sees of Magdeburg
and Halberstadt. These purely Protestant districts had already
been pounded by the breakers of the Edict of Restitution, and
their whole system of church government needed to be rebuilt
from its foundations. The task was entrusted to Johannes Botvidi,
in his capacity as senior army chaplain. The effects of this reform
have extended to our own day; apart from some alterations, the
ecclesiastical constitution which was then set up was still in force
in 1932. The form of service which was introduced at the same
time was in use until the third decade of the nineteenth century,
when the Prussian government replaced it by a new one; this in

its turn was part of that effort towards a real union between
North German Calvinists and Lutherans which had been stimulated by the Jubilee of the Reformation.

In some of the other areas which were by this time controlled
by Sweden the Lutheran faith had remained in the background,
struggling with the extremely difficult conditions which subjec-
tion to Catholicism involved. Here Gustav Adolf made it his
business to shape an organization which might support its
growth in the future. To this end Lutheran consistories were
established in Würzburg and Mainz. The educational system, in
particular, received his consideration. By all these measures the
king designed to lay the foundations of an order which should
subsist in years to come. To the three spiritual electors, the
archbishops of Mainz, Köln, and Trier, he sent a demand, while
he was still on the march in their direction, that they should
permit the Augsburg Confession in their territories. They seem
to have met this demand with frigid silence. And when, some
years after the death of the king, the Swedes were driven from
Mainz and Würzburg, the whole structure fell to the ground.

How Gustav Adolf intended to regulate the relations between
the three confessions in practice, appears from one of the very
last of his letters to Oxenstierna—an instruction despatched at
the end of October 1632. In the conquered lands in South Germany, Catholic, as well as Calvinist, the chancellor was to work to
maintain, with the help of God, the Christian religion according
to the *Augustana*. Those places in the Palatinate where Lutheran
congregations were to be found were therefore to be provided
with pastors. In Catholic regions where there were Lutheran
congregations, one or two churches, according to need, were
to be reserved and handed over to them. To these provisions the
king added a reminder to proceed cautiously and not to infringe
any man's freedom of conscience or his right to exercise his
religion: "Leaving others undisturbed in their conscience and
their service, wherever they are established already."

It is plain, then, that Gustav Adolf, even while he sought to
obtain advantages for his own faith, was becoming increasingly
persuaded that his mission was to act as a peacemaker.

[6]

MUCH has been written of Gustav Adolf's plans and purpose in Germany, and in dealing with this topic there have been writers who have fallen into the methodological error of confounding the earlier with the later phases of his ambition. Such a method of treatment presents an agreeable appearance of order to the eye, which is thus apparently able to view the scene as a whole. In reality, it is very largely true of Gustav Adolf's German policy that only an investigation which draws a distinction between evidence from different periods and judges it soberly upon its merits can provide an acceptable answer to the problem. The victory of Breitenfeld in September 1631 changed the whole aspect of affairs, and Gustav Adolf's attitude before that battle differed so essentially from his attitude after it, that even those who have come to see in him a far-sighted and profound statesman must reckon with a strong tide of new motives flowing thereafter through his policy.

With regard to the objects which the king had in view in respect of Sweden's interests in the Baltic region, it appears clear that they were designed to form part of a plan to assist German Protestantism. He demanded a return to the condition of affairs before the war, with such guarantees for the observance of the agreement as might be provided by a Swedish foothold in North Germany. So that if the question is put as to how Gustav Adolf envisaged his relations with Protestantism in the Empire, that program must serve as answer for the earlier and longer half of the war. The collaboration which he sought to bring about in one form or another was designed as a war measure, to last as long as the war lasted, and to fulfil the pressing need for union which the war imposed upon all. To attempt to read more than that into some of his remarks is to fall into a misapprehension; conditions on the coast cannot be applied by extension to Germany as a whole. All of which is surely no matter for surprise.

It is only some little time after Breitenfeld—not immediately —that there comes an alteration. The king directs his efforts to a more permanent organization, which is to be valid even when the war is over. He does so even while his diplomacy continues to work upon the old lines, and the alliance policy which had hitherto prevailed is broken off just when it is being fully developed, to take on bit by bit a new form. The war constitution gives way to a new arrangement, which, though it is still in the preliminary stages, is conceived as permanent. Gustav Adolf's design is so to organize cooperation between himself and the evangelical Estates that it may continue in time of peace. Naturally he thought of himself as the leading power in such a league—one might almost say as the main support of the *corpus evangelicorum*, and though he did indeed toy with other schemes and other solutions, he hardly ever gave them serious consideration. From start to finish Gustav Adolf was invariably anxious to keep the *directorium* in his own hands. Sweden was to enter the league in her new rôle of an "Estate" of the Holy Roman Empire, in virtue of her possessions along the north coast, to which she could lay claim as compensation for her intervention and as a pledge for her security. All who desired the welfare of the common cause were to be admitted as members of the league; if electoral Saxony, whom Gustav Adolf never more than half trusted, held aloof, it was probably neither a surprise nor a disappointment for him. The king apparently counted in the main upon those territories from which he had received pledges of fidelity either by reason of his right of conquest or in return for his powerful protection, and in particular upon the great Imperial cities of southwest Germany which he had favored in a variety of ways, and also upon the *reichsunmittelbar*[5] Protestant Imperial knights. The skeleton of the union, as it gradually took shape in his mind, was undoubtedly to have been the group of powers which after his death formed, under Axel Oxenstierna's leadership, the League of Heilbronn.

The evangelical union at which Gustav Adolf was aiming was to exist within the framework of the Empire. There is, however, good reason to question whether in the long run any such arrangement could have continued. And in fact we find that, in his last instructions to his chancellor, Gustav Adolf did not hesitate for a moment to interfere with the most venerable forms of the Imperial constitution. He considered that constitution to be "null and void"—a heresy which had not escaped notice, and had called

[5] i.e. Holding directly of the emperor and not by subinfeudation.

forth misgivings in more than one partisan of the traditional—
and rather arbitrarily interpreted—"liberties" of the Estates. And
although by his own account he intended to respect the old constitution of the Empire, and had no desire to introduce "new
laws," he made no secret, towards the end of his life, of his intention to provide the proposed evangelical union, in the interests
of public order, with its own representative institutions and its
own supreme court.

Was then his ultimate aim the crown of a Protestant Empire?

Although this question was debated with lively interest by
friend and foe alike, it is not easy to reach any tangible conclusion as to the king's own thoughts upon it. A consideration of
the habitual character of his policy would at first prompt the
supposition that the shadow of power, the empty title, had no
attractions for him. What he wanted was a real influence, which
would put him in a position to carry through his projects and
maintain his creation. In his hour of triumph Gustav Adolf probably did take into account the possibility of realizing his ambitions in this way, but only in so far as his elevation to Imperial
rank would effectively have forwarded his aims. The title dazzled
him not at all.

The first time that we can say with certainty that the idea
comes under discussion is immediately after the victory at Breitenfeld. It was then brought forward by none other than Johann
Georg of Saxony. Immediately after the battle (in which the
Saxons had certainly played no very distinguished part) the king
sent his trusted diplomat Salvius to the fugitive elector to invite
him to a meeting in Halle. Salvius must have known what passed
at that interview. In a letter written shortly afterwards he re-
counts that the king and the elector "drank to their friendship,
and became so cordial that he [the elector] represented himself as
being desirous of counselling His Majesty to place the Roman
crown upon his head, and said that he was prepared to assist him
to do so." It is generally, and quite rightly, assumed that Johann
Georg was not really serious in his offer. Either he acted upon
impulse in the intoxication of the moment, or, in his dissatisfaction at the part Gustav Adolf was now allotting to him—a
Saxon advance on the Imperial hereditary dominions—he was

trying by such baits to lure his ally to undertake the task which was so distasteful to himself.

At all events that scene in Halle (September 1631) became historic. In a political pamphlet (*Vindiciae secundum libertatem Germaniae*) which attacks Saxony's separate peace of 1635 from the point of view of the Swedish government, and incidentally refutes a number of counter-accusations, there is a clear and unmistakable allusion to the meeting. The author, who shows himself to be well informed, reminds the elector of his offer to the king at Halle, and of "what sort of an answer" he then received. He reminds him also of how Gustav Adolf always gave "an indignant and categorical refusal" when the German princes and their ambassadors raised this question. As eloquent proof of the king's desire to avoid anything which could possibly be construed as the expression of a wish for the Imperial crown, the author finally adduces the fact that during Gustav Adolf's stay in Nürnberg he declined an invitation from the town council to inspect the German Imperial regalia which were preserved in the castle there.

Gustav Adolf's reserve—which was, after all, easily explicable—naturally does not settle the question. It is true, however, that such of his contemporaries as bear witness to his ambition to become emperor are little worthy of credence. The opposite party did not shrink from fabricating and circulating rumors prejudicial to his position. In government circles in Bavaria, for instance, there was much talk at the beginning of 1632 of a scheme which was alleged to have formed the basis of negotiations at Frankfurt between the king and the Protestant Estates of the Empire, in which the creation of a new Empire for Gustav Adolf was said to have been the main feature. The hereditary Habsburg lands were to be given to Sweden, while Augsburg was to be made the capital of the Empire. It was a topic which offered splendid scope for political propaganda; and even the double-tongued diplomacy of France added its contribution.

Much more important, obviously, are such opinions as may be collected from the circle of Gustav Adolf's collaborators. That such a man as Salvius, thoroughly conversant as he was with the king's affairs, should have been convinced that the Imperial crown must be the ultimate solution, cannot fail to produce a strong impression. He was full of that conviction when he returned to his post in Hamburg from the Saxon headquarters. References to a great change in the future are not lacking even in his letters to the king, and to his colleagues in the royal service he spoke quite openly: all would be well if only the allied German princes would also become the king's subjects. It seems in fact to have been a general opinion among the Swedish diplomats active in Germany, that in the fulness of time Gustav Adolf would advance a claim to the Imperial power. Creilsheim, the court chamberlain—a near relative, incidentally, of that page Leubelfing who was a witness of the king's death—expressed himself with remarkable freedom about the king's intentions while on a visit to the court of the margrave of Bayreuth in the early autumn of 1631. Filip Sadler, too—one of Gustav Adolf's most trusted diplomats— was very frank about it when negotiating with Naumburg in the following summer. If his royal master should at some future time be elected king of the Romans, or emperor, he would certainly not sign the usual Capitulations upon election: on the contrary he would reserve to himself increased powers.

Axel Oxenstierna, who was in other respects so fond of speaking of the various aims of his late master, is silent upon this subject. His remark—still occasionally quoted—that Gustav Adolf never thought to be emperor, in fact comes from an obviously tainted source. We may note this silence without exaggerating its importance.

The idea of the Imperial title was acceptable not least because it would have done away with a number of difficulties in the king's relations to the princes of the Empire, and in his attitude towards the Imperial constitution. It seems quite certain that Gustav Adolf himself was well aware of this. His only known utterance in this connection points plainly to this conclusion. In January 1632, in the course of a tense interview with Duke Adolf Friedrich of Mecklenburg, he remarked, "If I were to become Emperor, then you, Your Grace, would be my prince." Moreover it does not seem possible to explain the conviction of the Swedish diplomats, to which allusion has been made above, except upon the supposition that they believed they knew the direction in which the king's thoughts were tending. There is, however, no need to assume that a definite plan had been made, and was being kept a secret. On the contrary, the balance of probability would seem to be against it. The immediate concern must be the great Evangelical Union. Yet it is very likely that towards the end of his career Gustav Adolf was reckoning with the altered circumstances which his election as king of the Romans would produce. If this conclusion is correct, the Imperial crown was to be the prize of the decisive victory which he was expecting. The majority of historians, although they reach their conclusion by very different roads, and express it with varying degrees of confidence, seem to be in agreement upon this point.

We are apt to ride our historical imagination upon a loose rein, and there are times when the animal is tempted to take the bit between its teeth. The prospects and the possibilities which are opened up if we assume that Gustav Adolf had been able to surmount the crisis which, in the closing months of his life, was clearly threatening, and that he had been able to carry his work to its conclusion—these fall outside the limits within which it is safe to dogmatize. An eyewitness has narrated how on the evening before Lützen the king complained bitterly of the "German princedoms" which refused to submit themselves to his "direction." He was nevertheless counting on an early and decisive victory. And this much appears certain: that Germany, disunited as she was in politics and religion, suffered an exceedingly heavy loss by his removal. But the work he had already achieved in his two years as champion of Protestantism in distress had assured his memory a permanent place in the history of the world.

GUSTAV ADOLF THE GREAT

GUSTAV ADOLF THE GREAT

[1]

THE AGE to which Gustav Adolf belonged delighted to honor men whom the accident of birth had destined for the governance of lands and peoples. Eulogies of princes comprise no inconsiderable proportion of its literature. We may be pretty certain that among those who obtained full meed of praise were some of relatively modest attainments. The trappings of majesty lent a splendor to qualities in themselves by no means splendid; and the full-blown baroque style was to bring the art of effective laudation to perfection. We are not likely nowadays to preserve the illusions which courtly flattery imposed upon contemporaries. Even Gustav Adolf in his latter years kept a court poet, by name Johan Narssius—who, incidentally, also practised as a physician—to sing his master's epic achievements in sonorous Latin verse. His dramas and odes have long lain buried in the dust-heaps of oblivion.

Gustav Adolf had learnt from Johan Skytte's "Short Instruction"—that "Mirror for Princes" of his youth—to appreciate the need to discount pretty speeches; had learnt also not to take jackdaws in peacocks' feathers at their own valuation. His life, moreover—and this was more important—had been anything but plain sailing. A keen and searching blast swept over his years of adolescence. He early grew to the knowledge that it was not smooth words, but bold partisanship, of which he stood mainly in need. The judgment of princes and potentates which he formed for himself as time went on was founded solidly upon this basis of realism. With all his ability to charm men, he had a sharp eye for their weaknesses. Of his dear brother-in-law at Berlin he once remarked that a new livery, a fine horse, or a couple of greyhounds meant more to him than all the world. His opinions of the foreign rulers with whom he dealt easily took on a tinge of irony—an irony perhaps in part induced by their frequent disinclination to follow the course he prescribed for them.

Gustav was himself the architect of his fame. The crown to which he succeeded was a perilous inheritance. He felt it to be a necessity to earn by his actions the right to wear it. And it was not long before he had convinced the world that it must take into account his wishes, and reckon with his ability. Foreigners who came to know him well saw in him a coming man. "As His Majesty is only twenty-one or twenty-two years old, great things are to be expected of him in the future, if he continues as he has begun." The testimony comes from a Dutchman, who has left us a description of the Swedish king as he was in 1616. Similar tributes from friend and foe alike grow ever more numerous as his reign proceeds. His fame spread far. After the battle of the White Mountain, Spinola, the foremost Spanish general of the age, observed that Gustav Adolf would be the only prince on the Protestant side whom they need take into their calculations. His view anticipated that of Wallenstein. Wallenstein, who in 1625 took over the supreme command of the Imperial armies, soon came to realize that the king of Sweden was to be his archenemy. He betrayed a passionate, half-superstitious interest in his person and projects, seeking uneasily to discover from the stars upon which of the two of them Fortune would ultimately bestow her favors. Wallenstein's early respect for Gustav Adolf, reluctant but irresistible as it was, is perhaps the most remarkable evidence of the king's reputation among his contemporaries, even before his intervention in Germany.

Innumerable expressions of opinion from his friends in the Protestant camp could be adduced as witness of their increasing confidence in him. The Palatinate statesman Rusdorf, who made his personal acquaintance when Gustav Adolf was visiting Germany in search of a wife, declared in 1624 that he placed him "above all other men." Rusdorf was a man of the world, not given to enthusiasm, or he might have been suspected of a certain partiality. Karl Karlsson Gyllenhielm, Gustav Adolf's own half-brother, was no doubt prejudiced in his favor, but what we know of his character seems to guarantee that he was serious in his hearty message of God-speed at the time of the first expedition to Prussia in 1626: "God grant His Royal Majesty good counsel and sufficient means," he says, "and then will the way lie open

GUSTAV ADOLF

From a Bronze Bust by Hans van der Putt,
done in Nürnberg in 1632

to victories exceeding Alexander's." Nor was Louis de Geer given to frivolous exaggeration. He met Gustav Adolf for the first time in 1627, and was soon completely won over. "So great is this king's genius," he wrote back to his home town in the Netherlands, "that not the hundredth part of it is to be expressed in words." More measured in his language, but equally convincing, is the Englishman Sir Thomas Roe, in a judgment uttered two years later. He speaks of Gustav Adolf as a soldier fortunate and victorious, the best disciplinarian in the whole of Europe, the possessor of the extraordinary gift of being able to content his men without paying them, the comrade of them all. Roe, a much-travelled and experienced diplomat, had come into contact with the king in Prussia, and remained ever afterwards his staunch admirer.

"We have got another little enemy on our hands." This remark, attributed to the Emperor Ferdinand, has, even up to our own day, been made to serve as an illustration of how grievously the adversaries of Gustav Adolf underrated him at the time of his entry into the German war. The remark was, indeed, never made; quite apart from the fact that it comes from a late and doubtful source, it lacks inherent probability. There was no disposition to despise the danger which his intervention would involve, though there was certainly a belief that he could be talked out of his plan. They knew him already, though it was with an imperfect knowledge. And the man among them who knew him best—Wallenstein—was withdrawn at that very moment from the scene of action, not to be recalled until the surprising Swedish successes put a premium upon good advice.

Very few historical personalities have so engaged the attention of their contemporaries as Gustav Adolf did at the climax of his victorious career. All eyes were turned towards him. A chorus of voices proclaimed the praise of the liberator. The poetry of the people paid him its simple homage; and a more cultured eloquence added its more elaborate tribute. In particular men vied with one another to draw comparisons with the heroes of classical antiquity and the Old Testament. Augustus was discovered to be an anagram of Gustavus. He was hailed as a new Gideon—a name, incidentally, which he had borne for some years back in the secret cypher of the exiled Palatine family. The name now took on a special significance for the common soldier, by reason of the fighting hymn to which Gustav Adolf was said to be particularly attached, and of which he later came to be considered as the author. He was likened almost equally often to Joshua. In a defense of their conduct addressed to the emperor in April 1632, the town council of Nürnberg spoke openly of "the evangelical Joshua, the king of Sweden." The process was almost complete: the distinction between pious imagery and practical reality had as good as vanished.

The news of his death at Lützen made therefore a proportionately strong impression. A tempest of lamentation broke out all over the Protestant world, silencing the dissensions of the moment. Even in the camp of his opponents there were not a few who heard the news with emotion. They knew that a great figure in world history had passed from them. What did the future hold, now that he was gone?

Anguish found expression in searing, despairing bitterness. Some lines from a "cry of woe" printed in Stockholm in 1633 may serve as witness: "Weep, ye priests and ye laymen, weep, young and old, rich and poor, great and small," cries the unknown author. "May the day be pitchy-dark, mist-shrouded, and forlorn. May God blast it from on high, may no light shine upon it, may thick cloud brood over it, yea, may it no longer rejoice itself among the other days of the month. Accursed be the hour in which the Christian, noble, heroic heart was stricken. Accursed be the hand that smote him, and the bullet which pierced his body, and the earth which sucked up his blood. Accursed be he who laid his hand upon the Lord's Anointed; accursed, all they who did compass against his life and welfare, and reft him from the light of life. Amen, Amen."

The people whispered of miracles on his deathday. "When His Majesty fell," we read in a contemporary notice, "the sun lost his splendor, and shone no more thereafter by the space of four weeks; a thick mist likewise continued several weeks." Legend could grow even on Protestant soil.

Johan Rudbeckius, who had seen the king in his moments of weakness no less than of strength, in a memorial sermon gave him a place next to, if not before, the Church's first martyr, St. Stephen. For if he who allowed himself to be stoned for the sake of Christ was a martyr, how much more so was he who bore so many wounds on his dead body!

Already the dead Gustav Adolf was threatening to obscure the living man. The apotheosis had begun.

[2]

THE news of the king's death came to Stockholm on December 8, 1632, by the ordinary "frontier mail"—a good month, therefore, after the battle of Lützen. For about a week beforehand rumors had been current as to a great battle with Wallenstein in which the Swedes were said to have come off victorious. The Råd was full of happy anticipation. Then came the news of his death, like lightning from a clear sky. According to the minutes of the Råd, the members spent the day in weeping and lamentation. But before they separated they had, as Per Brahe informs us, taken "an emphatic resolution to live and die together, for the protection, advantage, and defense of the fatherland." The next post brought them a letter from Axel Oxenstierna, which he had not been able to send off until a week after the disaster. It is a noble memorial to the two men who in close collaboration raised Sweden to the position of a great power, the one establishing that position, the other preserving it. Not even in that hour, when his emotions well-nigh overwhelmed him, did the chancellor lose that lucid dignity of utterance which was perhaps the foremost of his gifts. He acknowledges that what has occurred is in reality no surprise to him; the disaster to the fatherland, the monarchy, and the common cause, which he will mourn while life is left to him, is to be attributed to the king's "wonted impetuosity." In terms of unstinted admiration he salutes the departed as one of the great men of history. "In the world is now none that is his equal, nor has there been for centuries such an one; and indeed I doubt whether the future will produce his peer. Yea, truly we may call him King Gustaf the wise and great, the father of the fatherland, whose like never yet reigned in Sweden, as is acknowledged not by us alone, but by men of all nations, whether friend or foe."

The lords of the council in Stockholm were of the same opinion; the late king had fully made good his claim to the honorable title of "the Great." At the Riksdag which met in February 1633 the *lantmarskalk* and the speakers of the other Estates received a hint to this effect, and the epithet was accordingly introduced in a suitable context into the Estates' answers to the government's proposals. The Nobility and Clergy were careful to set forth the reasons why the name, henceforward and for ever, should be given to Gustav Adolf by his people. The Riksdag's resolution named him "King Gustav II the Great," and with that the matter was regarded as settled in a constitutionally binding form.

In virtue of this resolution, the government considered itself fully entitled to accord the hero his title even in its diplomatic correspondence, and to demand of friendly powers that they should employ it in their turn. The step was certainly highly unusual. However, in spite of the age's *penchant* for making all sorts of difficulties about questions of princely rank and titles, it seems to have been crowned with success. Gustav Adolf's greatness was given international recognition. Only from one side were there objections, and these came from Russia. This is hardly surprising in view of the tender susceptibilities of the Muscovites with regard to questions of this sort, and the naïveté of many of their ideas. When a Russian embassy visited Stockholm in 1633 some very curious negotiations were entered into upon this topic. The Russians, who were in other respects quite well disposed, raised the objection that the addition of the words "the Second and the Great" to Gustav's style and title was in clear conflict with earlier peace treaties, and these they had no power to alter, since they had been sealed by oaths and the kissing of the Cross. Per Banér tried to explain to them the significance of the question. "It is usual with us after the death of a king," he said, "to name him, according to how many of that name there have been already. We call His Royal Majesty *Great,* because he delivered Protestant Christendom in its hour of need, and did many other mighty works. In this we have but followed the example of others who have called their rulers after this fashion, as for instance Carolus Magnus. And at the last Riksdag it was decided, that we should do honor to His late Majesty by conferring this name upon him." The Russians were not to be persuaded. They hit at last upon an argument which is not without ingenuity. "It can be written in the chronicles," they pointed out, "otherwise it is irregular."

It was not only in chronicles or solemn orations that Gustav Adolf after his death was given the appellation of *magnus,* the Great. The phrase became generally current, and is heard even in everyday speech, though naturally not so often as the less cumbrous expressions "the late King," "King Gösta," and so forth. In Sweden, especially, men were long conscious of the fact that the honorable epithet was part of Gustav Adolf's full and correct title, accorded to him after his death to perpetuate his work in life. Queen Kristina speaks about it in the introduction to her uncompleted autobiography. "After Karl there succeeded to the throne Gustav Adolf, my father, who was called the Great," she writes. "He won the name through his devotion, his achievements, his blood, and finally his own life, through whose sacrifice he acquired an honor which others have won more cheaply. He was truly great by reason of his achievements and his good fortune. Nothing would have been wanting to the latter, if he had but died in the old faith of his fathers, instead of dying in the bosom of the Lutheran Church. But, not to do an injustice to so great a man, I decline to believe that he ventured his life in *that* cause. I prefer to believe that he cleverly used this pretext in order to reap glory from his vast designs. However that may be, it was his misfortune to be sacrificed, either to a lie, or to the chimera that men call glory. . . ." Such was the opinion of Kristina, of whom Axel Oxenstierna said, "After all she is the great Gustav's daughter."

There were many who did not stop at calling him "the Great," but placed him upon a pedestal, elevating him above any criticism from those that came after. It was accounted presumption to call in question what Gustav Adolf in his wisdom had ordained; no attempt to traverse his decisions was to be permitted. "The late King Gustav was so high and mighty a monarch (for by reason of his noble acts the whole world called him Great) that it will serve but little to examine his actions, inasmuch as he performed them to the admiration of all." This remark, which was made by the *lantmarskalk* Erik Fleming at the "Reduktion" Riksdag[1] of 1655, gives some idea of the extraordinary piety and veneration which hedged about Gustav Adolf's memory. It was, however, only natural that criticism should now and then have made itself heard, and that his aims, and the creations of his policy, should have been appraised very differently, according to the points of view of those who have cited them in support of their arguments. Such is always the fate of a living tradition common to all parties.

Of the strength and vitality of the tradition which Gustav Adolf left behind him in Sweden the minutes of the Råd are the best evidence. As long as Axel Oxenstierna lived he gave bounteously of his rich store of reminiscences. Some of these we have quoted already, but many others could be added. Even as late as in the time of Karl XI there sat in the senate one man— Per Brahe—who represented a direct link with the councillors of Gustav Adolf; and many others among the leading statesmen of that time—in particular, Magnus Gabriel de la Gardie—had been brought up in circles permeated through and through by the aura of the king's personality.

Nothing contributed more powerfully to preserve the authority of his memory among his successors than their consciousness of the success which had attended Gustav Adolf's enterprises in peace and war in such abundant measure. "All his life he was full of luck," as Axel Oxenstierna said on one occasion in his own inimitable fashion. How tempting it must have been to seek the rules of sound policy in the examples he had given! For the generation which had breathed the same air and which cherished early childhood memories of him, there must have been an irresistible tendency to such a line of thought. There can be no doubt that Karl X Gustav consciously modelled himself upon his famous uncle. The fact was noticed by contemporaries immediately after his accession in 1654, and a study of his methods of government and political principles confirms their impression in all sorts of ways. Thus in his relations with the Riksdag he

[1] The Riksdag at which it was decided that the Crown should resume those lands which, formerly the property of the State, had passed into private possession.

clearly sought to recur to forms of business which had been developed under Gustav Adolf, but which Kristina had found increasingly unsatisfactory, and had ultimately abandoned. The contention, for example, that his *Reduktion* policy involved a breach with Gustav Adolf's policy towards the nobles, will not hold water for a moment; Gustav Adolf would certainly have taken the same line under the altered circumstances. The similarity in aim and method would appear even more clearly if Karl Gustav's personality had not been in many respects so unlike Gustav Adolf's; for Karl Gustav mirrored but faintly the fascinating and brilliant qualities of his predecessor. Nor must it be forgotten that the younger man's road to power, long and testing as it was, helped to make him a statesman of rather self-contained character. But his attempt to imitate his great predecessor is none the less obvious, and without it the history of Sweden might possibly have taken a very different channel.

In course of time, Gustav Adolf's example began to lose its authority. Posterity's homage to his illustrious memory began to ring hollow, as adversity brought forth new men and new policies. Karl XI can be set with some show of reason at the opposite pole to Gustav Adolf, for he appreciated neither his statesmanship nor his personality. Johan Gyllenstierna, the creative statesman of this period, understood it better, though he too endeavored to strike out upon other lines than those preferred by Gustav Adolf's political executors. The precedent laid down by Gustav Adolf was eagerly cited in favor of the system of a French alliance, both in the seventeenth and the eighteenth century; but it proved a dangerous inheritance for Sweden. In reality, nothing could have been more alien to Gustav Adolf's spirit than thus to sell the kingdom into servitude. Without entering in detail into his shifting relations with Richelieu, it may be asserted with confidence that he saw his way clear all the time. Yet misconceptions of his policy in this matter have sometimes done injury to his memory at the bar of posterity.

In Germany his fame stood so high at the hour of his death that it was scarcely possible to raise it further. The unhappy prolongation of the war which, humanly speaking, was a consequence of his removal, necessarily caused a revulsion of feeling.

More than one who had in his life-time burnt the incense of devotion turned against him then. The poet Paul Fleming—who to be sure was a Saxon—may serve as an example: "Foe was he, not friend; and the sequel has laid bare his machinations." Respect for Gustav Adolf never indeed died out in the heart of the Protestant peoples, but the flood-tide of feeling had ebbed nevertheless. His work in Germany had filled scarce two years, and for hardly more than one of them was the part he played one of world importance. The sixteen years that followed before central Europe won to peace drew heavily upon her resources of enthusiasm, even though they left the hero's fame undimmed. Gustav Adolf's greatness was in fact never denied by the historians of the seventeenth century, even if they chanced to be Catholics. The story of Pope Urban VIII's grief for him is, however, a pure fable.

This is no place to tell how research, speculation, and poetry resuscitated his memory; how successive ages, tendencies, and modes of thought contrived to shape their conception of Gustav Adolf more or less to suit their own inclinations; how his personality and achievement called forth one interpretation after another by the magic of their inexhaustible richness. If few Swedes have taken so wide a scope, few have exercised such a power of attraction. Those who have at one time or another been fascinated by his character and have recognized the pioneer nature of his work include men of the most diverse mental horizons. The spokesmen of French enlightenment, as well as those of German idealism—Voltaire and Friedrich II, no less than Schiller and Ernst Moritz Arndt—have accorded him their admiration. Conversely, Gustav Adolf has also been a mark for suspicion and for open attacks, though less so perhaps nowadays than was formerly the case. Religious resentment, doctrinaire nationalism, historical materialism with its passion for revaluations—none of these has spared him. Even the scientific historians, who claim to make complete objectivity their watchword, have in their judgment of him varied through all the stages from coolness to enthusiasm. The picture of Gustav Adolf has changed and changed again; but the corrections which conflicting viewpoints have enabled us to make have only given us a deeper insight into the truth, and many of the thorny controversies of earlier days appear now to be settled in principle for ever; though no doubt there is still much to be done before Gustav Adolf's work is revealed and elucidated in all its aspects.

In the last resort we are brought back to the proof which his personality affords us of the ability of a single man to set his stamp upon an age. No one who honestly recognizes the importance of the personal factor in history, and the creative force of the human will, can ever remain indifferent to Gustav Adolf.

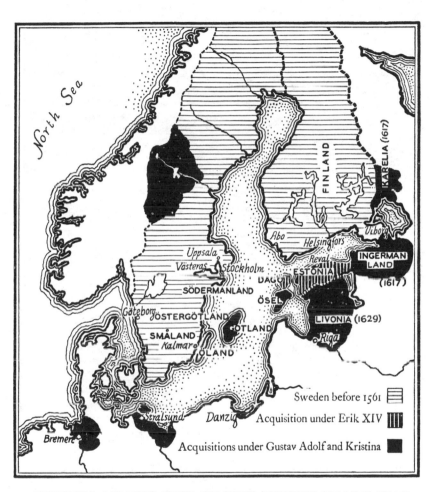

North Sea

KARELIA (1617)

FINLAND

Åbo

Helsingfors

Viborg

Uppsala
Västeras   Stockholm

Reval   INGERMAN
LAND

SÖDERMANLAND

DAGÖ   ESTONIA
(1617)

ÖSEL

Göteborg
ÖSTERGÖTLAND

GOTLAND   LIVONIA (1629)

SMÅLAND
Kalmar   Riga

ÖLAND

Sweden before 1561

Stralsund   Danzig   Acquisition under Erik XIV

Bremen

Acquisitions under Gustav Adolf and Kristina

SWEDEN AT THE END OF THE THIRTY YEARS' WAR

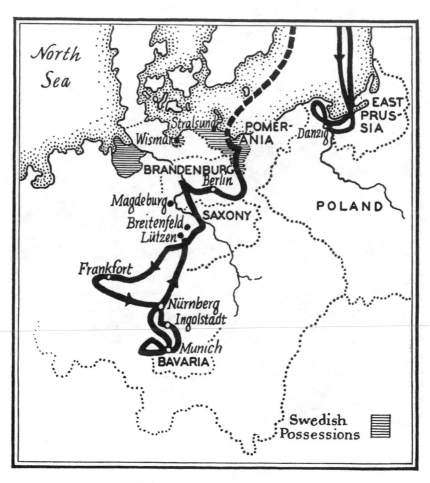

GUSTAV ADOLF'S CAMPAIGNS

GENEALOGY OF THE VASA FAMILY

SWEDISH RULERS OF THE VASA AND PALATINATE LINES

Gustav I Eriksson Vasa   Regent 1521–1523
                         King 1523–1560

Erik XIV   1560–1568 (deposed)
Johan III   1568–1592
Sigismund   1592–1599 (deposed)
Karl IX   Regent 1595–1604
              King 1604–1611

Gustav II Adolf   1611–1632
Kristina   1632–1654 (abdicated)
Karl X Gustav   1654–1660
Karl XI   1660–1697
Karl XII   1697–1718

2nd marriage
Kristina of Holstein

Gustav II Adolf — Maria Eleonora of Brandenburg

Kristina

Karl Filip
Duke of Södermanland

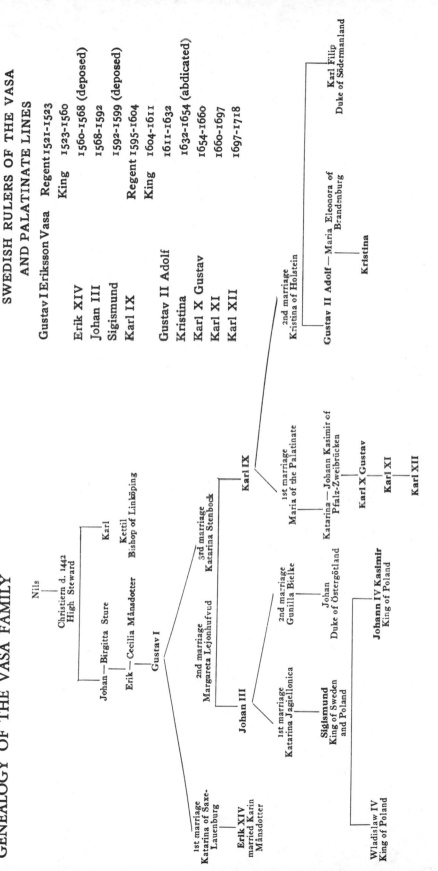

Nils

Christiern d. 1442
High Steward

Johan — Birgitta Sture   Karl

Erik — Cecilia Månsdotter   Kettil
                             Bishop of Linköping

Gustav I

3rd marriage
Katarina Stenbock

2nd marriage
Margareta Lejonhufvud

Karl IX

1st marriage
Maria of the Palatinate

Katarina — Johann Kasimir of Pfalz-Zweibrücken

Karl X Gustav

Karl XI

Karl XII

2nd marriage
Gunilla Bielke

Johan
Duke of Östergötland

Johan III

1st marriage
Katarina Jagiellonica

Sigismund
King of Sweden
and Poland

Johann IV Kasimir
King of Poland

1st marriage
Katarina of Saxe-Lauenburg

Erik XIV
married Karin
Månsdotter

Wladislaw IV
King of Poland

INDEX

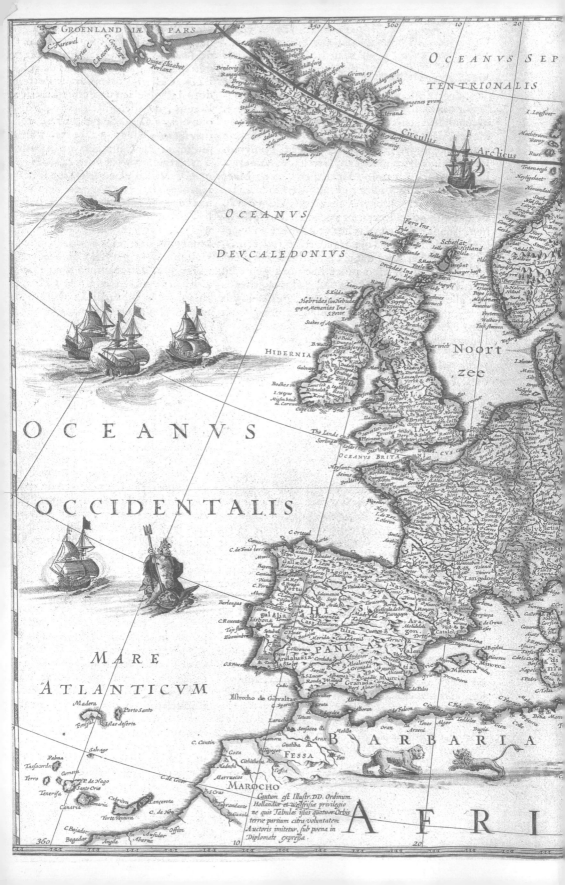